VICTORIA
THE UNKNOWN CITY

Ross Crockford

ARSENAL
PULP PRESS

VICTORIA

THE UNKNOWN CITY

Victoria: THE UNKNOWN CITY
Copyright © 2006 by Ross Crockford

Second printing: 2007

ARSENAL PULP PRESS
341 Water Street, Suite 200
Vancouver, BC
Canada V6B 1B8
arsenalpulp.com

Design by Electra Design Group
Production assistance by Judy Yeung
Editing by Derek Fairbridge
Front cover photograph by Brian Howell; back cover photograph by Stewart M. Wood

Printed and bound in Canada

Library and Archives Canada Cataloguing in Publication

Crockford, Ross, 1963-
     Victoria : the unknown city / Ross Crockford.

Revised follow-up to Victoria: secrets of the city, by Kevin Barefoot,
     2000.

Includes bibliographical references and index.
ISBN 1-55152-195-4

     1. Victoria (B.C.)–Guidebooks. I. Barefoot, Kevin, 1971- Victoria II. Title.

FC3846.18.C758 2006   917.11'28045   C2005-907779-4

ISBN-13 978-1-55152-195-4

c o n t e n t s

acknowledgments

Thanks to Brian Lam, Robert Ballantyne, and Shyla Seller at Arsenal for their tremendous patience, to Derek Fairbridge for the invaluable research and editing, and to Electra Design for the layout. Thanks also to Kevin Barefoot, David Leach, and John Threlfall, whose superb contributions to the previous *Secrets of the City* made me work harder to find new material. My gratitude also goes to Victoria's extraordinary historians, whose books (see Further Reading) provided details, especially John Adams, Danda Humphreys, and Martin Segger, along with Carey Pallister at the City of Victoria Archives. Much thanks also to Victoria's print journalists, who record history as it happens, especially Adrian Chamberlain, Malcolm Curtis, Mike Devlin, T.K. Demmings, Russ Francis, Jim Gibson, Norman Gidney, Alisa Gordaneer, Tom Hawthorn, Lyle Jenish, Dave Lennam, Shannon Moneo, Vivian Moreau, Briony Penn, Michael D. Reid, J. Sushil Saini, Shelora Sheldon, Andrew Struthers, and Sid Tafler. Further thanks to all those who put up with my inquiries, including Mark "Sparky" Adamson, Stephen Andrew, Allan Antliff, Ron Armstrong, Pat Martin Bates, Freda and Bus Bemister, Bill Blair, Peter Brand, Allan Cassells, Deirdre Castle, Lloyd Chesley, Chris Coleman, Allan Collier, Bill Crawford, Henry Ewert, Cynthia De La Hoz, Jennifer Drapeau, John Elliott, Art Farquharson, David Ferguson, Garry Fletcher, Gareth Gaudin, Barry George, Chris Gudgeon, Tom Henry, Shirley Hewett, Alan Hodgson, Lorna Jackson, Tony James, Susan Kerschbaumer, Niels Knudsen, James Lam, Mickey Lam, Brian Linds, Ricky Long, Miles Lowry, Liam Lux, Neil McAllister, Robert McCullough, John McFetrick, Ewan McLaren, Gene Miller, Bob Milne, Lynne Milnes, Andrew Murray, Philomena Pagaduan, Elida Peers, Chris Petter, Marcus Pollard, Phil Saunders, Dave Skilling, Nikko Snow, Godfrey Stephens, Clive Townley, Dave Unwin, Lynne Van Luven, Jo Vipond, Peter Walters, Liberty Walton, Al Wilcox, Glenn Willing, and David Wisdom. Cheers to the Oyster Club, who provided encouragement over drinks: Todd Davis, Mark Dusseault, Charles Tidler, Stephen White, and Tracy Yerrell. And most of all, thanks to my family and Dr. Jennifer Wise.

For more information about Victoria and updates to this book, visit the author's blog, *http://unknownvictoria.blogspot.com*.

introduction

The very idea of this book may seem absurd. As cities go, Victoria is just a baby; although the Songhees and Saanich Natives have been here for thousands of years, the tangle of infrastructure known as Victoria didn't really exist until it was incorporated in 1862. It's home to only 350,000 people, and a big share of them are government bean-counters, reporters, and ale-house gossips. So what about Victoria could possibly be "unknown"?

Plenty, as it turns out. Despite its size, Victoria is tremendously diverse.

Surrounded by seawater and rainforest, it's wild enough that whales swim past its shores and cougars prowl its streets. Occupying a strategic point at the mouth of the Pacific, its history is rich with tales of Spanish navigators, fur traders, gold-rush prospectors, and shipping tycoons. Located on an island just across the American border, its apparent isolation makes it an attractive hideout for fugitives and radicals, mystics and con artists. Travel a few minutes around here, and you'll find abandoned mines, waterfalls, organic farms, European streetscapes, salmon-spawning rivers, brewpubs, and world-class museums.

The consequence of such diversity is that it's often difficult to keep track of all its elements. Victoria is just large enough to nurture a thousand tiny subcultures, from cow-punk hootenannies to witches' covens, all harbouring their own codes and secret histories. Like many places, Victoria has also done its share of paving over the past — whether it's First Nations culture or streetcar tracks — in the name of progress. (Sometimes the suppression is psychological, too. Victoria has struggled to deal with its sewage for so long that it practically cries out for Freudian analysis.) In other words, Victoria is full of "unknown knowns," things we don't know that we know, the details that are remembered only by a select few, or have been forgotten altogether in the rush of modern life. This book aims to bring some of them back to light.

The trick with the unknown is that once you wade in, you quickly realize that it's bottomless. Victoria has always been richer than other cities its size — first in its natural bounty, subsequently in its wealth and influence, and today in its culture, producing global pop stars and athletes. Victoria always has one more trick up its woollen sleeve, one more story to tell, one more secret to reveal. In terms of economic and political heft, it will never equal New York, San Francisco, and the other burgs in the *Unknown City* series. But as you're about to see, if a place can be measured by its lore alone, Victoria is a metropolis.

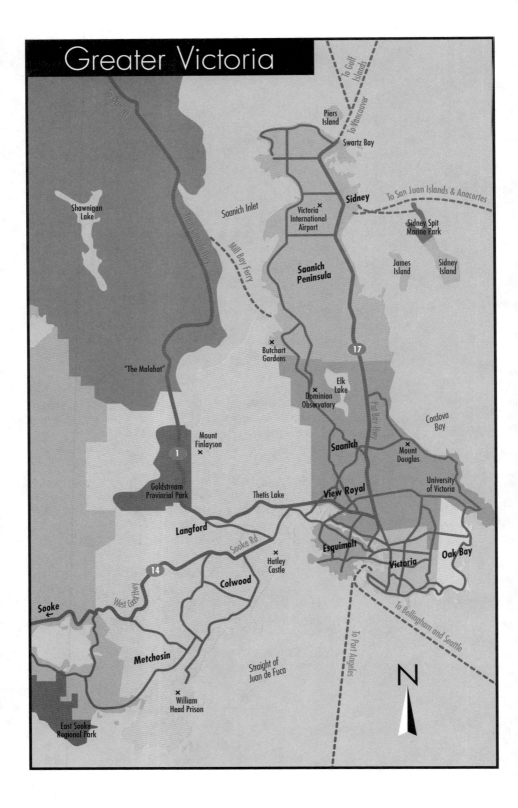

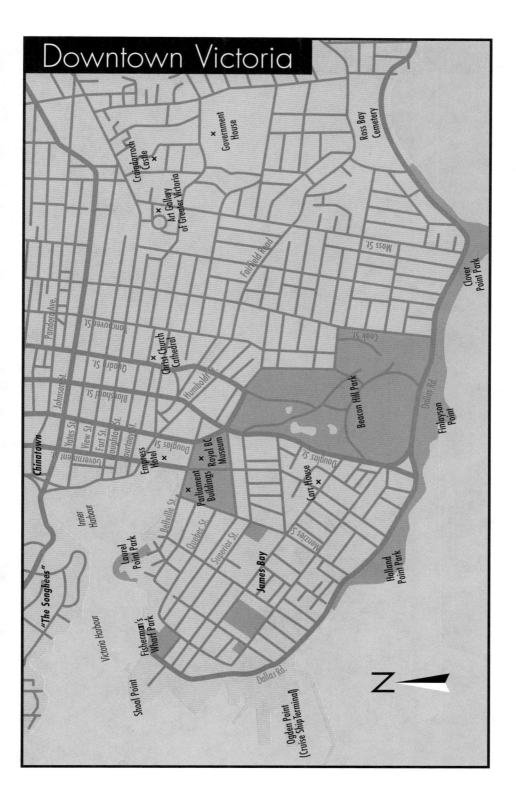

Downtown Victoria

"The Songhees"

Victoria Harbour

Inner Harbour

Chinatown

Shoal Point

Fisherman's Wharf Park

Laurel Point Park

Ogden Point (Cruise Ship Terminal)

Dallas Rd.

James Bay

Superior St.

Quebec St.

Belleville St.

Menzies St.

Holland Point Park

Empress Hotel

Parliament Buildings

Royal BC Museum

Carr House

Government St.
Yates St.
View St.
Fort St.
Douglas St.
Courtney St.
Broughton St.

Johnson St.

Blanshard St.

Quadra St.

Vancouver St.

Pandora Ave.

Christ Church Cathedral

Humboldt St.

Douglas St.

Beacon Hill Park

Cook St.

Fairfield Road

Art Gallery of Greater Victoria

Craigdarroch Castle

Government House

Moss St.

Ross Bay Cemetery

Clover Point Park

Finlayson Point

Dallas Rd.

N

As one of Canada's leading tourist destinations, Victoria has its share of must-sees. It's easy to find Miniature World, but what about old mineshafts, artillery batteries, and Chinese temples? Read on.

First Place Names

Photo: British Columbia Archives I-30804

For at least 4,000 years, most of the Victoria region was inhabited by the **Songhees people**. Their clans had dozens of settlements and food-gathering sites from Sooke to Gordon Head, and their largest settlement was on Cadboro Bay. But when the Hudson's Bay Company set up shop in 1843, most Songhees families moved to a village on the western side of the Inner Harbour (site of today's Ocean Pointe Resort), across from Fort Victoria. In their Lekwungen language, the location of the fort was *Ku-sing-ay-las*, "the place of strong fibre," home to a species of willow with an inner bark they spun into fishing line. James Bay (see photo), the site of today's Empress Hotel, was *Whosaykum*, "muddy place," where they gathered clams. The Gorge waterway was *Camossung*, "swift running water," from a legend about a selfish girl of that name who was turned to stone because she wanted to keep the ducks and oysters of the area for herself. (The stone is part of the rapids under the Tillicum Bridge.) And the rocky point south of their village was *Palatsis*, a sacred "place of cradles," where mothers put cradles after their children had outgrown them, to ensure the kids enjoyed a long life.

The Songhees did a brisk trade selling salmon and other goods, but as Victoria grew, the colonists started demanding that the "eye-sore" Native village be moved. In 1911, the federal government paid $10,000 to each of the 43 surviving families, and the Songhees relocated to a reserve in Esquimalt (the name derived from Whyomilth, the name of a clan that lived there). Railways and industries took over, and a roofing company built a water tower on Palatsis (its base is part of the lookout platform now on the rock). Today, the land is occupied by blocks of 1980s-built condo towers, collectively known as "The Songhees" – a rather backhanded tribute to the people who once lived there. To learn more, visit *songheesnation.com*.

In 1842, Hudson's Bay Company agent James Douglas scouted locations on Vancouver Island for a fort that would become the new base of the HBC's coastal fur trade. The site he chose would eventually become downtown Victoria. It was on a sheltered cove (today's Inner Harbour), next to a canal (The Gorge) that could provide water power and access to timber. It fronted vast fields (Beacon Hill Park) suitable for agriculture – mainly because the Songhees were already cultivating them for camas, the onion-like plant that was a staple of their diet. Douglas offered them work providing timbers for the fort's walls, and construction began.

There was confusion about the fort's name: at first it was called Fort Camosun, and then Fort Albert after Queen Victoria's husband, but officials in Britain ordered that it be named after the queen herself. When finished, **Fort Victoria** was about 100 metres square, with walls roughly where Bastion Square, and Government, Broughton, and Wharf Streets are today. The main path through the compound eventually became Fort Street.

The population outgrew the fort and it was dismantled in 1864, but subtle reminders of the structure still remain. A double row of bricks, engraved with names of the original settlers, outlines the fort's north and east walls, running along the sidewalk of Government Street and into Bastion Square. In the lobby of the Rithet Building (*1117 Wharf St.*, also notable for its cast-iron façade) you'll find a well dug in the 1860s behind the fort's west wall; a piece of the original pump equipment is inside (see photo). Also, several iron mooring rings are sunk into the rocks around the pink Customs House (*1002 Wharf St.*), where ships used to tie up. Look for one below the boardwalk at the water's edge (see photo), and another atop the rocky slope, hidden under a blackberry bush.

LEGISLATIVE FOLLIES

As you can imagine, the **Parliament Buildings** – that's their proper name, according to the 1893 act funding their creation – are home to numerous unusual facts:

• Francis Rattenbury was only 25 years old and fresh from Yorkshire when he won the competition to design British Columbia's seat of government. To keep it fair, the entrants submitted plans under pseudonyms, and Rattenbury wisely called himself "BC Architect"– while the losers used names like "Utile Dulce" and "Ta-ra-ra-boom-de-ay."

- The buildings, which opened in 1898, are fitted with many British parliamentary features, including the placing of government and opposition benches two-and-a-half sword lengths apart to prevent duels — but the topless nymphs adorning the legislative chamber's ceiling are likely unique.

- Beneath the granite steps of the buildings' grand entrance are three vaults that once held the province's gold.

- There are tunnels under the front lawn: on one occasion, NDP MLAs hid in them to trick the Social Credit government into thinking it didn't need all its members to vote on a crucial bill. (The strategy failed: the socialist NDP horde charged out when time came to vote, but their numbers weren't enough to defeat the motion.)

- The jail cell in the basement has never been used.

An authentic replica of one of Fort Victoria's **defensive towers** stands in the Fort Victoria RV Park, at 340 Island Highway. (The small tower overlooking Highway 1 is just advertising; the proper replica is inside the park.) The bastion was created by Dr. Herbert Plasterer, the German sculptor and architect who developed the campground in 1961. A stickler for detail, Plasterer built the bastion of timbers from the Cloverdale farmhouse (itself made of wood from Fort Victoria) and the former Point Ellice Bridge, using the same hand tools and nail-free construction employed in the original fort.

our imperial hotel

After Victoria was established as BC's capital in 1871, city fathers schemed to make it the leading health and pleasure resort of the Pacific Northwest. Trouble was, it didn't appear healthy. One of the first things visitors saw was James Bay – by then a fetid swamp, awash with town garbage. In 1901, the city started building a granite dam (the wall of today's Inner Harbour causeway) and filling the bay with gravel hauled on streetcars. (The gravel pit's huge divot remains, behind the Fernwood Community Centre.) The city planned to put a garden on the reclaimed mudflats, but Francis Rattenbury – an architectural star because of his Parliament Buildings – convinced the Canadian Pacific Railway (CPR) to build a hotel welcoming their *Empress* steamships from Asia. Work began on the **Empress Hotel** in 1904, driving hundreds of Douglas-fir pilings into the mud for the hotel's foundations.

As soon as it opened on January 20, 1908, the Empress was a hit. Demand for rooms was so great that by 1914 it had added north and south wings, and a Crystal Ballroom with 10 chandeliers each containing 8,000 crystal beads. The hotel welcomed numerous celebrities including Shirley Temple, Douglas Fairbanks, Katharine Hepburn, Spencer Tracy, Ginger Rogers, and Jack Benny. In 1931, King Prajadhipok of Siam and his 56-member party took over an entire floor, accompanied by 500 pieces of luggage. In 1944, a young Peter Lawford (later part of Frank Sinatra's Rat Pack) was

• The predecessors to today's legislative buildings were a set of wooden halls known as "The Birdcages." These witnessed one of the longest speeches of any legislature anywere on April 24, 1886, when Leonard McClure spoke for 16 hours non-stop – often with a glass of port in hand – so that a tax measure he opposed would expire.

• The Parliament Buildings' exterior was first illuminated with light bulbs in 1897 to celebrate Queen Victoria's Diamond Jubilee; there are 3,333 bulbs on the building today.

• The pieces of a stained-glass window (see photo) to commemorate the same jubilee were shipped from England in barrels of molasses. During a 1912 renovation the window was misplaced in the basement and stayed there for 62 years.

• In 2001, First Nations leaders demanded that the murals (painted by George Southwell in 1935) in the rotunda be removed because their depictions of bare-breasted Native women (see photo) were demeaning and historically inaccurate. That same year the Songhees — who once had a village on the site — filed a legal claim to the grounds, then estimated to be worth $46 million.

• The statue of Captain George Vancouver on top of the main dome (there are 33 domes in all) is made of copper and plated with gold.

To learn more, take a free tour or visit *legis.gov.bc.ca.*

thrown out for assaulting a girl delivering room service. Bob Hope and Bing Crosby were frequent guests in the 1950s; Hope chipped golf balls on the lawn and Crosby was so comfortable there that he was seen without his toupee. During Princess Margaret's stay in 1958, she worried Empress staff by climbing to the roof with her entourage to watch the Russian satellite Sputnik pass over the city.

By 1965, however, the Empress had become as shabby as the dowagers who lived in it year-round. The CPR seriously considered tearing the old girl down and turning it into a motor lodge or convention centre, but discovered it could save huge amounts of cash by switching to AC power instead of generating British-style direct current in the hotel's coal-fired power plant. The CPR overhauled the hotel in 1966 and 1988, moving the lobby, installing retail shops, and renewing such features as the Palm Court's stained-glass dome (see photo). Like any grand dame, the Empress still has quirks — there's no air conditioning, and the sub-basement floods at high tide — but it reigns over Victoria's newer hotels, and has become a tourist attraction in its own right. Check out its free tours and museum in the basement, and mark your calendar: the 2008 centennial should be quite the party.

Vintage Crystal

Once the Empress opened, the hotel needed a recreation centre. The CPR once again hired Francis Rattenbury — though his partner Percy James did all the work — to design the **Crystal Garden** at 713 Douglas Street. When it opened on June 26, 1925, it boasted the largest indoor saltwater swimming pool in the British Empire. On August 4 of that year, Johnny Weissmuller — later the star of *Tarzan* movies — broke the 100-yard world record in the pool with a time of 51.4 seconds. The building also featured dance floors, an art gallery exhibiting works by Titian and Gainsborough, and a palm-lined terrace where many Victorians took tea. (Not all were welcome, however; "No Orientals" signs were posted at the pool.) The Garden's glamour waned in the '50s: the huge glass roof leaked, salt corroded the pipes, and the weight at the deep end of the 232,000-gallon pool caused the building to settle off-kilter. In 1964, the City of Victoria took over operations, but the problems continued, and a chlorine gas leak that sent dozens of school kids to hospital in 1967 convinced the city to build a new facility (Crystal Pool) instead of renovating the original. After years of neglect, the Crystal Garden reopened in 1980 as a tropical conservatory and aviary. In 2006, it was taken over by The BC Experience, a $10-million tourist attraction that closed after 12 weeks and declared bankruptcy. Today, the Gardens is a wing of the Victoria Conference Centre across the street.

offbeat museums

Saanich Historical Artifacts Society

Beside the Pat Bay Highway is this tribute to the Saanich peninsula's rustic past, started by a collector of old farming equipment. The volunteer-run society has several relocated buildings from the area, including an 1860 iron house prefabricated in England, a 1913 schoolhouse, and an authentic smithy and sawmill. The property doubles as a working oat farm.
7321 Lochside Dr., 652-5522, shas.ca

Victoria Police Museum

Located in Victoria's police station, this tiny museum has a collection from the oldest Canadian force west of the Great Lakes, founded in 1858. Along with batons, handcuffs, parking meters, and uniforms, you'll find century-old books of criminal charges and mug shots. The museum also sells toy cars and Victoria Police caps and T-shirts — smart duds to be wearing if you're pulled over for a speeding ticket.
850 Caledonia Ave., 995-7654

COLLECTORS' ITEMS

The **Royal British Columbia Museum** isn't exactly unknown; one of the best museums in Canada, it has attracted some 30 million visitors since the current exhibit building opened in 1968. Several years ago its collection was estimated to be worth more than $50 million, although many of the artifacts are irreplaceable. Notable items include:

• An antique Spanish dagger, purportedly used to kill Captain Cook in Hawaii in 1779.

• A bonnet owned by Queen Victoria. The museum's extensive clothing collection also has a gold rush prospector's moose-hide shirt, and a top hat worn by explorer Simon Fraser.

• A 1968 Rolls Royce owned by John Lennon, and decorated with psychedelic artwork. It's so big that it can only be displayed in the lobby, usually in the wintertime when there are fewer crowds.

• Specimens of 230,000 plants from across the province, some dating back to the 19th century. Many are so rare and unusual that they're loaned around the world for study.

- Thirteen (and counting) specimens of Humboldt squid, a species usually found off the Pacific coast of Mexico but now turning up as far north as Alaska, providing further evidence of climate change.

- Eight thousand stuffed shrews, gathered for a study of subspecies on different parts of the Queen Charlotte Islands.

- Fifty-seven specimens of woolly mammoths, many of them found by the museum's archeologists in gravel beds on the Saanich peninsula. The oft-photographed mammoth in the natural history section is a foam model covered with musk-ox hair.

675 Belleville St., 356-7226,
royalbcmuseum.bc.ca

Photo: Courtesy of the Royal BC Museum

Victoria's earliest Chinese immigrants arrived on boats from San Francisco in 1858. Many continued on to the Fraser River gold fields, but some stayed and built Canada's first **Chinatown**, which remains Victoria's most intriguing neighbourhood to this day.

The Gate of Harmonious Interest

Freestanding gateways known as *paifang* were originally symbolic entrances to temples or palaces, and later were built to honour visiting dignitaries and decorate scenic places. The first permanent *paifang* in Canada was erected on Fisgard Street in 1981, and visited by Queen Elizabeth II in 1983. The gate is topped by a symbolic bottle-gourd, a charm to protect against evil spirits. (But apparently not against the weather: the roof's glazed tiles started breaking off in the cold, creating a hazard for pedestrians, and in 1996 the gate was refurbished for twice its original cost, leading some to call it "The Gate of Compound Interest.") The large ideograms on the eastern side read, from right to left, "To work together / with one heart," and on the western side, "To help each other / achieve harmony." The two granite lions, donated by Victoria's sister city of Suzhou, China, weigh three tons each. The female *(yin)* has a baby between its paws, and the male *(yang)* has a ribboned ball.

Tam Kung Temple

Hidden on the top floor of the Yen Wo Society building *(1713 Government St.)* is Canada's oldest Chinese temple. Therein lies a shrine to Tam Kung, a patron saint of seafarers worshipped by the Hakka

people of southern China. The shrine was built on this site in 1876 and moved into the current building in 1911. If you visit, take an offering (oranges are popular) and coins for joss sticks to place around the temple, decorated with vibrant silk banners. You may also seek Tam Kung's advice via the ritual of *qui quan* — shake a bamboo tube of numbered sticks until one falls out, and the temple custodian will match the number to a verse guiding your future. Even if you aren't among the faithful, the temple is a trip into another time and place.

Fan Tan Alley

In the 1880s, opium was BC's third-largest export to the United States, after fur and coal. Much of it was made in small factories in the courtyards behind the practical brick buildings facing Cormorant (now Pandora) and Fisgard streets. By 1908, opium was outlawed and the courtyards filled in with more buildings, creating an alley that became home to a different vice. In 1910, there were at least eight clubs along the alley where gamblers played *fan tan*, a game

of placing bets on the number of buttons tipped out of a cup. The cops occasionally raided Chinatown, so club owners sealed both ends

Victoria's subdivisions have intriguing histories of their own.

Broadmead

One of Canada's largest residential developments, consisting of some 4,500 housing units on 280 hectares (692 acres), Broadmead was cobbled together on various Saanich properties once owned by R.J. Rithet, a merchant who prospered during the Klondike gold rush and used his wealth to build steamship wharves at Shoal Point and to breed horses. ("Broadmead" was his favourite racing horse.) The development got underway in 1965, but didn't boom until 1970, when the Guinness brewing empire started bankrolling construction, and was completed in the early 1990s.

Fairfield

"Fairfield" was the name of civil engineer Joseph William Trutch's manor house, appropriately at 601 Trutch Street. Fairfield the neighbourhood took off after 1912, when engineers drained the swamp just east of today's Cook Street Village. Hundreds of houses (including Arts and Crafts numbers like the one in the photo above) were quickly built on and around it to satisfy the demands of Victoria's emerging middle class.

Harris Green

Named for Thomas Harris, Victoria's first butcher and mayor, Harris Green is the long grassy strip that parallels Pandora Avenue from Chambers to Quadra. Established in 1920, Harris Green was originally designed to be reminiscent of European boulevards, but the only formal mention of it is on a small memorial stone at the corner of Pandora and Cook, and in the name of the plaza anchored by London Drugs.

of the alley with doors, and posted watchmen to check visitors. You can still see a watchman's peephole (see photo on page 20) in a wall near Fisgard, and signs for the clubs on brick columns and doorway transoms. Tourism promoters say Fan Tan Alley is the narrowest commercial street in North America.

Chinese Public School

In 1907, the Victoria school board caved in to the demands of racist parents, and passed a law stating that Chinese kids couldn't attend public school until they understood English well enough to take orders. So the Chinese Consolidated Benevolent Association raised money and built a school of its own at 636 Fisgard Street. The school was designed by David Frame (he also did the machinery building occupied by Chintz and Company), who mimicked elements of Oriental style, visible in the roof's upturned eaves and corners. The second floor is occupied by the Palace of Sages, a shrine to Confucius, the Queen of Heaven, and to the gods of wealth, medicine, and the military. Tread carefully to see it: the school welcomes anyone interested in taking courses on Chinese culture, but it's not open to tourists.

Hidden Floors

A feature of many Chinatown buildings is a "cheater storey," an extra level built into a high-ceilinged ground floor. These date from the days of simpler taxation, when assessments were based on the height of a building and not square footage, so an owner could create an extra storey and keep the income it generated. An example is the Loo Tai Cho building *(549-555 Fisgard St.)*, which only had three floors and arched entrances when it was built. The owners later squared out the entryways and installed a cheater storey, now home to a busy social club.

Street Characters

Chinatown's street signs are bilingual, but they're not exact translations: Herald Street is rendered in Chinese as "announcing good news" and Government is "wealthy Canadian families." More Chinese words are at your feet: the sidewalks on Government are inlaid with red bricks forming *shou*, the character for "longevity," and Fisgard's sidewalks have the character for "centre," because China called itself the Central Kingdom.

Gardening Tips

Saturdays in July and August are fireworks nights at **Butchart Gardens** (see next page), and the show is more spectacular than you'll see anywhere on Canada Day. Dress warmly, arrive early, get a picnic basket from the dining room (book ahead at 652-8222) or sneak in your own and feast on the lawn beside the Italian Garden. Stick around after the fireworks to smell the 250 varieties in the rose garden, free of the daytime crowds.

Spring Ridge / Fernwood

Spring Ridge, the original name of the Fernwood region, was Victoria's first principal source of water. The water was transported in barrels, and later piped downtown in hollowed-out logs, from two springs located near Pembroke Street and Spring Road. Governor James Douglas declared the springs public property, but in 1861 the Hudson's Bay Company sold them to water barons — including George Carey, the colony's first attorney-general — who fenced them off and posted armed guards. Riots ensued, and Carey resigned. (He returned to England and died, insane, five years later at the age of 34.) In 1875, the city started piping water from Elk Lake, and Spring Ridge became known as "Fernwood," the name of a 15-room stone manor built by surveyor Benjamin William Pearse at Begbie and Vining, and bulldozed in 1969. But the ridge springs eternal: recently a public well was reopened behind the Fernwood Community Centre.

The Uplands

In 1907, three Winnipeg businessmen purchased 465 acres of farmland near Cadboro Bay, and hired John Charles Olmstead to turn it into Victoria's most exclusive neighbourhood. (His stepdad, Fredrick Law Olmstead, designed Vancouver's Stanley Park and New York's Central Park.) The Uplands became Olmstead's self-acclaimed masterpiece, consisting of radiating boulevards following the land's contours, lined with cast-iron lampposts, specifically placed trees, and stately homes – no one could build unless their house was worth more than $5,000. University of Victoria geographer Larry McCann says Olmstead's design influenced suburbs across North America, and changed the rest of Oak Bay, too. Originally, Oak Bay was a mix of farms, estates, and working-class residences, but in the 1930s, it aped the Uplands and became one of the first municipalities anywhere to enact bylaws requiring a minimum square footage for houses – a rule created to keep out the shacks of Hindu and Chinese market gardeners, then common in Victoria and Saanich.

Blooming Benvenuto

Anyone who has wrestled with a sack of manure can understand the perennial appeal of **Butchart Gardens** – it's the ultimate green thumb fantasy of what one could do with 22 hectares (54 acres), a million bedding plants, and 250 full-time employees. Canada's largest private garden, and BC's biggest tourist attraction, first sprouted in 1904. Robert Butchart, a cement manufacturer from Ontario, bought the area for its limestone deposits, and once he'd quarried most of it, his wife Jeanette started developing gardens using soil from nearby farmland. Trained as a chemist, she didn't know much about plants, but she hired respected designer Isaboru Kishida to develop the Japanese Gardens, and W.J. Westby to create the famous Sunken Garden (see photo) in the quarry's largest crater. (You can still see one of the cement works' huge chimneys poking up from the far side of the trees.) As the gardens grew, the Butcharts got architect Samuel Maclure to expand their house, named it "Benvenuto" ("Welcome" in Italian) and offered tea to all visitors, serving 18,000 in 1915. The Butcharts travelled the world to collect unusual plants, but as the gardens became more elaborate, they started running huge deficits, and in 1939 the Butcharts actually offered to sell the attraction to neighbouring municipalities for a dollar. (The governments declined, so the Butcharts started charging a 25-cent admission.) The Butcharts died not long after that, and their ashes were scattered on the property in 1950. The business has stayed in the family: today, the Butcharts' great-great-grandchildren run the gardens, which are now illuminated at night and pesticide-free. More than 50 million people have visited, including Indira Gandhi, King George VI, and newlyweds Bill and Hillary Clinton – and a million more come every year. *800 Benvenuto Rd., 652-4422, butchartgardens.com*

Canadian Forces Base (CFB) Esquimalt

Victoria seems like a peaceful place, but the truth is that a part of the city's always been getting ready for war. As early as 1848, Royal Navy warships started anchoring in Esquimalt Harbour. After the British attacked Russia's Pacific coast in 1854 during the Crimean War, they built three hospital huts on Esquimalt's shores to treat possible wounded soldiers. The British increased their military presence in 1858 when Americans flooded into Victoria on their way to the Fraser River gold rush, and reinforced it a year later when US troops landed on San Juan Island. (British and American troops faced each other for 12 years on the disputed island – after an American shot a stray Hudson's Bay Company pig – until the San Juans were awarded to the States.) In 1865, the Royal Navy officially made Esquimalt the headquarters of their Pacific Squadron. The harbour bristled with their ships until 1910, when they turned the base over to the new Royal Canadian Navy.

Today, Esquimalt is the operations centre for Maritime Forces Pacific, Canada's $4.5-billion west coast fleet consisting of five frigates, one destroyer, a second-hand British submarine, numerous smaller vessels, and a squad of worn-out Sea King helicopters. (Built in the 1960s for anti-sub warfare and search and rescue, Sea Kings need 30 hours of maintenance for every hour they spend in the air.) More than 6,400 military and civilian

Vic West

Originally called Gorge Inlet, Vic West started out colonial life as an "attractive recreational amenity" for wealthy families – the sole intact survivor being the 1861-built Point Ellice House *(2616 Pleasant St., 380-6506)*. But after the Songhees resettled in Esquimalt in 1911, the remainder of Vic West was thrown open to industrial development, and as the gravel piles grew, many of the large old estates were subdivided.

Battle Stations

Fort Rodd Hill

During the Crimean War and for decades afterward, Britain feared that Russia would attack its Pacific colonies. Britain decided Victoria needed permanent defences, and built the largest of them on a slope facing the entrance to Esquimalt Harbour. The navy started construction on Fort Rodd Hill's upper and lower batteries in 1895, fitting them with three six-inch guns on pneumatic "disappearing" carriages that could drop out of enemy sight. The guns were manned and upgraded during both World Wars, but never actually saw combat. Jets and missiles rendered coastal artillery decommissioned obsolete, and the guns were in 1956. Historical societies still use Fort Rodd Hill to re-enact battles: the bunkers, turrets, and rifle-slit walls make it the closest thing around to a real military castle.
603 Fort Rodd Hill Rd., 478-5849, pc.gc.ca/fortroddhill

employees work at the base, doing everything from explosives training and salvage diving (the Pacific Dive Team was recently in New Orleans cleaning up after Hurricane Katrina), making it the region's third-largest employer, annually pumping $400 million into Victoria's economy. The base offers free daily tours during the summer, and the rest of the year by appointment. *363-4006, navy.forces.gc.ca/marpac*

Basic Education

If you want to learn more about the history of CFB Esquimalt, visit the **Naval and Military Museum**, located in a former hospital near the Naden entrance on Admirals Road. Artifacts include Royal Navy uniforms and weapons, mockups of a sailors' mess and sleeping quarters, and a Nazi flag from the U-boat that torpedoed the HMCS *Esquimalt*, the last Canadian ship to be sunk during World War II. Open weekdays. *363-4312, navalandmilitarymuseum.org*

Incoming!

On August 29, 1996, residents of View Royal heard what sounded like a gas explosion in the vicinity of Pete's Tent and Awning at 254 Island Highway. They went to check it out, and discovered that a garage had been demolished by a **20-kilogram missile**, fired by the HMCS *Regina* during a test in nearby Esquimalt Harbour. Fortunately, the missile was only loaded with metal "chaff" to distract enemy warheads, and no one was injured – although a day care centre was only half a block away.

there is a light that never goes out

Fisgard Lighthouse

By 1858, the Fraser River gold rush was bringing merchant ships into Victoria, and the Royal Navy was increasingly using Esquimalt as a base of operations. But if ships entered the Strait of Juan de Fuca at night, they were immersed in darkness, fumbling their way along a coastline peppered with deadly rocks. Governor James Douglas wrote to the British government, demanding money for lighthouses, and the first one on Canada's west coast went up in 1860 at the mouth of Esquimalt's harbour, using local stone and a lantern and lens from England. Since the light was close to shore — though not close enough for one poor keeper, who drowned rowing back from Esquimalt's pubs — the federal government automated it in 1928. A causeway built in 1951 lets visitors amble from Fort Rodd Hill out to the lighthouse, where you'll find exhibits and great spots for a picnic. *603 Fort Rodd Hill Rd., 478-5849, pc.gc.ca/fisgardlighthouse*

Race Rocks

One of the most extraordinary environments near Victoria is this cluster of islets, a mile offshore at the narrowest point of the Strait of Juan de Fuca. Tidal currents rip past Race Rocks at speeds up to eight knots, drawing an incredible variety of creatures to feed, and creating a terrible hazard for boats. The lighthouse went into service on December 26, 1860 — three days after the British ship *Nanette* crashed on the rocks. In subsequent years there were other disasters, the worst being the nearby sinking of the steamer *Sechelt*, killing 18 people in 1911. Nor were the lighthouse's residents spared: the first keeper and his wife watched in horror as their relatives drowned while trying to land for a Christmas Day visit in 1865; the second keeper had to

Bay Street Armoury

This imposing fortress, built in 1915, is home to the 5th (BC) Field Regiment, a descendant of the gunnery unit created in 1878 that manned Victoria's defensive batteries, and the Canadian Scottish Regiment (Princess Mary's), a descendant of the Victoria Fusiliers. Lieutenant-General Sir Arthur Currie, Sidney's first schoolteacher and a legendary commander of the CScotR, led Canadian forces to victory at key battles in World War I. A cross erected by the regiment at Vimy Ridge stands on the armoury's north wall. Visitors can watch the 5th drill on Tuesday evenings *(363-3626, 5fieldband.ca)*, and the CScotR on Thursdays *(363-8753, islandnet.com/~csrmuse)*. Both units have museums in the armoury, but call ahead to see if they're open. *715 Bay St.*

Macaulay Point

To protect Victoria's harbour, in 1878 the Royal Navy built temporary gun batteries at Esquimalt's southernmost piece of land, Macaulay Point. (Guns also stood at Finlayson Point south of Beacon Hill Park, which is how nearby Battery Street got its name.) The navy began work on permanent emplacements in 1896, installing three six-inch guns on disappearing carriages. The guns were removed in 1949. Today, Macaulay Point is a public playground of bunkers and tunnels, and a great place to take the kids or walk the dog – although the Capital Regional District is considering it as a site for a sewage treatment plant. To get to the point, park at Fleming Beach at the south end of Lampson Street.

Ashton Garrison Museum

Located in an industrial area in Saanich, this military museum has the largest collection of functioning antique fighting vehicles in the country, plus guns, uniforms, Canadian Women's Army Corps memorabilia, and a large collection of "trench art" made by soldiers and prisoners of war.
724 Vanalman Ave., 363-8346 or 415-5902

dive for shellfish and gold coins from earlier shipwrecks to help feed his six children. The lighthouse is automated now, but a family still lives there, maintaining an environmental education centre for school groups and guarding the rocks' status as Canada's first marine protected area. Check out the centre's Internet site (racerocks.com), which has live webcams.

Discovery Island

The Songhees had a village on this island roughly three kilometres east of Oak Bay, which became a refuge in 1862 when smallpox swept through their principal village near town. The island's first lighthouse was built in 1886. When the keeper died in 1902, his daughter Mary Ann Croft took up the job, becoming the first female lighthouse keeper in Canada; she retired in 1932, after living on Discovery for 46 years. Today the island is uninhabited, but the northern half has been returned to the Songhees and the southern half is a marine park, popular with kayakers. The lighthouse was automated in 1997; one of its earlier cast-iron lanterns stands outside the coast guard station at Shoal Point.

Trial Island

Perched just 100 metres off Gonzales Point, this chunk of rock seems close enough to swim to from shore, but don't try it. Strong currents surround Trial Island – so named because naval vessels repaired in Esquimalt would make test runs to it and back – and it's been the site of at least one fatal shipwreck. (The tug *George McGregor* sank here in 1949, killing six.) The lighthouse was built in 1906, and is staffed today. Its original lantern stands outside the Maritime Museum. The radio antennas with the glowing red lights are operated by the coast guard and the radio station CFAX 1070.

Sheringham Point Lighthouse

Rumours have circulated that a developer is angling to buy land around this automated 19.5-metre concrete lighthouse, built in 1912 on a spectacular point 20 kilometres west of Sooke. Locals are petitioning the feds to turn the property into a park. It's currently fenced off, but you can get close enough for a look if you take the road next to the community hall in Shirley.

Towering Overhead

Several decades ago, one of Victoria's most visible landmarks was the 350,000-litre **Rockland Water Tower**, just off Laurel Lane. Built in 1909, the 40-metre tower really got noticed in 1962, when it was topped with a 7-metre neon candle flame donated by sign companies to mark the city's 100th anniversary. The light was so strong that Americans could see it on the far side of the Strait of Juan de Fuca. The neon was removed in 1990, but the tower still supplies Rockland with water at times of peak demand. Many early farms had water towers – one is the **Hamsterley Farm Jam Factory** (see photo) on Sinclair Road, next to the University of Victoria's Alumni House. The Pease family built the factory in 1910 to turn fruit into preserves – and wine, some of which turned up at the swanky Union Club during Prohibition. Vandals recently burned part of this redwood "tower of jam," which has been empty for many decades.

Other pillars are used for communication, such as the **CNCP Tower** at the corner of Langley and Fort Streets, on the site where Fort Victoria's wooden bell tower once stood. The 1978 brick structure is far larger than the original, but its purpose is similar: it signals citizens using cell-phone transmission equipment concealed inside. And there's the **Netherlands Centennial Carillon** (see photo), outside the Royal BC Museum. Donated by Dutch immigrants in 1967, the carillon holds 62 bells (the biggest is 1,500 kilograms), the largest number in any tower in Canada. Rosemary Laing, a minister of metaphysics, plays concerts on Sundays at 3 p.m. by striking her fists on a keyboard of levers that hit the fixed bells. Her repertoire is mainly classical, but she's mixed in jazz and "Stairway to Heaven" – a title she must ponder when climbing the 75 steps to the playing booth.

Secret Passages

Freud would have something to say about our fascination with dark and forbidden passageways. Channels to the subconscious? Evidence of shadowy conspiracies? Here are some of the famous ones around Victoria.

Skirt Mountain Copper Mines

Until the summer of 2006, few knew there were caves on the forested peak overlooking Langford Lake. But when the fancy Bear Mountain golf resort up top announced that it was going to bulldoze a new road down the southern slope to Highway 1, the Songhees Natives threatened to blockade the work because it would disturb a sacred water-filled cave used by their ancestors. The developers bulldozed over it anyway, and now they're mired in a standoff with the Songhees over remaining ancestoral sites in the way of the unfinished road.

There are other notable cavities on Skirt Mountain. Between 1897 and

1903, a copper-mining company expanded the limestone caves on the western slope, and dug more than 500 metres (1,800 feet) of shafts. The company gave up after learning the ore was contaminated with magnetic iron oxide, but the mine shafts remain. Several are big enough that you can walk right inside them (see photo) and still see the old drill holes in the rock. Be careful stumbling around here, though: some of the unmarked shafts also plunge straight down 20 metres (65 feet) or more.

Victorians understood that punctuality is a virtue – which is why the city has several prominent timepieces. Most visible is the massive clock at **Victoria City Hall** (see photo) *(#1 Centennial Square)*, installed in 1891 after it was sent from England to Victoria, Australia by mistake. The mechanism must be wound by hand daily to keep time, and rings a 984-kilogram bell every half-hour. Another distinctive clock is in **Athlone Court** *(2187 Oak Bay Ave.)*, adorned with characters from Charles Dickens stories (see photo below) which sits over a restaurant that was called Pickwick's when it opened in 1985. The characters used to rotate, but the English-built clock proved expensive to maintain and hasn't worked for years. Also no longer ticking is the **Time Ball** that stood above the Belmont Building *(614 Humboldt St.)*, enabling sailors to synchronize their watches. Activated by a telegraph line from the Gonzales Observatory, a large metal ball would ascend a mast on the cabin atop the Belmont, and then drop at precisely 1 p.m. The ball stopped in the 1930s and was removed – but the cabin is still there, waiting for virtue to return.

Dippy Fountains

Victoria has many natural springs – and several curious artificial ones. The ornate **three-level drinking fountain** at the south entrance of Market Square (see photo) originally stood at the corner of Hillside and Douglas, and was built in 1887 by a compassionate resident who wanted to provide water for travellers, horses, and dogs on their way into the city. Their likely destination, the Victoria Public Market, once stood on the site of the gaudy **Egyptian-themed fountain** in Centennial Square, adorned with gold-glass mosaics – in fact, some of the market's bricks are part of the surrounding paving. A more pleasing **Centennial Fountain** is the one unveiled in 1962 behind the Parliament Buildings, adorned with otters, seagulls, and other BC critters. Its spray has been known to soak visitors standing downwind, but the water shuts off if the breeze gusts above 24 km/h.

Alas, other fountains have been permanently stoppered. All that remains of three Italianate beauties in front of **Jameson Motors**, a car dealership at 754 Broughton Street from 1922 to 1966, is the tile work of one (see photo) on the wall facing the adjacent parking lot. Dried up too is a **concrete battleship** that shot water from its cannons, built about 80 years ago by a Dutch priest (and now badly eroded) near the northwest corner of St. Ann's Academy.

Chinatown Tunnels

One of Victoria's persistent urban legends is that there is a network of tunnels under Chinatown, purportedly used to smuggle opium or booze up from the harbour during Prohibition. The tunnels are pure myth, says UVic geography professor and Chinatown expert David Lai: the Chinese people of that era were mostly poor labourers who had neither time nor the heavy equipment to dig through solid rock foundations. There *were* secret passages – but above ground. Narrow, gated corridors connected the courtyards behind Fisgard Street (you can see them from Fan Tan Alley), and several Chinatown buildings had closets with hidden back doors, so an insider fleeing the police (or a racist mob) could duck through them and escape.

Castles Dunsmuir

No Victoria family saga tops that of the Dunsmuir clan. Robert Dunsmuir came from Scotland in 1851 to oversee the Hudson's Bay Company's coal operations, opened his own mines near Nanaimo, and steadily became the richest man on Vancouver Island. To show off his daughters to naval officers and show up his partners in the E&N Railway, he built **Craigdarroch Castle** *(1050 Joan Crescent, 592-5323, craigdarrochcastle.com)*, a huge fairy-tale mansion overlooking Victoria. He never got to live in it: Dunsmuir died in 1889 before the castle was finished. After an ugly legal battle involving most of the family, the mansion passed to Dunsmuir's wife Joan, and then to her five daughters. They sold it to an accountant who subdivided the surrounding land – and offered the castle in a lottery to woo buyers. The winner mortgaged it, and when his investments failed, the bank foreclosed. Craigdarroch became a military hospital after World War I, then a college, a music school, and eventually the grand tourist attraction it is today. Packed with chintz, it's not to everyone's taste – especially members of trade unions. Dunsmuir used the militia and low-wage Chinese labourers to break unions at his deadly mines (an 1888 explosion killed 77 workers), and to this day many union members refuse to set foot in his mansion.

Dunsmuir's son James felt much the same way about it. After serving as premier and inheriting all of his father's businesses, in 1908, he used the riches to build an even larger palace: **Hatley Park**, a 22-bedroom medieval fortress with Tudor additions, surrounded by 600 acres of forested waterfront west of the city. He spared no expense, recruiting pre-eminent residential architect Samuel Maclure for the design, importing exotic woods and William Morris glass for the ballrooms and offices, and building a feudal village with a dairy, stable, slaughterhouse, refrigeration plant, and conservatory for exotic fruits and orchids. But his plans to become a gentleman farmer never panned out, and he died

Empress Laundry Tunnel

Empress Hotel employees used to cart linens from the hotel's sub-basement along a tunnel under Douglas Street to a laundry and power plant on the corner at Humboldt Street (now a Budget car rental lot). Though the plant was torn down in 1968, parts of the tunnel remain. One section (see photo) runs all the way under the hotel to its parkade. The other, hidden behind a locked red door on the parkade's lower level, continues under Douglas.

brokenhearted; one of his sons was a hopeless alcoholic, and another had perished in the 1915 sinking of the *Lusitania*, so James's estate eventually went to his six daughters, who blew most of it during the Roaring '20s. They sold the castle to the Canadian military, and it became an officer training centre – and possible home for the Royal Family during World War II if the Germans invaded Britain. Today, the castle is home to Royal Roads University, the only Canadian university located in a national historic site. See *royalroads.ca* for information about summer tours.

Modernist Influence

Samuel Maclure and Francis Rattenbury get all the press, but Victoria's other seminal architect, **John Di Castri**, designed most of the interesting modernist structures in the city, including the University of Victoria's Interfaith Chapel, St. Patrick's Church *(2060 Haultain St.)*, and the lobby of the Royal BC Museum. Influenced by Frank Lloyd Wright, Di Castri used bold lines and angles to advantage: he designed the McCall Brothers funeral chapel *(1400 Vancouver St.)* so that daylight could enter through window slots and illuminate the altar without revealing mourners to the street. Arguably his most influential building is the airframe-inspired Canadian Trend home *(3516 Richmond Rd.)*, built in 1954. Di Castri deplored the mass-produced "crackerbox" houses filling Victoria after World War II and replied with this one-bedroom masterpiece that drew thousands of open-house visitors and awakened BC's forest industry to the creative possibilities for its wood.

Designing Woman

Esther Marjorie Hill, Canada's first registered female architect, did most of her pioneering work here in the Garden City. After graduating from the University of Toronto in 1920 (the chairman of the architecture department refused to attend the convocation because Hill was a woman), she moved to Alberta, and then to Victoria in 1936. She couldn't get work as an architect at first, so she earned her bread as a master weaver.

Government Retreat

Some say there's a tunnel from the Parliament Buildings, under the grounds of the Empress to the Belmont building, for the purpose of transporting "sensitive" documents. That's another myth – but a tunnel does run from the Parliament Buildings to the Douglas Building across the road at 617 Government Street. Built in the 1950s, the tunnel was a popular way for legislature employees to reach a cafeteria in the Douglas building basement without getting wet. Post-9/11 worries have closed off the tunnel, and today it's merely a conduit for pipes and wiring.

HBC Arches

Across from Bastion Square, the sidewalk along Wharf Street is lined by a brick wall that drops straight down to a parking lot. This wall was once part of the lower levels of the Hudson's Bay Company warehouse, built in 1858 and torn down in 1937. Several archways in the wall accessed chambers under Wharf Street, providing extra storage for the warehouse, but they've been sealed up. Further along Wharf at Ship Point are more concrete arches, but there were never tunnels behind these – they were added in 1984 to support the crumbling retaining wall.

Vanished Broad Street

Before the Bay Centre (formerly the Eaton Centre) was built in the late 1980s, a tunnel under Broad Street connected the Eaton's department store to an annex. The tunnel is gone (it now forms the mall's first level) and so is that part of Broad — even though its access was supposed to be preserved. To get the city's approval for the mall, the developers created the Broad Street Arcade, a passage mimicking the vanished roadway.

According to the deal, a citizen walking up Broad Street could buzz a security guard and demand to be let through to the other side, between 7 a.m. and midnight. In the 1990s, city councillors thought this passage so important that they threatened to install signs indicating the hours. But a few years ago, when the mall was struggling, the city quietly retired the agreement. A giant mosaic announcing the arcade entrance was torndown, and all that's left of the once-public space is an old street sign on the arcade wall.

After World War II, commissions to create houses for returning vets came her way. Hill designed the first purpose-built seniors' housing in Canada (Glenwarren Lodge, at *1230 Balmoral Dr.*) and prominent homes (*1905 Mayfair Dr., 2368 Queenswood Dr.*), but the best example of her work is the apartment building at 1170 Fort Street (see photo on previous page). Built in the 1950s, its clean lines, overhanging eaves, and prominent windows prove that Hill was in step with modernist thinking, back when many Victorians were still doing mock Tudor.

Uplifting Experience

New owners don't have to destroy old homes. **Nickel Brothers House Moving** (656-2237, *nickelbros.com*) lifts or moves about 300 buildings a year, propping them up on hydraulic jacks and delivering them to a waiting list of buyers. The Nickels' unique recycling business, possible because wood-frame houses hold together even in mid-air, is especially popular with Americans. The Nickels have shipped dozens of old Victoria houses across the border to the San Juan Islands.

Temporary Setback

Fans of "New Urbanism" say that houses with front doors and porches **close to the street** make for friendlier neighbourhoods. But good luck getting such designs approved in Victoria, where planners require new homes to be 25 feet from the road. Fortunately, the town's full of old examples proving the New Urbanists correct; check out cozy Lewis Street in James Bay, which city planners deemed "substandard" because its century-old houses are set back only 10 or 15 feet.

mystery properties

Janion Hotel

The most prominent undeveloped site in the city is this derelict edifice at 1612 Store Street, across from the Swans Hotel. It opened in 1891 as a 48-bedroom inn for passengers on the adjacent Esquimalt and Nanaimo Railway. Despite having two parlours, a huge skylight, and a dining room – newspaper ads assured that "only white cooks" worked in its kitchens – the hotel was a bust. The railway took it over in 1895 and turned it into offices. In 1933, the Janion became a warehouse, which it remained until it was shuttered in 1978. Currently, it's owned by an elderly widow, who'll sell only if the building is preserved. She also owns the boarded-up Northern Junk store at 1314 Wharf Street and the Morley's Soda Water factory in Waddington Alley.

Carnegie Library

Another sadly underused building is this *bibliothèque* at 794 Yates Street, built in 1904 with cash from Andrew Carnegie, the Pittsburgh steel baron who funded construction of more than 2,500 libraries around the world. The Yates library served bookworms for more than seven decades, and appeared on a 1996 postage stamp as well as in movies, but for the past couple of years the BC government has leased it and let it sit vacant. You can still appreciate its Romanesque exterior of Saturna Island sandstone, carved with whimsical details (see photo), but the art nouveau interior and stained glass are locked away from view.

Hidden Drive-Thru

One curious public thoroughfare apparently still in place runs under the Victoria Regent Hotel at 1234 Wharf Street. The alley beside Reeson Park once continued all the way around the Yates Block (home to Chandler's restaurant) to the old HBC loading docks at the water's edge. To get the city's approval to build the hotel over the roadway, the developers agreed to let any driver who buzzed at the parkade entrance continue through to the other side. You can still drive through today, although you'll merely end up in a tiny parking lot.

Masonic Temple and Odd Fellows' Hall

Secret societies have always been prominent in downtown Victoria. The grand Freemasons' lodge at 650 Fisgard Street was designed by John Teague (he also did the nearby City Hall) and opened in 1878. Its most intriguing room is the second-floor meeting hall, which has plush carpet with Masonic symbols (see photo), and a blue domed ceiling adorned with stars in the same pattern that appears over Jerusalem during the summer solstice. Teague also designed the lodge for the International Order of Odd Fellows at 1315 Douglas Street, which opened in 1879 and was the first building in Victoria to have running water, piped from the creek that ran along today's Johnson Street. Its original arched façade was later covered by a blank wall for structural reasons, but the frescoed, mahogany-throned meeting hall upstairs remains the grandest room in town outside the Parliament Buildings. Both societies are still active: there are nearly 2,000 Masons in Victoria today, and around 400 Odd Fellows.

E&N Roundhouse

Just west of the Johnson Street Bridge is the only completely intact railroad roundhouse in western Canada, built for the Esquimalt and Nanaimo Railway in 1912. Although it was designated a national historic site in 1992, for the past two decades the roundhouse has sat practically empty. Recently it was purchased by Calgary developer Ken Mariash, who's hoping to turn it into retail for the $1.2-billion Bayview condo complex (former eastern Canada premiers Mike Harris and Brian Tobin own units) that he's building next door.

Sidewalk Glass

Several downtown sidewalks (the 500-block of Johnson Street, the 700-block of Yates Street, or around the Yarrow building at 645 Fort Street) are embedded with purple glass blocks suggesting that tunnels lurk below, but they're merely extended basements. Daylight filtering through the glass blocks, installed in the early 1900s, helped illuminate the underground storage areas — many of which were filled in by owners after the city started charging tax on the spaces.

Photo: Busby Perkins + Will architects

Several gigantic projects are underway to turn former industrial land into condos and offices. The biggest is **Dockside Green**, on the west side of the Inner Harbour and north of the blue bridge: Windmill Developments and the VanCity credit union are spending $300 million over the next decade, erecting 26 buildings with state-of-the art environmental features (see photo) including on-site sewage treatment, water recycling, and heat and electricity from a waste-wood incinerator. More work is going on north of Chinatown at **Rock Bay**, cleaning up tar from a plant that turned coal into gas and heated city homes until 1952. (Rock Bay is the hidden cove fronted by the LaFarge cement works; there used to be a bridge across it, which is how Bridge Street got its name.) Developers hope to create a "design district," incorporating the 1862 gas works control station at 502 Pembroke (one of the oldest industrial buildings in BC), and the adjacent 1893 coal-burning power plant that ran the city's streetcars. If you're at Butchart Gardens, across the water you'll see **Bamberton**, a World War I-era factory that dominated the region's cement-making business until 1987. Hundreds of workers lived on the site, and its recreation hall was as large as the Empress Hotel. In the 1990s, a developer spent $30 million trying to turn Bamberton into a town of 12,000, but gave up after battling complaints about possible environmental damage and traffic on the Trans-Canada Highway. In 2005, a local Mercedes dealer bought the 592-acre waterfront property for $10 million and is hatching his own plans for a mixed-use development.

Imaginary Victoria

In 1909, a business association announced plans to construct a replica of the Parthenon atop Beacon Hill, made entirely of Douglas-fir logs. (Despite the *Colonist*'s endorsement that "such a structure would be invaluable for conventions," the plan was abandoned.) No development proposal has since matched its audacity, but that hasn't stopped boosters from trying. Here are some recent projects that never got off the drawing board:

West Victoria Freeway

In its 1965 *Overall Plan for The City of Victoria*, the regional planning board cooked up auto-erotic fantasies that would've made Henry Ford blush. The centrepiece was network of overpasses blasting through Vic West and across the harbour to James Bay, and feeding into a 250,000-square-foot department store and parkade replacing the entire block occupied by Market Square. Fortunately, heritage fans prevailed.

Skydeck Tower

In 1966, a company announced plans to build a 100-metre pillar on the site of today's Laurel Point Inn. The attraction would've had glass-sided elevators carrying tourists to an observation deck and snack bar overlooking the harbour. Opposition to altering the city's skyline killed the project.

oddball houses

Sailors' Quarters

Two distinctive homes celebrating Esquimalt's maritime heritage are located next to the West Bay Marina. One is "The Swallowed Anchor" (*464 Head St.*), a 1912 house decorated with nautical bric-a-brac – salvaged ship lights, a whaling boat's steering wheel, and fibreglass-and-styrofoam creatures including dolphins, piranhas, a mermaid, and a pirate flying the skull and crossbones from the roof – all created by "Barnacle" John Keziere, an old salt who died in 1999. The other is a gorgeous 1893 mansion at 507 Head Street, built in "Steamboat Gothic" style for Victor Jacobsen, a Finnish captain who settled here in 1880 and made a fortune on seal pelts. Jacobsen designed and carved the house's ornate wooden details himself. His wife used to pace the rooftop "widow's walk," waiting for his ships to return from the Bering Sea.

Revolutionary Design

The Dominion Observatory isn't the only structure on Saanich Mountain that rotates. Just down the slope is a dream house built in the 1960s by Barney Oldfield, a mechanical genius who worked on the observatory's dome and ran a welding shop near Prospect Lake. Constructed out of steel, the entire house can spin at two speeds plus reverse, doing a full panoramic turn once a day in low gear, and once every three minutes in high gear. The current tenants want to keep the address a secret, but at the Save-On gas station on West Saanich Road (run by Barney's nephew, Rob) you can see a photo of a streamlined "teardrop" car Oldfield built in 1938.

Property Squeeze

Thanks to an old planning loophole, Victorians have been able to plunk dwellings on odd-shaped lots — including ones so skinny they're only suitable for growing spaghetti. One slender home is a two-bedroom unit at 244 Cadillac Avenue (near the Town & Country Shopping Centre) that's only 10 feet wide and 62 feet long, built in 1994 despite complaints that it resembled an "overgrown doghouse." Ten years later, another obstinate owner wedged a house 11 feet wide — into a lot 15 feet by 135 feet — at 2245 Shakespeare Street in Fernwood (see photo). After neighbours staged a protest rally, Victoria's council tied off the loophole, and now owners can put only sheds and garages on lots less than 25 feet wide.

Philosophical Observations

Fifty years ago, one of Oak Bay's notable personalities was William Alfred Scott, "the lighthouse philosopher," so nicknamed because he built lighthouses on the coasts of Africa and China before moving to Victoria in 1946. A self-confessed crackpot, Scott ran a pawn shop,

Reid Centre

When the federal government told Victoria in 1970 that it had no cash for urban renewal, developer Sandy Reid stepped in with a $25-million scheme for a three-tower, nautical-themed hotel on the Wharf Street waterfront. Yacht owners could moor at the marina and then step into elevators whisking them to the Gangplank Mall, Mermaid Honky-Tonk Room, or Crow's Nest restaurant. The Centre died when the province froze harbour development in 1974.

Songhees Living Historic Village

In 1984, a society proposed turning the harbour's western shore into an anglo Frontierland, containing a perfect replica of Fort Victoria, a town of relocated old farmhouses and residences, and reconstructions of the vanished Dallas, Driard, and Mount Baker hotels, all for $17 million (brothels and opium dens not included). The society couldn't show us the money, however.

Civic Square

As developer Cadillac Fairview bulldozed two blocks of downtown for the controversial Eaton Centre in 1988, UVic's chancellor, several mayors, and author Peter C. Newman proposed turning the space into a huge public square instead. Despite polls showing that citizens favoured the square, the developers refused — and in an eerie twist of fate, their point man died soon afterwards in a car accident.

Mile Zero

In 1999, the city approved a plan for a huge redevelopment at the foot of Douglas Street, including a concrete observation "prow" sticking out over the Strait of Juan de Fuca, a "monument plaza," a free "unity phone" connected to the other end of the Trans-Canada Highway, and (most importantly) toilets and parking for tour buses. The millennium grant for the project never came through.

Harbour Arts Centre

As an alternative to sinking money into the Royal Theatre, in 2001 arts mavens unveiled plans for a $45-million centre at Ship Point (next to the tourist info centre), containing an 1,800-seat theatre for the opera and symphony. Again, a vital grant failed to materialize, letting visitors continue to enjoy one of North America's most scenic parking lots.

addressed countless public meetings, and caused officials grief — he once billed Oak Bay the price of a lawnmower, claiming the municipality's street lights were responsible for his grass growing 24 hours a day. You can still see a big glassed-in room, reminiscent of a lighthouse keep, he built to store artifacts atop his home at 1066 Newport Avenue.

Heavy Metal

Shahn Torontow's house satisfies the building code, but it is nonconforming in every other respect. In 1996, the artist and welder constructed his 1,600-square-foot home entirely out of steel — appropriately at 3112 Steele Street, just north of Burnside — and outfitted it with steel furniture, a bathroom resembling a laboratory, and an elevator to an underground pool. Officials gave Torontow the gears, so to get around a rule against three-storey houses he sank the ground floor, and to dodge a ban on balconies he erected a freestanding tower instead. If you're into metal, Torontow has put the place on the market (www3.telus.net/victoriahouse) along with his 17-ton steel motorhome, which gets five miles per gallon.

Transportation

British Columbia wouldn't exist without extraordinary means of transportation. Monumental bridges, ships, railways, and roads have all been built here, just to overcome the landscape. Is it any wonder that Victoria is home to sailing and navigation records, a gigantic dry dock, and the site of the worst streetcar accident?

Vessels of Spirit

In the shed next to Ivan Morris's home there are half a dozen canoes – and hundreds of trophies. Morris, a Saanich elder, had the idea in the 1970s to form a canoe team – consisting mainly of members of his extended family, including his son Wayne, the former Tsartlip chief – and train them to race, as he had. They carved an 11-man canoe from a 47-foot western red cedar and named it *Geronimo*, after the family's chihuahua. "Everyone laughed," Morris recalls. "Then the team won. No one was laughing after that." The **Geronimo canoe team** captured the Coast Salish Championship seven years straight in the late 1980s, and since then the men's and women's Geronimo crews have won countless other regattas throughout the Pacific Northwest.

Traditionally, Saanich dugout canoes had a wide bow and flat stern for carrying reef nets and salmon, and were often equipped with sails woven from cattails or cedar bark. (A typical Saanich dugout rests in the lobby of the ŁAU,WELṈEW̱ Tribal School at 7449 West Saanich Road.) Long, narrow canoes were an invention of necessity: the Saanich started building them for defence against similar boats used by raiding tribes from the north. That's why they're called "war canoes" today, though the name also fits because they suffer tremendous battle scars as teams fight them around the turns on a triangular course. Their construction has changed: tall, clean logs of western red cedar are rare and expensive, so racing canoes are now built of laminated cedar strips and coated with fibreglass. Paddles were once made of solid yellow cedar, with diamond-shaped blades (hunters could keep the point in the water, preventing drips that alerted prey); today they're rounded and laminated. Wayne and his brother, Leonard Morris, have pushed the design further, making curve-shafted paddles that provide tremendous thrust – and continue to give Geronimo teams a competitive edge. If you want to see them in action, call the Tsartlip Band Council at 652-3988 for a schedule of summer races.

Considering Vancouver Island's penchant for radical politics, it's appropriate that the most distinctive – and debated – form of transportation here is the product of a labour dispute. In the spring of 1958, workers for the companies providing ferry service to the island (Canadian Pacific Steamships and the Black Ball Line) threatened to strike for higher wages. Fearing an economic disaster, then-BC premier W.A.C. Bennett invoked the Civil Defence Act and got court orders forcing the employees to stay on the job. They walked out anyway, and Bennett stunned the public by announcing that the province was starting its own ferry company. **BC Ferries** was born.

Bennett knew the other lines were unwilling to improve their aging fleets, especially for cars and trucks. His advisors suggested a terminal at the tip of the Saanich peninsula for the shortest route to the mainland so the boats could make numerous crossings a day. Local shipyards were hired to build unique "roll-on, roll-off" vehicle ferries, and the first two, MV *Sidney* and MV *Tsawwassen*, started sailing on June 15, 1960. BC Ferries quickly became a success: so much traffic shifted to its boats that Air Canada slashed its number of Victoria-Vancouver flights by two-thirds, and rival ferries struggled. (Rubbing it in, the government renamed its boats *Queens* to one-up CP's *Princesses*.) In 1970, BC Ferries enlarged seven boats by cutting them in half and adding midsections, and in 1981, it sliced five lengthwise and inserted additional vehicle decks – an incredible feat of engineering, and a faster way of increasing capacity than building from scratch. After buying up private routes on the coast (including the 507-kilometre [314-mile] run from Port Hardy to Prince

PLANNING AHEAD

If you're driving, *bcferries.com* shows how long the wait is at all terminals in the ferry system. Even if you're walking aboard, or driving at off-peak times, check the online reservation system to find out which boat you'll be taking. If you value comfort, time your trip for the *Spirit* vessels, which have decent buffet food and roomier seats. If you get one of the *Queen* boats from the 1960s, you'll face huge lineups in the cafeteria, proletarian seating, and oppressive fluorescent lights. One upside: at the stern of the top deck of the old vessels, you'll find a former dining room with comfortable chairs and tables worthy of a shag-era tavern. Make a beeline for it while everyone else is drifting around in steerage.

Rupert), BC Ferries was the largest ferry system in the world, in terms of distance covered.

But such glories may be all in the past. As of 2005, the average ship in the system was 32 years old, and prone to breakdowns. BC Ferries is spending $542 million on three new German-built vessels – when they start sailing in 2008, they'll be the largest double-ended ferries in the world – but the system will remain oriented to auto traffic. (Critics say up to 30 percent of passengers on the run between Swartz Bay on the Island and Tsawwassen, south of Vancouver, aren't in cars – so it's time for downtown-to-downtown service.) On top of that, the government privatized BC Ferries in the wake of the PacifiCat fiasco (see page 48), and now the company's selling off unprofitable routes and squeezing cash from the rest. A nearly $20 reservation is practically a necessity for anyone driving on at peak times (along with the nearly $50 for car and driver). Recently the company's added a $7 "privacy lounge" on its spacious 1990s-built *Spirit* boats – from which protesters have been forcibly ejected, arguing that the once-public ships are reviving the class distinctions of Victorian times. Welcome Aboard! Even today, BC Ferries is the embodiment of the province's ship of state.

FOR BLOWHARDS ONLY

Here are some ferry facts, to impress fellow passengers:

• One long blast of the ship's horn means the vessel's leaving its berth, or alerting others as it rounds a bend.

• One short blast: turning to starboard.

• Two short: turning to port.

• Three short: reversing.

• Four short: warning of potential collision.

• The correct pronounciation of Tsawwassen uses both *t* and *s*, so the oft-heard "Tah-wassen" and "Sah-wassen" are wrong.

• "Swartz Bay" is a mistake, too: that bit of waterfront was originally called Swart's Bay, after an American named Swart, who owned it in the 1870s; a careless cartographer used a "z" and the spelling's been stuck ever since.

• Active Pass is named after the USS *Active*, an American ship that surveyed the international boundary nearby in 1857.

Harbour Ferry Ballet

Photo: courtesy of Victoria Harbour Ferries

Imagine 20-foot, diesel-powered ballerinas pirouetting to the strains of *The Blue Danube*, and you've got the most unique ballet performance in town – the dance of the **Victoria Harbour Ferries**, gracing the waters in front of the Empress Hotel, Sunday mornings from June to September. The sturdy little 12-passenger vessels, designed and built in BC, also perform a valuable service year-round, carrying tourists and commuters to points all over the Inner Harbour. For a great jaunt, walk out to Fisherman's Wharf or West Bay Marina, and then catch a ferry back. The certified skippers include former airline pilots, navy officers, and CEOs. *708-0201, victoriaharbourferries.com*

Faulty Connection

There are high-speed passenger boats from Victoria to Seattle, and from Nanaimo to Vancouver. Why not Victoria to Vancouver? It's been tried: one company ran jetfoils between BC's two biggest cities in 1986, and another ran catamarans in the early '90s. Both failed because of poor management, and because winter seas pummelled the lightweight vessels, making passengers sick or cancelling sailings altogether.

God Save the Queens

When 10,000-ton ships have an accident, the results are hard to ignore. These are some of the worst that have befallen BC Ferries near Victoria:

August 1970:
A Russian freighter slices into the *Queen of Victoria* in Active Pass, killing three passengers. The Soviet government pays only 60 percent of the $1-million bill.

August 1979:
The *Queen of Alberni* hits a reef in Active Pass and nearly capsizes, damaging many cars and trucks and killing a race horse on board.

February 1992:

The *Queen of Saanich* smacks a catamaran operated by Royal Sealink Express in foggy Active Pass, injuring 23. An inquiry says the catamaran's excessive speed was the cause.

September 2000:

The *Spirit of Vancouver Island* runs over a yacht that turns into its path near Swartz Bay, killing the yacht's two elderly American occupants while they were on a romantic reunion voyage.

July 2003:

The *Spirit of Vancouver Island* crashes into its berth at Swartz Bay, injuring four. An investigation says the captain was going too fast.

Ferrying to America

British Columbia's government isn't the only one that got into the ferry biz after private ships were paralyzed by strikes and price increases: the same thing happened south of the border in the late 1940s. **Washington State Ferries** *(206-464-6400, wsdot.wa.gov/ferries)*, the largest ferry system in the US, connects Sidney to Anacortes, Washington, twice daily each way in summer and once in winter. Between Victoria and Port Angeles on the Olympic Peninsula, take the **MV *Coho*** *(386-2202, cohoferry.com)*, which makes the 90-minute crossing up to four times daily each way in summer, twice in winter. The *Coho* was launched in 1959 to carry its owner's fleet of trucks, but it isn't uncomfortable; the vintage bench seats let you stretch out for a nap, something you can't do on BC Ferries. Go out on deck to enjoy the roller-coaster swells in the middle of the Strait – but have your Gravol handy, just in case. The Port Angeles route is also travelled during the summer by the passenger-only **Victoria Express** *(361-9144, victoriaexpress.com)*. Between Victoria and downtown Seattle, you need the zippy passenger-only catamarans of **Victoria Clipper** *(800-888-2535, victoriaclipper.com)*. Tickets are pricy, but cheaper off-season or if you buy a month in advance. The *Clipper IV* was the fastest cat in the western hemisphere when it was fitted with 10,000-horsepower gas-turbine engines in 1996, but it's recently been replaced with cheaper-to-run diesels. Nevertheless, the Clippers can still hit top speeds of 32 knots, and reach Seattle in less than three hours. Allow 90 minutes before boarding any of these ships to clear customs.

Float Your Boat

If you want to learn how to build a ship of your own, the **Cowichan Bay Maritime Centre** offers courses by qualified boatwrights on the art of constructing wooden vessels. The facility, located on a picturesque pier (originally used by Chevron to unload oil), also houses a fine museum of local maritime history.
1761 Cowichan Bay Rd., 250-746-9989, classicboats.org

To protect the American passenger-ship business, in 1917 the US government passed the Jones-Shafroth Act, which lets foreign ships sail between American ports only if they stop at a foreign port on the way. Since nearly all cruise ships are owned outside the US, if they sail from the lower 48 to Alaska they've got to stop in Canada – and Victoria's been a major beneficiary. In 2005, more than 140 cruise ships landed at **Ogden Point**. The tourism industry's thrilled, of course, but the neighbours aren't: James Bay residents gripe that cabs and buses clog their streets, and that the ships run their diesel engines when they're tied up here instead of plugging into the local electrical grid. But don't fret, passengers: hearing locals complain is just another part of the Victoria experience. For a schedule of arrivals, see *victoriaharbour.org*.

LONG-DISTANCE *TREKKA*

In September of 1955, British-born **John Guzzwell** sailed out of Victoria in the *Trekka*, a 6.5-metre yawl he'd built in the boiler room of the downtown YMCA and in back of a fish-and-chip shop. Four years and 53,000 kilometres later, he cruised into the Inner Harbour on September 12, 1959, greeted by 3,000 cheering fans – congratulating him for circumnavigating the globe in the smallest vessel to ever do so at the time. Guzzwell sold the *Trekka* in 1964 to an American couple (who also sailed it around the world) but it's now owned by the **Maritime Museum of British Columbia** and displayed at local boat shows. *28 Bastion Sq., 382-2869, mmbc.bc.ca*

Around the World in a Canoe

On May 21, 1901, Captain John Claus Voss and young journalist Norman Luxton sailed out of Oak Bay on one of the most fantastic voyages to ever begin in Victoria. A few months earlier, Luxton had met the barrel-chested captain in a waterfront bar, and they got talking about sailing. Luxton proposed they attempt to circumnavigate the globe in the smallest vessel on record, and offered to finance the trip if he got exclusive rights to the story. Voss agreed. He procured a 38-foot Native dugout canoe, and had it fitted with a deck, a tiny cabin, water tanks, a new keel, half a ton of ballast, three masts, and sails constructed on a friend's sewing machine.

They named the boat *Tilikum*, the Chinook word for "friend," but the journey was hardly amicable: after six months enduring spoiled food and terrible storms, the two threatened to kill each other, and Luxton got off in Fiji. Voss sailed on to Australia and New Zealand, across the Indian Ocean and up to Europe, arriving in London three years later. Although he traversed three oceans and arrived with his boat unharmed (he burned through 11 other mates, one of whom was swept overboard), he hadn't crossed all the meridians necessary to technically claim that he'd sailed around the world.

After displaying the *Tilikum* at an exhibition at Earl's Court, London in 1905, Voss sold the boat. He published an account of its odyssey in 1913 as *The Venturesome Voyages of Captain Voss*, and its appendix of sailing tips, such as "how to manage a small vessel in a typhoon," has been cited by mariners ever since. (Luxton's bitter account was published by his daughter in 1971 as *Luxton's Pacific Crossing*.) Voss died in 1922; some say he drowned at sea, others claim he spent his last days driving a taxi in Tracy, California. The *Tilikum* itself sat on the banks of the Thames until the Victoria Publicity Bureau arranged to have it shipped back here in 1929. Today, it proudly resides in the Maritime Museum of BC.

WIND AT HIS BACK

Another sailing record was set in March 25, 2003 when Tony Gooch, a 63-year-old former financial planner, cruised into the marina at the Royal Victoria Yacht Club in his 13.3-metre sloop *Taonui*, escorted by a coast guard vessel and a flotilla of fellow sailors. At that moment, Gooch became the first person to make a nonstop solo voyage around the world from a west coast port, a journey that took him only 177 days.

ships of yore

A few of the important vessels that launched or landed here are commemorated with streets: *Fisgard* and *Pandora*, for example, were British warships that first surveyed Esquimalt Harbour. But others loom so large in the city's mythology that no strip of asphalt can do them justice.

SS Beaver

Photo: British Columbia Archives A-00010

In 1834, the Hudson's Bay Company decided it needed a steamship to navigate the narrow, rocky inlets of the Pacific Northwest and win control of the fur trade over the Russians and Americans. It built the *Beaver*, which arrived from England in 1836, and carried James Douglas, the colony's governor, to Clover Point when he chose the site of Fort Victoria. In the ensuing decades the venerable paddlewheeler "saved the west" for the HBC, visiting remote Aboriginal villages, surveying much of the coastline, and ferrying logs and coal – right up to 1888, when it crashed on the rocks next to Vancouver's Stanley Park. (The ship was considered so important that a bit of wood salvaged from it was turned into the legislative gavel that opened the Parliament Buildings in 1898.) The *Beaver* now rests directly under the Lions Gate Bridge, where it's used by the Underwater Archeological Society of BC to train new divers.

FAT CATS

It doesn't take battleships to bring down a government. In 1994, BC's employment and investment minister Glen Clark launched an initiative to build three **high-speed catamarans** for BC Ferries, in the hope of renewing Victoria and Vancouver shipyards with a flashy export product. Clark promised they'd cost $210 million, "right down to the toilet paper," but by 1999, when he was premier of the province and the PacifiCats started running, the bill was double that. Though well-built, the ships were ill-conceived – they couldn't carry big trucks or handle rough seas, and their huge wakes demolished Gulf Island docks – and they became floating symbols of Clark's blustering incompetence. He resigned, but the New Democratic Party he once led got creamed in the 2001 elections anyway, and two years later the vindictive Liberal government sold the ships for only $19 million, as if to remind voters how empty Clark's promises had been. The PacifiCats are tied up in North Vancouver while the owner decides what to do with them.

BC Submarines

Psst. Buddy, you need some subs? BC did in 1914. The Brits had pulled out of Esquimalt, near Victoria, the first World War looked inevitable, and a German naval squadron was in the Pacific. So premier Richard McBride bought two submarines from a Seattle shipbuilder for $575,000 a piece. McBride's agents handed over the cheque in the middle of the Strait of Juan de Fuca, and sailed the subs to Esquimalt – where they were nearly shelled by surprised troops. The new submariners trained in the Crystal Gardens pool and performed test dives and torpedo firings for crowds on the Dallas Road waterfront, but the urgency faded when the German squadron was destroyed by the British, and in 1917 the subs were ordered to Halifax. They were the Empire's first ships to pass through the Panama Canal, but were plagued with mechanical problems and fires, and several crew members deserted en route. Canadians haven't learned: recently the feds bought four as-is British subs, and they turned out to be defective too. One of them, HMCS *Victoria*, is in repairs at Esquimalt until 2007.

The Princesses

Photo: British Columbia Archives A-06272

Our elders say life was classier in their day, and the *Princess* ships were proof. In 1901, the Canadian Pacific Railway bought the largest ferry company working the BC coast, and spent millions building smaller sisters of the giant *Empress* steamers travelling to Asia. The *Princess* boats quickly became the most beloved vessels in BC. They were fast – in 1908, the *Princess Victoria* cruised from the Inner Harbour to downtown Vancouver in three hours, nine minutes – and their dining halls and lounges (see photo on previous page) rivalled those of the best hotels. (Many Victorians would spend all night carousing on the "triangle route" to Seattle and Vancouver, and return hungover the next morning.) During World War II, several *Princesses* served as troop ships in Europe. But after the war the CPR failed to upgrade the ships to handle increasing car traffic; the BC government launched its own car-friendly ferries in 1960, and the uncompetitive *Princesses* were eventually sold abroad or scrapped. All that remains of them is the **Princess Mary** restaurant *(358 Harbour Rd., 386-3456)*, incorporating the superstructure of a CP ship that worked the Gulf Islands from 1910 to 1952. That, and architect Francis Rattenbury's neoclassical 1924 steamship terminal on Belleville Street – currently occupied by a wax museum.

MV Kalakala

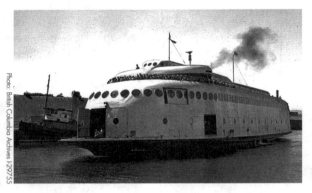

Photo: British Columbia Archives I-29755

For a few years, Victoria's waters were regularly visited by a floating Art Deco masterpiece. The motor vessel *Kalakala* ("flying bird" in Chinook) was a burned-out ferry rebuilt in 1935 with a modernist superstructure of gleaming electro-welded steel. It was the most stylish boat in Seattle: swing bands did live radio broadcasts from its ballroom, and it appeared in newsreels around the world. The *Kalakala* mainly serviced Puget Sound, but it also connected Port Angeles to Victoria from 1955 to 1959, when it was replaced by today's *Coho*. When the *Kalakala* was retired in 1967, it became a floating crab cannery in Alaska and then a rusting hulk on a beach, but fans had it towed back in 1998 and now it's anchored in Tacoma, where a foundation *(kalakala.org)* is raising money to rebuild it.

CHINESE JUNKS

In the summer of 1999, four dangerously rusted freighters appeared off the coast of British Columbia, carrying nearly 600 desperate immigrants from China's Fujian province. Most of the passengers were sent back, but the ships remained. Where are they now? Three were submerged near Port Alberni to create artificial reefs for scuba divers. The fourth, a freezer-packer named *Black Dragon*, sank near Cadboro Bay in 2003 while being towed to a scrapyard.

Photo: British Columbia Archives I-26660

GAS LIGHT

Victoria's swankiest gas station used to be the **Causeway Garage** — now Tourism Victoria's info centre on the Inner Harbour — designed by the same architects who did Vancouver's Art Deco city hall. When it opened in 1931, the garage had a Spanish tile roof and its 25-metre tower was topped by an airplane navigation beacon that beamed a 10 million-candlepower light a distance of about 95 kilometres. Eight huge floodlights illuminated the words "Imperial Oil" on all sides of the tower, but they were turned off just before World War II. The garage's lower service bays are now Milestone's restaurant.

One of the first major shipyards in North America was the Esquimalt Marine Railway Company, which started servicing Royal Navy ships in 1893 on the Esquimalt Harbour; later renamed **Yarrows Shipyards**, it boomed during World War II, when it employed up to 3,500 people building freighters to supply England. (Yarrows went out of business in the 1990s: its shipyard is now the municipal works yard next to CFB Esquimalt. The Yarrow building on Fort Street held the company's offices.) Another major firm was **Victoria Machinery Depot**, which had a shipyard just north of today's Bay Street Bridge, and took over wharves at Shoal Point to build freighters during World War II. VMD constructed 11 of the first 14 BC Ferries vessels, and in the mid-1960s built the world's largest semi-submersible oil drilling platform, a 17,000-ton, 15-storey monster that towered over James Bay until the rig was shipped off to Alaska. The Shoal Point yard closed and the wharves were demolished in 1975 – the timbers were used in Market Square – to make way for today's coast guard base. VMD's Bay Street yard closed in 1994, but many of the steel manhole covers forged there are still in use all over town.

Ship work continues today. Many yachts are built in Sidney, and the Point Hope Shipyard just north of the Johnson Street Bridge repairs smaller commercial vessels, but the heavy labour occurs at the legendary **Esquimalt Graving Dock** (see photo on previous page). When the Royal Navy started using Esquimalt's harbour, it had to sail ships to San Francisco for repairs; Vancouver Islanders felt it was so important that the Canadian government build a dry dock here that they made it one of their terms of joining confederation. The dock was completed in 1887 and decommissioned in 1927 (it's now used by the military) because an even larger one was dug into the solid rock nearby: at 361 meters long, it was the second-largest dry dock in the world at the time. The huge *Queen Elizabeth* liner secretly used this dock in 1942 – fearing sabotage, naval authorities urged residents not to mention the ship's name – to be refitted as a troop ship. Today, the dry dock is rented by various companies to repair and refit commercial vessels and cruise ships, with the help of one of the biggest cranes on the west coast, handling loads up to 150 tons. Take a peek on a tour of CFB Esquimalt, or call 363-3914 for a group visit.

Riding the E&N

Photo: British Columbia Archives NA-06158

Every story about the building of a railroad is one of power, guile, and marvel; the **Esquimalt & Nanaimo Railway** is no different. When BC joined Canada in 1871, one of its conditions was that the federal government build a railway to the west coast. Not knowing BC's geography, Prime Minister Sir John A.

air pressure expelled passengers out the broken windows. Horrified onlookers pulled out survivors ("class distinctions were forgotten," noted the *Colonist*) and lined up corpses on the shore. In total 55 people died, 12 of them children. An inquiry determined that the bridge timbers were rotten. The City of Victoria was found negligent for failing to maintain the bridge, and had to pay more than $150,000 in claims. The Point Ellice disaster remains the worst streetcar accident in North American history.

Macdonald declared the tracks would end in Esquimalt to service the Royal Navy – and then changed his mind when surveyors said it would cost $20 million to bridge the Strait of Georgia. British Columbians threatened to secede, but Macdonald calmed them down by announcing that coal baron **Robert Dunsmuir** (who'd already built railroads for his mines up-Island) would construct a railway to Esquimalt from Nanaimo. Dunsmuir's men did the job in three years, erecting several magnificent trestles and bridges across the Malahat canyons (see photo on previous page); Sir John A. himself drove the last spike on August 13, 1886, at Cliffside near Shawnigan Lake. Dunsmuir was rewarded handsomely: the railway gave his Victoria foundry full-time work, and provided a direct route for his coal to Esquimalt's warships. To thank him for helping build the nation, Macdonald granted Dunsmuir a fifth of Vancouver Island.

In 1905, the Canadian Pacific Railway bought the line from Dunsmuir's son James, and got the land too. After the 1950s, they let the E&N's passenger service deteriorate to the point that it was nearly cancelled, and most of the Island's industries switched to shipping by truck. But the line's still in use, and gas prices and carnage on the Trans-Canada Highway may give it a future; a non-profit is taking over management of the track, in the hope of renting it to more operators. (Commuter rail, anyone?) Currently VIA Rail runs a one-car day-liner called the Malahat on the route, between Victoria and Courtenay. It leaves Victoria from the eastern end of the Johnson Street Bridge in the morning and returns in the evening, so you can stop in downtown Duncan or Nanaimo, spend a few hours, and catch the train back in the afternoon – on a line as spectacular today as when it was finished. Go to *viarail.ca* or call 1-888-842-7245 for reservations.

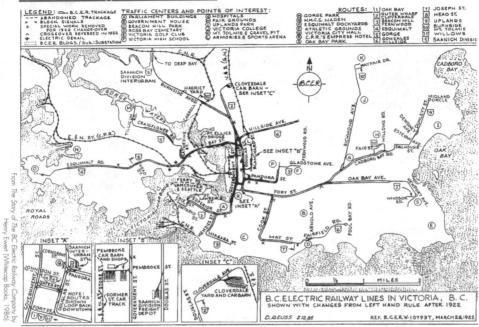

From *The Story of The BC Electric Railway Company* by Henry Ewert (Whitecap Books, 1986).

B.C. ELECTRIC RAILWAY LINES IN VICTORIA, B.C.
SHOWN WITH CHANGES FROM LEFT HAND RULE AFTER 1922

D. REUSS 2.12.85

REF. B.C.E.R.W-10793T, MARCH 28,1922

"Victoria has a genius for inertia," a local developer famously once said, and there's no greater evidence of it than the city's fuddling over **rail-based transit**. Since 1986, countless meetings, consultants' reports, and newspaper editorials have debated the merits of building a streetcar from Chinatown to Ogden Point. (In 1993, the province earmarked millions to improve traffic in the capital, but downtown businesses actually refused cash for a streetcar, fearing it would become a sinkhole for property taxes.) More recently, discussions focused on building light rail to downtown from the western communities. Many politicians say it's "inevitable" – although few are really doing anything to make it happen.

This sluggishness was inconceivable when the city installed streetcars 120 years ago. In September 1888, Victoria's council heard applications to establish a streetcar system; within a year the approved company was laying tracks, and on February 22, 1890, it began service. (Victoria was the third city in Canada to have streetcars, after Windsor and St. Catharines, Ontario.) By Christmas of 1891, *six* streetcar lines were running in the city, to Esquimalt, Spring Ridge (Fernwood), and Oak Bay. By 1922, rails reached every corner of the

MODEL CITIZENS

Guys love to play with their technology, regardless of its size. The **Victoria Radio Control Modelers** (members.shaw.ca/vrcms) fly airplanes many mornings of the year in a field on the Lochside Regional Trail, just north of Martindale Road. The field is reportedly the first zoned aerodrome for model aircraft in Canada. The **Victoria Model Shipbuilding Society** (members.shaw.ca/vmss) meets Sunday mornings at Harrison Pond — purpose-built for model sailboats in 1953 at the waterfront end of Government Street, thanks to former mayor Claude Harrison. On certain days of the summer, the **Vancouver Island Model Engineers** *(pacificcoast.net/ ~trainman)* let the public ride on their large-scale trains. The three-and-a-half-horsepower engines haul 29 passengers along an impressive seven-and-a-half-inch-gauge track (with a bridge!) that winds around the **Saanich Historical Artifacts Society** *(7321 Lochside Dr., horizon.bc.ca/~shas)*. **Finbar's Forest R.R.** is a front-yard model railroad at 2609 Cadboro Bay Road in Oak Bay that delights kids, weekends from April to Halloween. If you want to erect a set of your own, contact the **Vancouver Island Garden Railroad Club** *(vigardenrailway.com)*, or look for the model railway show in town every September.

region (see map on previous page), bearing BC Electric streetcars, the Victoria & Sidney railway, and Canadian National's noisy "Galloping Goose" to Sooke.

So what went wrong? Railways took a beating competing with each other and "jitneys" (unlicensed taxis) and buses working their routes. Plus, the Depression and World War II kept investment money away. In 1945, BC Electric reported that it would have to switch to buses to compete with automobiles and reach expanding suburbs, and two years later Victorians voted for the change. (American cities were already dismantling streetcars, partly because of lobbying from bus, tire, and gasoline companies, and we followed the trend.) On July 5, 1948, the last streetcar, draped in black, ran through town. The cars were sold off for $150. One became a diner in Langford, another a children's theatre in Saanich, and others were turned into chicken coops and outhouses.

Reminders of Victoria's streetcar era still exist. The BC Electric depot designed by Francis Rattenbury stands at 502-508 Discovery Street, occupied by Sports Traders and the Evolution nightclub. A former passenger shelter sits outside the Jubilee hospital. The old rails poke up through the grass near the Midland Road roundabout (see photo) in the Uplands. And, incredibly, one Victoria streetcar still runs — #400, which sat at the Royal BC Museum for several years — in Nelson, a BC interior town with only 10,000 citizens, but a whole lot more get-up-and-go.

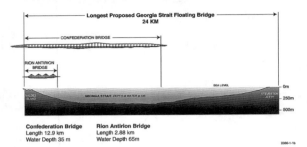

Confederation Bridge
Length 12.9 km
Water Depth 35 m

Rion Antirion Bridge
Length 2.88 km
Water Depth 65m

Every time there's ferry trouble, somebody asks, "Why isn't there a f#%*ing **bridge to Vancouver Island**?" The question was raised as early as 1873, when Prime Minister Sir John A. Macdonald pondered a crossing north of Campbell River for Canada's transcontinental railway. Since then, countless governments have come to the same conclusion he did: it would cost too much money. Most recently the subject was brought up in 2001, when the province considered its options after withdrawing the troublesome PacifiCat ferries from service. The problem is, the water between the two points is 24 kilometres across and up to 365 metres deep. That's too much for a conventional bridge: the 13-kilometre Confederation Bridge to Prince Edward Island, by comparison, sits in water only 35 metres deep – and PEI doesn't have to worry about earthquakes. The Strait of Georgia's also too deep for a tunnel, which would have to be 50 kilometres long to clear the sea floor, and would end up emerging near Abbotsford. A floating bridge is more feasible, but it would impede the 45,000 ships that use the Strait every year, and could be demolished by heavy tides and waves. Those problems might be avoided with a floating tunnel – but such a thing's never been built, and a rupture would kill everyone inside. In any case, even if a link could be constructed, the province calculated it would cost between $8 billion and $12 billion; based on projected traffic, they'd have to charge one-way tolls of $180 to

WHIRLYBIRDS

Though it's mainly used by white-collar types travelling on expense accounts, **Helijet** *(800-665-4354, helijet.com)* flies Sikorsky S76 helicopters from Ogden Point to downtown Vancouver and Vancouver International (free shuttle to the terminal) for as little at $125 one-way. If you've got real dough, consider buying a chopper of your own: Transport Canada says you can turn your lawn into a landing pad, as long as your helicopter's not for commercial use and you don't fly over built-up residential areas. Increasingly, high-flying property owners in the Gulf Islands are taking advantage of this *laissez-faire* policy, much to the annoyance of their neighbours.

$260 just to break even. But proponents argue the price would be offset by the travel time saved, and the development boom that would come from turning the Island into a Vancouver suburb. So you can count on parking-lot debate about this one for the foreseeable future – or at least until the next ferry shows up.

YOU'VE GOT AIRMAIL

North America's first regularly scheduled international airmail service started in Victoria. On October 15, 1920, an enterprising floatplane pilot began meeting the *Empress* liners from the Far East when they arrived in the Inner Harbour, and then flying the America-bound mail to Seattle. The service was so valuable to Seattle businesses that it continued until 1937.

The Blue Bridge

It may not look it, but the edifice on Johnson Street has a classy pedigree: Victoria's blue **Johnson Street Bridge**, which opened in 1924, was designed by Joseph Strauss, who later created San Francisco's Golden Gate Bridge. And that's not its only interesting detail. The 780-ton concrete blocks that counterbalance the parallel spans (one for road, one for rail) are partly hollow; back when the bridge had wooden decks that absorbed rain, extra concrete was put inside the counterweights so the spans could be lifted. Why is it light blue? That particular shade looks the same as it oxidizes and "chalks" with age, so the bridge doesn't have to be repainted frequently. If you need to get a tall ship up the Gorge, call 385-5717 (24 hours a day) or use VHF marine-band channel 12 to arrange a bridge-lifting. Lifts are free during the day – but not available at rush hour – and $75 after midnight weekdays or 4 p.m. on weekends.

Why do you have to schlep all the way out to Sidney to catch a plane? Blame Adolf Hitler. In 1936, during the run-up to World War II, the Canadian government decided it needed a military airport on Vancouver Island. It bought 700 acres of north Saanich farmland, and by the time fighting started it had begun building the Patricia Bay Air Station to train pilots, navigators, gunners, and ground crews. During World War II, Pat Bay became the third-largest airport in the country, housing as many as 3,500 recruits, its skies abuzz with Hurricanes, Kittyhawks, Mosquitos (built of BC Sitka spruce), and other warplanes. More than 100 trainees died in accidents. The worst occurred in 1942, when a B-24 Liberator crashed in Sansum Narrows, killing 11.

After the war, commercial traffic took over the airport, renamed **Victoria International Airport** in 1959. The most famous planes to use its runways in the 1960s were World War II-era flying boats converted into water bombers; one slammed into Skirt Mountain near Langford while fighting a forest fire in 1967. Now YYJ deals with 650 arrivals, departures, and overflights a day, making it one of 10 busiest airports in Canada — and a challenge for air-traffic controllers, who juggle airliners, small private planes, military aircraft, and logging helicopters. (The airport is dark between midnight and 6 a.m., but pilots can activate runway lights by tuning to a particular frequency, and land with direction from Vancouver's control tower.) YYJ has just completed a spiffy five-year makeover that cost $30 million. Check *victoriaairport.com* to see if your flight's on time.

AIRFIELDS OF DREAMS

Early in the 20th century, Victoria's busiest airfield was at Deans Farm (today occupied by Lansdowne Junior Secondary School), the site of several key moments in Canadian aviation history. On September 8, 1910, inventor **William Wallace Gibson** flew his "twin plane" — it had front and back wings, and an engine with propellers facing fore and aft (see sketch above) — over the farm a distance of 25 feet, marking the first successful flight of a Canadian-built aircraft. Gibson flew 200 feet two weeks later, but totalled the plane flying into an oak tree. In 1928, BC Airways bought the

land and started flying a tri-motor plane daily to Seattle, thereby creating western Canada's first international airport (a monument to it stands in the schoolyard). Tragically, a month after the service started, the plane crashed en route to the US, killing all seven on board. Later another airfield appeared just up the hill. In 1931, an aviation club established an aerodrome on the Finnerty farm (today's University of Victoria campus), and held an acrobatic air show in 1932 for huge crowds. Enthusiasts tried to turn the field into a commercial airport after World War II, but the neighbours opposed it.

Newcomers who've paid big coin for a condo or hotel room overlooking Victoria's harbour are often surprised to discover they're sitting in the middle of a busy airport. **Floatplanes** make as many as 120 takeoffs and landings a day at the harbour, certified as the first "water aerodrome" in North America. Incredibly, no plane has ever hit a boat or building – a few have crash-landed on the water – even though there's no air-traffic control. (The flight station at Shoal Point only provides weather info.) The harbour is regulated, however: pilots must have prior permission to land from the harbourmaster *(380-8177)*, and all boats must stick to lanes designated by the traffic scheme at *victoriaharbour.org*

Harbour Air *(800-665-0212, harbour-air.com)* and **West Coast Air** *(800-347-2222, westcoastair.com)* offer numerous flights daily to downtown Vancouver; both also fly to Vancouver International, although you'll need a cab to the get to the main terminal. Harbour Air says it's the biggest seaplane airline in the world – a title also claimed by **Kenmore Air** *(800-543-9595, kenmoreair.com)*, which makes up to seven trips daily to Seattle. All fly DeHavilland Beavers and Otters, classic bush planes designed and built in Canada. DeHavilland stopped making the planes in the 1960s, but Kenmore fixes and refits them, and they're still going strong – providing quick transport, great sightseeing, and a history lesson at the same time. Work your itinerary to include a flight: travelling in a floatplane is a quintessential Pacific Northwest experience.

Photo: British Columbia Archives G-05364

In 1913, two of the best-known barnstormers around were **Alys McKey and John Bryant**, a wife-and-husband flying team from California. In August of that year, they travelled to Victoria to exhibit their skills at a festival of waterfront events, and set a few flying records. They'd already set one on their tour: on July 31 at Vancouver's Lulu Island, McKey became the first woman to fly a plane in Canada. She flew again in Victoria on August 5, but had to land prematurely because the ocean winds kept thumping her plane. The following day her husband attached a float to the undercarriage and attempted the same flight. He piloted the aircraft over downtown — becoming the first person to fly over a Canadian city — and landed in the Inner Harbour, to the cheers of thousands.

A few hours later, Bryant took off from the harbour and circled back over downtown. He'd only been in the air a few minutes when the craft went into a steep dive over City Hall — and, to the crowd's horror, smashed onto the roof of a building in Chinatown. Bryant was killed instantly. Tragically, he'd set another record: he was the first person to die in a plane crash in Canada.

Alys McKey saw everything from a building nearby. Though she later did important work for US aviation plants during both world wars, she was so heartbroken by her husband's death that she never flew again.

What's in a Name?

Some of the region's important thoroughfares have unusual monikers. Here are the origins of a few of them:

Admirals Road

Originally a trail from the Craigflower farm to a mansion known as the "Admiral's House," rented to Royal Navy commanders serving at the Esquimalt base.

Burnside Road

Like Hillside or Craigflower, a road named for the farm it once serviced. The Burnside farm was owned by Matthias Rowland, the Hudson's Bay Company's well-paid hangman. In the late 1800s Rowland also ran the Burnside Hotel, a popular watering hole.

Dead Man's Curve

Photo: British Columbia Archives D09536

Canora Road

This back route to Sidney follows part of the old track line for the *Canora*, a railcar ferry that operated from 1918 to 1968. The ferry docked at Patricia Bay; railway cars then rolled off the boat and down to Victoria.

Cedar Hill Road

To help build Fort Victoria, Natives cut timber on "Cedar Hill" (now Mount Douglas) and dragged it along this path into town. After the fort was completed, up-Island tribes wanting to trade would beach their canoes at Cordova Bay and take the path to town instead of fighting the tricky waters at Ten Mile Point.

Around Victoria, nothing gets the pulse racing like a drive up the Trans-Canada Highway — especially the steep, narrow section locals call "**The Malahat**," referring to the massive ridge the road traverses between Shawnigan Lake and the Saanich Inlet. More than 24,000 vehicles blast along the Malahat daily, and every year there are several dozen serious accidents — often shutting down the entire highway, and effectively sealing off Victoria from the rest of Vancouver Island. The most spectacular occurred in July 2000 when a drunk driver fatally rolled his truck full of propane, closing the road for 19 hours and forcing nearby residents to evacuate.

The highway was first surveyed in 1903 by J.F. Lenox MacFarlane, a retired artillery officer who was ticked off after he'd spent three days on an old wagon track getting from Victoria to a farm he'd bought at Mill Bay. MacFarlane bullied politicians into building his road, and was the first to drive its snaking, muddy route when it opened in 1911. The road's been straightened and widened since then (especially before 1962, when the Trans-Canada Highway was completed), but not much more can be done because it passes through the sensitive lands of Goldstream Provincial Park. In 1990, the BC government approved a plan for a bypass near Sooke Lake, but shelved it because of potential damage to Victoria's water supply. Since then, all sorts of solutions have been bandied about — drilling a tunnel, double-decking the lanes, constructing a toll bridge to the Saanich Peninsula — but no one wants to pay for them or encourage more car traffic, so the wrecks and delays continue. For current info, check road reports on the Ministry of Transportation website (drivebc.ca), which also has a webcam so you can see whether the Malahat's backed up.

Sidewalk Scrabble

Dead ends, one-ways, streets that change names three times in as many blocks — it's always been difficult to find your way around Victoria. This was even truer a century ago, when it was popular for hooligans to steal street-name signs from utility poles. In 1907, the city solved the problem by spelling the names in **ceramic tiles**, and embedding them in concrete sidewalks. You can still see the earthenware tiles (made by a long-defunct company in Zanesville, Ohio) at corners in James Bay, Fairfield, and Oak Bay. But theft and vandalism have continued, and public works departments have nearly run out of the antique tiles. They've tried knockoffs by various companies and local potters, but none have weathered well. If you're a master of ceramics, come forward! This is a chance to cement your place in history.

Alley Cats

One of the most European aspects of downtown Victoria is its narrow, car-free alleys. Several have vanished (Theatre Alley, Poodle Dog Alley) but others remain — and many of them were initiated by developers. One is **Waddington Alley**, created by a grocer who cut a lane through his property from Yates to Johnson in 1858 to provide more frontage for new businesses, including dance halls and gambling houses. Much quieter today, this byway is the only place where you can see the Douglas-fir paving blocks that once covered many Victoria streets. **Trounce Alley** was the result of a dispute: in 1858, surveyors suggested that View Street would be open between Government and Broad, but the colonial administration sold the right-of-way, enraging owners who'd counted on the frontage, and one of them replied by opening his own alley through the block. In 1910, a fire destroyed all the surrounding buildings and View Street was put through as originally promised, but the alley survived. It is still privately owned today, and gated and locked up every evening.

Foul Bay Road

Despite its name, this street dividing Oak Bay and Victoria is quite pleasant. But where's the bay? Gonzales Bay, at the road's end, used to be called Foul Bay, perhaps because ships fouled their sails in its calm waters. (Another story says it was called Fowl Bay because thousands of geese and ducks congregated there.) In 1934, the city changed the bay's name because residents complained that "Foul Bay" lowered property values. In 1962, municipalities considered renaming Foul Bay Road as University Way to acknowledge the UVic campus at the other end, but a new generation of residents threatened a nude Godiva ride in protest, so the original name remains.

Interurban Road

Named for BC Electric's Interurban streetcar line, which ran along this straight stretch of Saanich between downtown Victoria and Deep Cove.

Motorcycle City

If life is a highway, it's best travelled on two wheels — a sentiment that seems to be shared by many in Victoria. Given the low levels of rain and the cheaper ferry price, travelling by motorcycle may be the most logical choice of Island transportation. Certainly that's the view held by *Canadian Biker*, the national motorcycling monthly, which is based in the Garden City and hosts such events as the Ride for Sight and the Christmas Toy Run, both of which get more than 1,000 riders annually. Publisher Len "Layback" Creed started the mag with lottery winnings over 25 years ago, and he's been riding tall in the saddle ever since. (You can find him at *735 Market St., 384-0333, canadianbiker.com*)

Need servicing? For Japanese bikes, seek out **SG Power** *(730 Hillside Ave., 382-8291, sgpower.com)*, or **Adrenalin Motorcycle Co-op** *(6-721 Pembroke St., 480-7874, adrenalinmotorcycle.com)*: a $100 Adrenalin membership gets you discounts on certified repairs, access to do-it-yourself garage space, and a club room for socializing. For Harleys it's **Steve Drane Harley-Davidson** *(735 Cloverdale Ave., 475-1345, stevedraneharley.com)*, the Island's centre for all things "hog." Don't own but still want to ride? **Cycle BC Rentals** *(747 Douglas St. and 950 Wharf St., 380-2453, cyclebc.ca)* has a variety of cruising and touring bikes, and scooters for the kids. Once you've got your machine, the best rides in the city include the scenic Dallas Road/Beach Drive route, the scream along Old West Saanich Road to East Sooke Park, the Malahat (watch for speed traps), and the Pat Bay highway straightaway.

The Name Game

Where do **street names** come from? When a new subdivision is created, its roads are labelled by its developers and their appellations are often as thrilling as their architecture. A.H. Phelps built a corner of Langford (around Phelps Road, of course) in the 1960s and named streets after his friends and family, giving us such exquisite cul-de-sacs as Trudie Terrace and Coralee Place. The wise men who created Broadmead in the '70s thought the suffix -wood was stylish, so their roads comprehend such paradoxes as Boulderwood Drive and Pondwood Lane. To deter such clunkers, municipalities maintain lists of potential street names (of pioneer families, etc.) that don't need the time-consuming approval of their planning departments.

Old Esquimalt Road

BC's very first road, cut and paved by sailors in 1853 because several of their compatriots had died navigating between Fort Victoria and the Esquimalt naval station in small boats.

Tillicum Road

This street dividing Esquimalt and Saanich used to be a property line separating two estates. The neighbours called to each other over the fence with the Chinook greeting *Klahowya tillicum* ("Hello, friend"), and the second word stuck.

Veyaness Road

Yet another avenue built upon a section of vanished rail line — in this case a Central Saanich section of the "V an' S," the Victoria and Sidney Railway.

Why do locals call Highway 17 the **Pat Bay** highway if it ends at the Swartz Bay ferry terminal? That's because the highway was destined for the Patricia Bay airport (today's Victoria International) when the road was first surveyed in 1948; the stretch to Swartz Bay wasn't finished until the ferry terminal opened in 1960. The highway was rammed through the Tsawout reserve without compensation to the Natives, so in 1975 they started allowing **billboards** on their land facing the road. The signs have been used for birthday greetings and marriage proposals, but the statements that really get attention are often political, like the anti-consumerist Christmas message (see photo) a couple of activists posted in 2002. Got a beef? Rates are $1,050 per month for a south-facing sign and $1,250 for one facing north, hitting the tourists headed into town.

Terminal Traffic

Victoria's a small town, but expect big-city fares if you cab it to the airport – it can be $40 or more from downtown. That's why locals love YYJ's long-term parking, $12 per day for the first four and $4 a day after that. If you do take a taxi, you may notice only Yellow cabs waiting at the airport. Yellow has an exclusive deal for the taxi stands, although other companies can drop off passengers. Another option is the Akal Airporter *(386-2525, victoriaairportshuttle.com)*, $15 per person to and from downtown hotels. Yellow also commands the Swartz Bay ferry terminal; for a cheaper alternative, try the #70 city bus.

WHAT PARKING PROBLEM?

Contrary to popular local belief, downtown Victoria is a **parking oasis**. According to a 2005 Colliers survey, parking here costs about $10 per day, less than the national average (it's $17 in Ottawa). In 2004, the city issued 200,000 parking tickets – 50,000 fewer than it handed out five years earlier. On top of that, parkades are free on Sundays, and many of the city's 1,900 meters take smart cards, sold at City Hall; if you use a meter for less than 90 minutes, you insert the card and get a refund for the unused time. So c'mon downtown. Sure, parking's free at the mall – but a special circle of Hell is reserved for those who pave farmland, and you really don't want to associate with such people.

Make It a Double

In 2000, Victoria's transit system became the first in North America in more than 30 years to put **double-decker buses** into service. Today, it runs 36 of the British-built machines, worth more than $700,000 apiece. But they aren't just for show. Londoners created double-deckers so they could increase a bus's passenger capacity while keeping its wheelbase short enough to navigate winding streets, and some of Victoria's are just as intricate. (Perhaps too intricate: Victoria's doubles take a beating from overhead foliage, and they have to stop away from downtown curbs to avoid bashing heritage lampposts.) Look for them on long-distance routes, especially #14, 50, 61, and 70. If you're keen on sightseeing, **Gray Line of Victoria** (grayline.ca, 388-6539) uses British double-deckers from the 1960s — with authentic diesel fumes — on tours departing in front of the Empress. .

Here Come Da Bus

Victoria Public Transit reaches all corners of the capital region, from Swartz Bay to Sooke. (You only need buses #70 and 61 to do that trip, but it takes nearly three hours.) Many buses have bicycle racks, and can hydraulically "kneel" to the curb to allow wheelchairs to roll aboard; look for "access" on the web schedules (busonline.ca, 382-6161). To get to Vancouver, board **Pacific Coach Lines** (pacificcoach.com, 800-661-1725), which times buses to get on every ferry, without the waits or reservation fees suffered by car drivers. PCL buses leave from the station at 700 Douglas Street, behind the Empress. That's also where you can catch a bus to Duncan, Nanaimo, and towns further north with **Island Coach Lines** (385-4411). To get to points west of Sooke, including Port Renfrew, use **West Coast Trail Express** (trailbus.com, 477-8700).

MECHANIC TO THE STARS

The ultra-rich owners of Mercedes-Benz 300SL gullwings and roadsters — built from 1954 to 1963, and worth an average of $250,000 — ship them from places as far off as Venezuela and Thailand to the secluded Saanich workshop of **Rudi Koniczek**, the world's best restorer of such vintage vehicles. Koniczek's clients tend to keep a low profile, but occasionally well-known personalities seek his services: Seattle glass artist Dale Chihuly has two such Mercedes. Recently, Koniczeck restored the 1960 roadster that Pierre Trudeau famously raced off Ottawa's Parliament Hill, leaving reporters in the dust; Trudeau's son Justin got the car fixed so he could drive it at his wedding.

The Unbearable Rightness of Cycling

Non-motorized transport is a big deal in Victoria. Thanks to the city's fair weather, up to 10 percent of all trips around town are made by bicycle – a stat that's led local politicians to brand Victoria as "Canada's Cycling Capital." Whether the title is warranted or not, there's no doubt that Victorians are seriously into pedal power.

More and more public facilities are built for Victoria cyclists every year, and much of the credit goes to the **Greater Victoria Cycling Coalition**, a growing (819 members at last count) and influential lobby group. Aside from needling politicians, the GVCC also organizes social rides and seminars on legal rights and traffic planning issues. To join, visit their resource centre at #12 Centennial Square *(480-5155, gvcc.bc.ca)*.

Traffic Tune-Up

Already Victorians make more than six percent of their trips to work by bicycle (it's only two in Vancouver), but the number spikes to 15 when local businesses rally their employees during summer's **Bike to Work Week**. The organizers give free one-day courses on bicycle commuting *(920-5775, biketoworkvictoria.ca)*. You can also learn the fundamentals – be visible, signal, make eye contact with drivers (hey, why isn't one-way auto glass illegal?) – from Allan Dunlop's year-round Can-Bike courses for kids and adults *(721-2800, cyclingsolutions.ca)*.

RULES OF THE ROAD

According to BC's *Motor Vehicle Act*, a cyclist has "the same rights and duties" as a driver. That means cyclists are entitled to use the streets, and just as subject to their regulations. Head to *bikesense.bc.ca* and bone up. As of this writing, fines for moving violations (riding on the sidewalk, etc.) are $86; it's $29 for not wearing a helmet (not applicable to pedicabs) plus insurers will automatically cut 25 percent off any award you might get for a head injury. Respect signs and signals, too: In 2005, a Victoria judge ordered a cyclist to pay $130,000 for knocking down a pedestrian in a crosswalk and breaking her collarbone. Ignorance is no excuse – and it's expensive.

THE OTHER NATIONAL DREAM

If you want a serious two-wheeled journey, Victoria is a starting point on the 18,000-kilometre **Trans-Canada Trail** — the world's longest recreational path, due to be "substantially complete" by 2010. The official TCT route starts from Mile Zero, follows the Galloping Goose until Langford, and then suicidally continues up Highway 1, but plans are afoot to use paths through the Sooke Hills. (In the meantime, take the safer alternative along the Lochside Trail, across Central Saanich to the Mill Bay ferry, and then up Shawnigan Lake-Mill Bay Road.) Just north of Shawnigan Lake, you'll come upon the spectacular Kinsol Trestle: at 187 metres long and 40 metres tall, it was reputedly the largest wooden structure in the British Empire when it was built in 1921. Motorheads torched it a few years ago, so you'll have to detour to carry on to Nanaimo — but if you're on the TCT, you shouldn't be in a rush anyway. For more info, see *tctrail.ca*.

Trailing Wheels

The most important car-free route in Victoria for getting around is a regional trail network built atop a former railbed owned by Canadian National Railway. The 55-kilometre section from downtown west to Sooke is known as "**The Galloping Goose**," the name of a clattering gas-engine bus (on train wheels) that chugged the tracks from 1922 to 1931. The 29-kilometre **Lochside Trail** from downtown to Swartz Bay follows rails that mostly shipped freight. Highlights on the Goose include swimming at Thetis or Matheson lakes, or a visit to Royal Roads University or Fort Rodd Hill; on Lochside, try tea at Matticks' Farm or watch the radio-controlled airplanes near Martindale Road. Most impressive are two old bridges en route that were rebuilt for cyclists: the Selkirk Trestle that dates back to 1920 and reopened in 1996 with a counterweighted drawbridge; and the Blenkinsop Trestle, dynamited by a logger in 1954 so he could land his floatplane on Blenkinsop Lake (!), and reconstructed in 2000. The trails are popular with pedestrians and rollerbladers too, so get a bell for your bike. For more info, see *crd.bc.ca/parks*.

Two-Wheel Touring

Surveys say that cycling equals golf as visitors' most-preferred activity on Vancouver Island. But where to go? The website *cyclevancouverisland.ca* provides numerous links to tours (e.g., "Pedalling for Pinot" and other visits to local vineyards), and bicycle-friendly places to stay. Also look for the Victoria Cycling Map (which shows paths not indicated on regular road maps) for sale at most bike shops.

conveying the past

You can learn more about Victoria's transportation history at these **museums**:

British Columbia Aviation Museum
Every week, veterans of the aviation industry gather in the restoration hangar of this museum near the international airport to reassemble classic planes. Their work, displayed in the main hangar, includes a Bristol Bolingbroke MK IV training bomber that flew at Pat Bay during World War II, and a Fleet Model 2 biplane that worked the northern bush from 1930 to 1981, when it was deemed the oldest active registered aircraft in Canada. Current projects include a T-33 Silver Star jet (see photo). Also check out the memorial room, which extensively documents the airport's war years.
1910 Norseman Rd., Sidney, 655-3300, bcam.net

Maritime Museum of British Columbia
Located in a magnificent 1899 courthouse, this museum's highlights include a working steamship engine, numerous models (its HMS *Temeraire* was constructed of chicken bones by prisoners of the Napoleonic wars), a torpedo from 1900, an Enfield machine gun, a heritage courtroom renovated by Francis Rattenbury. If you draw the velvet curtain aside on the room's right-hand side, you'll see his sketches for the moulding. The ornate birdcage elevator (see photo) is the oldest functioning one of its kind on the continent. Keep an eye out for the museum's marine garage sale every spring, when it sells off artifacts, tools, lights, books, and model boats.
28 Bastion Sq., 385-4222, mmbc.bc.ca

GETTING IN GEAR

Numerous downtown shops rent bikes, but if you're a newbie and you want to get on the Galloping Goose Trail without riding through traffic, try **Selkirk Station** *(800 Tyee Rd., 383-1466, switchbridgetours.com)*, right next to the trail. If you're in the market for something exotic, go to **Fairfield Bicycle Shop** *(1275 Oscar St., 381-2453, fairfieldbicycle.com)*, which sells and services recumbents, adult tricycles, and other specialty bikes.

Horsing Around

Victoria has travelled a ways since 1886, when there were 10 livery stables downtown and, as artist Emily Carr wrote, "the smell of horse manure was so much a part of every street that it sat on your nose as comfortably as a pair of spectacles." **Horse-drawn hack (taxi) and stagecoach lines** served parts of town well after streetcars started running in 1890, and horses were the only real private transport around until cars appeared here in 1903. (Bicycles weren't practical on unpaved roads.) You can still see the effect horses had on architecture of the late 1800s: Grimm's carriage works (731-733 Johnson St.), and former Hart stables (532-539 Herald St.) have high-arched, equine-sized entrances.

The Tally-Ho carriages (on the cover of this book) started ferrying sightseers in 1903. They were heralded as a boon to tourism – until a team bolted and dumped passengers into the Inner Harbour in 1913. Tally-Ho revived during World War II because of gas shortages, and their carriages have been on the road ever since, carrying more than four million visitors. Single-horse carriages were allowed back on the roads in the 1980s. So the age of the horse continues – and when oil hits $200 a barrel, our streets might look and smell like they did in Emily Carr's day.

LOCKING UP

In 2004, Victoria was the third-worst city in Canada for bike thefts, a problem many blame on the growing use of crystal meth. (Its addicts love to tinker while they're agitated.) Fernwood and UVic are high-theft areas, as is downtown at night. If you're hoping to reconnect with a stolen steed, the Victoria Police regularly put unclaimed bikes for auction at Kilshaws.

RIDE SHARE

Cars are like dogs: you've got to keep them clean and well fed, and find a place for them to stay at night. That adds up to a lot of trouble, and expense. You can live without a dog. But can you live without a car? You don't have to make that choice, thanks to the **Victoria Car Share Co-op**. After paying a refundable entry fee of $400 you can rent one of four cars, a minivan, or pickup truck for three dollars per hour and 20 cents per kilometre plus get access to similar networks in Vancouver, Nanaimo, Courtenay, and Tofino. It's convenient and cheap, especially since you don't pay extra for maintenance or insurance. *995-0265, victoriacarshare.ca*

Kooky Kabuki

To some tourists, the finest sights in town are the tight buns of Victoria's pedicab riders. Pamela Anderson, Halle Berry, and Jennifer Love Hewitt have all hailed **Kabuki Kabs** (385-4243) on the Inner Harbour, and even at the rate of a dollar a minute, some passengers have insisted on being carried all the way out to Butchart Gardens (about $300). The largest fare was an American realtor who took an all-day tour of the city's bars and then gave his astonished rider $1,250. The strangest fare was a dead salmon, which got a ride around downtown paid for by a group of drunken fishermen.

Sports & the Outdoors

Southern Vancouver Island is home to the world's fastest cyclist, the oldest lawn tennis club in North America, basketball and triathlon superstars, and several Olympic medal winners – plus busy parks, beaches, and hiking trails. Truth is, recreation is often the hardest work Victorians ever do.

The Pioneering Patricks

Victoria is a pioneer hockey town. On Christmas Day 1911, Lester and Frank Patrick (the sons of a BC lumber baron) opened the 2,500-seat **Patrick Arena** at the corner of Epworth Street and Cadboro Bay Road, across from today's Oak Bay High School. It was the largest wooden structure ever built on Vancouver Island, and was Canada's first artificial ice surface. In the building's first game, the New Westminster Royals skunked the Victoria Senators 8-3. The arena burned down in November 1929, but while it stood the Patricks invented many features of Canada's national game still in use today: numbers on jerseys (1911), blue lines (1913), post-season playoffs (1918), and line changes on the fly (1925). In addition to coaching his hometown Cougars to a win in the finals in 1925, Lester Patrick (namesake of the NHL's Patrick Division) coached the New York Rangers to three Stanley Cups. His sons Muzz and Lynn also won the cup with the Rangers.

Victoria Wins the Stanley Cup!

Believe it or not, in 1925 the **Victoria Cougars** beat the Montreal Canadiens to win the Stanley Cup. Victoria took the series 3-1, despite the presence of such legends as Howie Morenz and Georges Vezina on the Canadiens. (Victoria's new innovation, line changes on the fly, consistently gave the Cougars fresh legs against the exhausted Montrealers.) But the glory didn't last long: the following year, Victoria coach Lester Patrick departed to lead the New York Rangers, and the Cougars franchise moved to Detroit. They played as the Detroit Cougars for four more seasons, and eventually changed their name to the Detroit Red Wings.

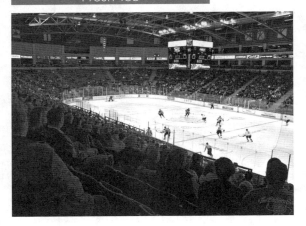

Downtown Victoria's arena, the 7,300-seat **Save-On-Foods Memorial Centre** *(1925 Blanshard St., 220-2600, saveonfoodsmemorialcentre.com)*, is a controversial new addition to the city. During its construction mysterious gas leaks twice forced the evacuation of the police station next door, and when the rink finally opened in 2005 (a year late) it was tied up in contractors' lawsuits, leaving many of its details unfinished. (Rod Stewart jokingly wore a construction helmet onstage at the building's first concert.) Nevertheless, it's open for public skating (a schedule is at *city.victoria.bc.ca*) and the games of the **Victoria Salmon Kings**, an AA semi-pro hockey team. Another new rink is the 2,300-seat **Bear Mountain Arena**, behind Colwood's Juan de Fuca Rec Centre *(1767 Island Hwy., 478-8384, jdfrecreation.com)*. It too offers public skating, and is home to a team in BC's Junior A League, the **Victoria Grizzlies**. (There aren't any grizzly bears on Vancouver Isalnd, so why the name? The team is owned by the wealthy Bear Mountain golf resort, looking for a promo tie-in.) For tickets to games, see *salmonkings.com* and *victoriagrizzlies.com*.

City of Champions

Maybe it's because our mild climate enables year-round training, or perhaps it's our propensity for clean living. Whatever the reason, the Garden City has produced many great athletes. Here is a list of some; see the Greater Victoria Sports Hall of Fame display at the downtown arena or *gvshof.ca* for more.

Norm Baker (Basketball)

He led the Victoria Dominoes to four Canadian national basketball championships, and scored 33 points in that team's 1939 victory over the Harlem Globetrotters in a game at Victoria High School. Baker was also the only non-US player selected for a "stars of the world" team in 1950.

Lori Bowden and Peter Reid (Triathlon)

This former husband-and-wife team dominated the Ironman world championships in Hawaii: Bowden won in 1999, and Reid in 1998 and 2000. Two weeks before the 2003 race they split up, but both won again that year.

Art and Chuck Chapman (Basketball)

An unusual number of Victoria's legendary athletes are siblings. These two played for Victoria's Blue Ribbons and Dominoes (five-time national champions), and took silver with Canada's 1936 Olympic team.

Dawn Coe-Jones (Golf)

The Lake Cowichan native holds the title for the most career money won by a Canadian woman on the LPGA tour.

Geoff and Russ Courtnall (Hockey)

Geoff played 18 seasons in the NHL, winning the Stanley Cup with the Edmonton Oilers in 1988. Brother Russ played for NHL teams in Toronto, Montreal, Los Angeles, and Vancouver.

Luck of the Irish

Victoria hasn't won a Stanley Cup since 1925, but it continues to clean up in Canada's "other" national sport. Victoria's Foundation Lacrosse Club first won the Mann Cup, the national prize in senior lacrosse, for the Garden City back in 1919, and since the **Victoria Shamrocks** team was created in 1950, it's won eight more, most recently in 2005. The 'Rocks play from May to August at the Bear Mountain Arena; for a game schedule and news, see *victoriashamrocks.ca* or the fan site *rockslax.com*.

Hyper Links

Victoria's snowless winters have always made it a popular place for golf. The city's first course is at the **Victoria Golf Club** *(1110 Beach Dr., 598-4321, victoriagolf.com)*. The 6,015-yard, par-70 links were laid out in 1893, making it the oldest course in the country still on its original site. Seven holes play beside the ocean, which is why some call it the "Pebble Beach of Canada." Green fees are $125, and you have to be a member of an affiliated private club. Another historic 18 is at the **Royal Colwood Golf Club** *(629 Goldstream Ave., 478-8331, royalcolwood.org)*, initiated by James Dunsmuir when he carved up his land behind Hatley Castle. Dunsmuir's pal the Prince of Wales played the 5,912-yard, par-70 course, and assented to the "royal" title. The green fees can be princely too: $125 for duffers, $60 if you're a guest of a member. The new **Bear Mountain Golf and Country Club** *(2020 Country Club Way, 391-7160, bearmountain.ca)*, on the other hand, caters mainly to the *nouveau riche*. Part of a huge development financed by NHL hockey players, the 7,212-yard, par-72 course designed by Jack Nicklaus is one of the toughest layouts on the continent. Green fees from $75 to $130 include a power cart with GPS, and valet service. The trickiest hazards to avoid on the course are realtors; based on talk that Bear Mountain is the next Whistler, the resort recently sold $130-million worth of condos in a single day.

Without a doubt, Victoria's most famous son at the moment is basketball superstar **Steve Nash**. Born in South Africa and raised here in Gordon Head, Nash led Arbutus Jr. Secondary to a British Columbia basketball championship in 1990, and carried St. Michael's University School to the provincial high-school championships in 1992. (Like many Victoria athletes, he was also a formidable all-rounder: Nash was named MVP in BC's high-school soccer championships, played superb lacrosse, and won his school's annual chess tournament.) In 1995, while studying sociology at Santa Clara University in California, the six-foot-three point guard was recruited by the Phoenix Suns, becoming the first Canadian to be chosen in the first round of the NBA draft. A consummate playmaker with a Gretzky-like ability to wait for opportunities, Nash tallied over 400 assists with the Suns in his first two seasons. By 2004-2005, he was number one in the league in assists. That season he led the Suns to the NBA championship finals, and was named the league's MVP.

Although he's now signed to a $66-million deal, Nash remains a class act. He reads Dostoyevsky, and plays pickup ball in city parks. At the 2000 Olympics, he gave every non-NBA player on Canada's team $2,500 so they could enjoy Sydney; when a popular BC youth basketball program was about to fold, Nash funded the program himself. Victoria couldn't ask for a better ambassador.

Billy Foster (Auto Racing)

In 1965, the brother of music producer David Foster became the first Canadian to race in the Indianapolis 500. (He dropped out in the 90th lap due to a broken water line.) Sadly, Foster died later in a practice-lap crash at Riverside, California in 1967.

Paul and Gary Gait (Lacrosse)

Arguably two of the greatest players ever of the game. Gary is the all-time leading scorer in the professional National Lacrosse League, and Paul is the fourth-highest. Together they led the Victoria Shamrocks to the team's 1999 win of the Mann Cup (Canada's national title), and shared the MVP award.

Rich Harden (Baseball)

The Claremont Secondary grad was drafted to pitch for the Oakland A's in 2003. An impressive right-hander, he signed a $9-million, four-year deal with the A's in 2005, and is now #2 in their pitching rotation.

Silken Laumann (Rowing)

Two single-sculls world championships, bronze in the 1984 Olympics, bronze in 1992, and silver in 1996. Perhaps best-known for her remarkable comeback following a terrible rowing accident in 1991.

Ed Murray (Football)

The English-born Mount View (now Spectrum) Secondary grad started out playing rugby and soccer, then spent 18 seasons in the NFL as a place kicker, becoming the seventh-leading scorer in league history and winning a Super Bowl with the Dallas Cowboys in 1994.

Lynn and Murray "Muzz" Patrick (Basketball, Hockey, Football, Boxing)

Both of these multi-talented brothers won national basketball titles with the Victoria Blue Ribbons/Dominoes dynasty, and a Stanley Cup with the 1939-40 New York Rangers. Lynn also played football for the Winnipeg Blue Bombers, and Muzz held the Canadian amateur heavyweight boxing title.

Tennis, Anyone?

Dozens of free outdoor courts are scattered across town, and a good way to find them is through **Victoria's Virtual Tennis Club** *(vvtc.bc.ca)*; their online ratings say the best courts include those at Juan de Fuca Recreation Centre, the Ernest Todd playground in James Bay, and Stadacona Park. For an unforgettable game, visit the **South Cowichan Lawn Tennis Club** *(2290 Cowichan Bay Rd., 250-746-7282, scltc.bc.ca)*: founded in 1887 (see photo), it's the second-oldest existing lawn tennis club in the world after the All England Club at Wimbledon, established 10 years earlier. The poet Robert Service used to read under the maple trees overlooking the seven grass courts. Membership is $250, but they take drop-in players for $20, and the place is a mecca for some of the best on the west coast. (Grass courts were in Victoria, too, at the corner of Fort Street and Foul Bay Road, but they were replaced in the early 1960s by a Safeway.) Organizers of the annual **Victoria Open** tournament *(victoriaopen.ca)* are planning to build French-style clay courts at the former Beaver Lake school. If they persuade the cranky neighbours, look for the facility *(theclaycourts.com)* to open in 2006.

The Physics of the Felt

If you're looking for a game of eight-ball and don't want to deal with lager louts and loud music, line up a shot at **Peacock Billiards** *(1175 Douglas St., 384-3332, peacockbilliards.com)*. David Peacock's new downtown establishment has 30 professional tables – including several he built himself – and carpet and commissioned artwork throughout, instead of the usual fluorescent-lit lino and motorcycle posters. Foosball, internet terminals, and a full restaurant too. Another class hangout is **Noble Billiards** *(1010 Craigflower Rd., 381-2225)*, which has a dozen pro tables and a liquor-licenced café.

Smash-Up Derby

Since 1954, Langford's **Western Speedway** *(2207 Millstream Rd., 474-2151, westernspeedway.bc.ca)* has been the region's home of full-throttle auto racing, and the training ground for many great drivers, including Billy Foster (see page 74), who won many big races at the track in the early '60s. Stock cars, drag racers, and wing-tipped sprint cars are just some of the types of vehicles that take to the Speedway's 4/10ths-of-a-mile oval every weekend. Its biggest draw, however, is "hit-to-pass" demolition racing, a sport unique to the Pacific Northwest. While regular demolition derby cars chug around an enclosed pit, in hit-to-pass they're racing flat-out at highway speeds, guaranteeing plenty of rollovers, engine fires, and pulverized metal. It's like a *Mad Max* movie come to life.

Doug Peden (Everything)

The ultimate all-rounder, he was on Canada's 1936 Olympic silver-medal-winning basketball team, won seven international cycling races, played on the national junior tennis squad, hit over .300 in Class A Eastern League baseball, and was the only Canadian to score against New Zealand's All Blacks during their 1936 rugby tour. He later became the *Victoria Times* sports editor. His brother William "Torchy" Peden (nicknamed for his red hair) was a national cycling champion, and competed in the 1928 Olympics.

Derek Porter (Rowing)

A chiropractor with a back of steel, he won Olympic eights gold in 1992, singles silver in 1996, and a single-sculls world championship in 1993

Gareth Rees (Rugby)

Canada's leading points scorer in international rugby, he also competed in a record four World Cups in the 1990s and captained Team Canada in two of them.

Alison Sydor (Mountain Biking)

She reluctantly entered a bicycle race for the first time when she was a UVic student, and went on to win three world championships and a silver at the 1996 Olympics.

Cliff Thorburn (Snooker)

Winner of the 1980 world snooker championships, and a member of the Order of Canada. Nicknamed "The Grinder" for his methodical style of play.

Luraina Undershute (Kickboxing)

Ranked number one in the world in 1999, she's since become an actress, appearing in such B films as *Sometimes a Hero* and *G.O.D.* — as an assassin.

Simon Whitfield (Triathlon)

Winner of an Olympic gold medal (the sport's first) at the 2000 games in Sydney.

The World's Fastest Man

Photo: John Cassidy

Next time you're driving on a highway, try to imagine achieving the same speed, or faster, on a bicycle. **Sam Whittingham** has: in October 2002, the theatre stage designer and Victoria racing cyclist pedalled to 130.36 km/h (81 mph) on a flat, windless road in Nevada — the fastest any human has travelled entirely under their own power. Of course, Sam wasn't riding any ol' Raleigh. His machine was the Varna Diablo II, a recumbent bicycle encased in an aerodynamic kevlar shell designed by Georgi Georgiev, a Bulgarian-born sculptor living on Gabriola Island. Georgiev also makes hand-powered bikes for disabled riders; see his handiwork at *varnahandcycles.com*.

Over Hill, Over Dale

The **South Island Mountain Bike Society** *(simbs.com)* has the dope on where to ride. The only official mountain-bike park on Vancouver Island is on the slope of Mount Work, next to the Hartland landfill. SIMBS maintains its extensive trail network, which includes a technical area for advanced riders. Look for a map at bike shops, or join a guided introductory ride the first Sunday of every month. Development has put the squeeze on unofficial trail areas, but try Burnt Bridge near Shawnigan Lake, Mt. Tzouhalem near Duncan, and the Broom Hill area near Sooke, which has its own chat site at *sooketrails.com*.

Best Gym

Of all the places to work out, the gold medal goes to **Saanich Commonwealth Place** *(4636 Elk Lake Dr., 475-7600, gov.saanich.bc.ca)*, the city's most visible legacy from the 1994 Commonwealth Games. National-calibre athletes train alongside housewives in the state-of-the-art strength and cardio area, the aquatic facilities (50m competition pool, dive tank, play area with water slides and wave pool) are considered the finest in Canada, and runners can do a 10k loop around nearby Elk Lake. The building also contains a branch of the public library.

Mile Stone

More than 30 tour buses per day stop at **Mile Zero** at the corner of Douglas Street and Dallas Road marking one end of the 7,821-kilometre (4,849-mile) Trans-Canada Highway, the longest national highway in the world. Here you'll find a statue for Terry Fox, the one-legged athlete who tried to run the length of the highway in 1979 to raise money for cancer research, and then died of cancer himself. Across the road is Fonyo Beach, named after Steve Fonyo, who completed Fox's run and dipped his artificial leg in the Pacific here in 1985. Fame took its toll on Fonyo: a decade later he pleaded guilty to 16 charges for criminal offences including assault, fraud, theft, perjury, and possession of a handgun.

Well, Hit My Wicket

In keeping with the city's old-empire roots, it's easy to find a cricket match here.

Beacon Hill Park

Cricket has been played on this ground since 1866. The clubhouse (see photo) was built in 1909. Fans often watch from cars parked on Circle Drive.

Metchosin

The ground is at the end of Happy Valley Road, behind the Metchosin council chambers. The tree in the middle of the pitch is in play: hit it on the fly it's a six, a roller it's four.

Get in Gear

Downtown Victoria has several sporting-goods stores to help with your next adventure. For camping and hiking gear, **Robinson's Outdoor Store** *(1307 Broad St., 385-3429, robinsonsoutdoors.com)* is a good bet. This venerable outfitter has been in business since 1930, and there are still bullet holes in the basement wall from the days when it sold guns. Technical hiking and climbing equipment and clothing can be found at **Valhalla Pure Outfitters** *(615 Broughton St., 360-2181, vpo.ca)*. Also look for an outlet of the phenomenal **Mountain Equipment Co-op** *(1450 Government St., mec.ca)* to open in 2006. **Frontrunners** *(1200 Vancouver St., 382-8181, frontrunnersfootwear.com)* is the city's best running-shoe store; owner Rob Reid directs the Royal Victoria Marathon, and offers clinics out of his shop. **HtO** *(1314 Broad St., 920-5511, hto.ca)* is best for bathing suits and other watery accessories. For surf, skateboard, and snowboard gear, check out **Coastline** *(1417 Broad St., 382-2123, coastlinesurf.com)* and **ThreeSixty** *(506 Herald St., 382-0360, threesixtyboardshop.ca)*. **Sports Traders** *(508 Discovery St., 383-6443, sportstraders.ca)* has new and used gear, from hockey equipment to golf clubs. And if you're just visiting or trying out a pastime, **Sports Rent** *(1950 Government St., 385-7368, sportsrentbc.com)* loans out tents, snow and water skis, bicycles, wetsuits, roof racks, and much more.

St. Michael's University School

A pristine pitch located on the campus of one of the city's elite academic institutions, at 3400 Richmond Road.

Windsor Park

The pitch at Windsor Road and Newport Avenue in Oak Bay has been in use since 1906. An expensive new pavillion — which neighbours say resembles a highway rest-stop — is due to open for the municipality's centennial in 2006.

For the Birds

If you're in Beacon Hill Park near Douglas and Simcoe Streets and you hear a lot of commotion overhead, don't be surprised. The surrounding trees contain the biggest **Great Blue heron nesting site** in the region, often housing more than 200 birds. Sadly for the herons, Bald eagles also frequent the area, and prey on heron chicks. The nests are busy from February to July. You can also watch them on *heroncam.com*, a webcam on the 12th floor of an apartment building on the other side of Douglas Street.

a walk in the park

The city's most historic green space is **Beacon Hill Park**, but if you wander through it you won't find many markers indicating its intriguing details. Here are a few. For more, see Janis Ringuette's superbly comprehensive website, *islandnet.com/beaconhillpark*.

Signal Hill

How did the park get its name? Just off the Ogden Point breakwater stands a beacon marking Brotchie Ledge, a shallows that once caused havoc for ships trying to enter Victoria's harbour. In the 1840s, the Hudson's Bay Company strategically placed two masts on the grassy hill of today's park. When a ship's captain could line up the masts in his sights, he knew it was time to turn to avoid the submerged rocks – and thus the masts' location became known as Signal or Beacon Hill.

Burial Cairns

Just down the grassy slope from Signal Hill are several clusters of large rocks. They're what's left of several dozen Native gravesites that used to be spread across the hilltop. Finlayson Point (across Dallas Road) once was a defensive fort, which the local Songhees peoples used to protect themselves from raiding parties of rival tribes. The Songhees buried their dead on this slope, and covered each body with earth and a pile of stones. (Most of those buried here were probably victims of smallpox rather than warfare, however.) After the white colonists moved in, they broke up or moved many of the rocks. Four of the 300-year-old cairns have since been reconstructed.

Photo: Tony Austin

THE GAME OF KINGS

Horsemanship was once an essential skill in western Canada, as much for British cavalry officers as for cowboys, and the best way to practice it was by playing polo. The first recorded match in Victoria occurred in 1889, and the tradition is continued by the **Victoria Polo Club** *(carriagehousebandb.ca/polo1.html)*, which plays Sunday afternoons on a regulation turf field at 7161 Wallace Drive in Central Saanich, and breaks out the tea and cakes for invitational tournaments several times a year.

Wayward Statues

In the middle of the putting green stands a statue of the Scottish poet Robbie Burns and his lover "Highland Mary" Campbell, installed in 1900 by the William Wallace Society. In 1998, the auld statue suddenly disappeared, and turned up several days later in a driveway after police received an anonymous phone call insisting the reward money go to a cancer charity and the Robbie Burns Society in Scotland. Next to Goodacre Lake (artificial, by the way) deeper inside the park, you'll come across a bust of Queen Elizabeth II, commemorating her 1959 visit. The bust is a replacement: the first one was stolen in 1960 and thrown into the Inner Harbour.

PLACE YOUR BETS

Victorians once raced horses all over town. Beacon Hill Park's Circle Drive was first trod as a race track in the 1850s, and between 1899 and 1948 locals played the ponies at Oak Bay's glorious but now-vanished Willows Exhibition Grounds. Today, the only remnant of the city's racing heritage is North Saanich's **Sandown Park** (656-1631, sandownpark.ca), built in 1954. Sandown's harness racers drive their steeds around a 5/8-mile limestone track on weekends from July to September. Lately horse owners have been allowing visitors to take the reins for free after racing is over to get a feel for the sport.

Blue Camas

If disaster strikes and all the Thrifty Foods supermarkets are closed, don't panic. You can always eat the bulbs of the blue camas, a type of lily that flowers on the dry grasslands of Beacon Hill Park every spring. For many centuries the Songhees peoples cultivated these plants, harvesting the sweet bulbs and roasting them in pit ovens. But if you're ever tempted to do the same, collect them only when the blue camas is in bloom. The bulbs look identical to that of the white-flowering death camas, which was often responsible for killing the grazing sheep of Victoria's pioneers.

pristine parks

At these free outdoor oases of concrete you can 'board without fear of bylaw officers or rough patches in the road.

West Shore Skatepark
Behind Belmont Secondary School, across from the CanWest Shopping Centre. Boxes, rails, banks, flat bars, fun box, hubbas, bowls, quarter pipes.

Saanich
At Lambrick Park Sports Centre, 4115 Torquay Drive. Fun boxes, pyramid, quarter pipe, railings, ramps.

Beacon Hill isn't the only green space in town. There are 48 regional, provincial, and federal parks in greater Victoria, totaling more than 7,600 hectares (18,780 acres). It's impossible to mention them all here but these are local favourites.

Rithet's Bog

A trail circling the only intact bog in the region provides great birdwatching. More than 120 species have been spotted here, including loons, hummingbirds, and owls. Access off Chatterton Way in Saanich.

Sidney Spit Marine Park

Kayak or take a water taxi (call 474-5145 for the schedule, May to September) from the foot of Sidney's Beacon Avenue out to this island, with one of the largest salt marshes on the BC coast, and more great birding. An osprey nest is next to the overnight campground.

Goldstream

Along with its famous fall salmon run, and access to Mount Finlayson, a walk through an old-growth forest leads to BC's own Niagara Falls. Access off Highway 1, five kilometres west of the Millstream interchange.

Esquimalt Lagoon

A federal bird sanctuary, thick with herons, eagles, cormorants, and mergansers. Plus a beach, and views of Hatley Castle. Access from Ocean Boulevard.

Witty's Lagoon

A spectacular waterfall, lots of birds (kingfishers, warblers), and seals frolicking around the Haystack Islets, especially in summer. Access from lots along Metchosin Road.

Sidney

Eighth Street and Pat Bay Highway. Pyramid, play boxes, ramps, stairs, quarter pipe, rails, railings.

East Sooke Park

More than 1,400 hectares (3,400 acres) of spectacularly craggy waterfront, plus abandoned mine sites, petroglyphs, and picnic areas. Hundreds of raptors circle overhead in late September. Easiest access from the end of Becher Bar Road.

Sooke Rotary Skatepark

Next to Journey Middle School, 6522 Throup Road. Has lights for nighttime skating. Quarter pipes, pyramids, flat rail, round rail, 5 set.

To learn more about these parks and the creatures in them, join the **Victoria Natural History Society** (vicnhs.bc.ca), or take a free interpretive walk with **CRD Parks** (crd.bc.ca/parks) or the **Sierra Club** (sierra.ca/bc, 386-5255).

Vic West

On Esquimalt Road, next to the Victoria West Lawn Bowling Club. Biggest park on Vancouver Island. Boxes, big bowl, quarter pipes, big and small hubbas, rails down banks, flat bar rails, fun boxes, pyramids. Closed after 10:30 p.m.

Ultramarathon Man

Countless people have started or finished cross-Canada journeys at Mile Zero, but the most incredible physical specimen of them all has to be Victoria runner **Al Howie**. Fifteen years ago, Howie was the *ne plus ultra* of marathoners: in 1991, at the age of 45, he ran across the country in just 72 days, averaging more than 103 kilometres (64 miles) a day. Two weeks after that, he travelled to New York, and set a record in a 1,300-mile (2,092-kilometre) race. In 1996, while working as a treeplanter, he was diagnosed with diabetes. But that didn't stop him. In 1997, he ran up and down Mount Douglas 25 times, a distance of 100 kilometres (62 miles), in just over 10 hours, and continued to enter ultramarathons. Howie, who now lives quietly in Duncan, earned several entries in the *Guinness Book of World Records*, but for some reason all you'll see at Mile Zero is a small plaque acknowledging his amazing cross-country sprint.

wild wild life

Victorians have unusual relationships with some of the other species that call this place home.

Bullfrogs

They've been common back east for millennia, but bullfrogs didn't exist on Vancouver Island until the 1930s, when Depression-era residents imported them to build frog farms and sell the legs to French restaurants. But Victoria didn't really *have* French restaurants at the time, so the farmers let the bullfrogs loose, and now the croakers have taken over many of the city's lakes. This wouldn't be a problem, except that the big frogs (weighing up to five pounds each) eat everything that moves, including snakes, rodents, fish, small birds, and the tiny Pacific tree frogs native to the island. A six-year program is underway to eradicate the bullfrogs by stunning them with electroshock devices and then freezing them to death.

Cougars

Whenever a police report goes out that a cougar has been sighted, a shiver of excitement goes through town. The big cats are usually spotted out in the 'burbs, but sometimes they come into the heart of the city; in 1992, a cougar was caught and tranquilized in the parkade of the Empress Hotel. That's a better fate than many cougars have faced. Until 1958, they were considered no-good varmints (there was a bounty of $40 on their heads), and though there are only approximately 800 left on Vancouver Island, around 60 are killed every year by hunters and conservation officers, especially if the cat has attacked a farm animal or a pet. Domestic dogs, though hardly endangered, rarely suffer the same fate for the same crime.

Sporting Life

These are the city's big annual sports and outdoors events.

Highland Games

Clans from across the Pacific Northwest converge for dance contests, sheepdog displays, drumming, piping, and tossing the caber — one of many games Scots played to keep them battle-fit and ready for war.
May; victoriahighlandgames.com

Luxton Rodeo

The western communities celebrate their rural roots and pro-circuit cowboys show their stuff. Bronco and bull riding, barrel racing, steer wrestling, a midway, and lots of grilled beef to boot.
May; 478-4250, members.shaw.ca/luxtonrodeo

Royal Victoria Marathon

This event, which first occurred in 1980, has grown to include 55,000 entrants, and was recently branded one of the 10 best "destination" marathons by *Runner's World* magazine. The scenic course follows the waterfront; you can walk the full distance if you prefer, or compete in a

half-marathon or eight-kilometre race.
October; 658-4520,
royalvictoriamarathon.com

Swiftsure
Victoria's premier sailing event started in 1930, and now draws the best crews on the west coast. It consists of three distinct races, the longest being the 223-kilometre (138.6-mile) run from Clover Point to Swiftsure Bank (at the mouth of the Strait of Juan de Fuca) and back. Weather is always a factor; some years the seas are so calm that competitors give up and power to shore, and in others the seas are deadly. The worst year was 1976, when a Seattle yachtsman drowned after swells up to seven and a half metres swamped the cockpit of his boat. Watch the action from Dallas Road or the Ogden Point breakwater.
May; 592-9098, swiftsure.org

Garry Oaks

Legend has it that Walt Disney got the idea for the scary forest scene in *Sleeping Beauty* from these jagged trees, but that's not what makes the Garry oak important. The only type of oak indigenous to western Canada, it grows best in dry grassy meadows alongside dozens of unique species, including food plants (chocolate lily, nodding onion) once harvested by the Songhees natives. Garry oak meadows also are endangered; though they exist in Canada only on southeast Vancouver Island and a few Gulf Islands, they're steadily being wiped out. (Langford's big-box stores on Millstream Road sit atop a former Garry oak meadow.) To see Garry oaks in their proper environment, visit the grounds of Government House, or Mill Hill Regional Park.

Rabbits

There are as many as 1,000 bunnies on the University of Victoria campus, descendants of cottontails introduced in the area in the 1950s and other breeds (e.g. Himalayan giants) later abandoned by pet owners. The rodents are cuddly, but hardly benign: they debark trees, tear up gardens, and undermine sidewalks. More rabbits hop around the Victoria General Hospital, giving the staff headaches because visitors track bunny poop into the wards. In 1999, VGH hired exterminators, but animal lovers thwarted the massacre by capturing 500 rabbits on the grounds and shipping them to a refuge in Sooke.

Salmon

Every October and November, when the rivers swell with rain, Victorians migrate to Goldstream Provincial Park to witness the spectacular return of up to 60,000 salmon. Nearly all the fish are the chum species, guided by smell back to the place they were born four years earlier. After laying and fertilizing some 3,000 eggs apiece, they die, providing food for bald eagles and (as University of Victoria studies have shown) vital nutrients for the surrounding forest. The Goldstream Visitors' Centre *(2930 Trans-Canada Hwy., 478-9414)* provides informative tours during the salmon run.

Urban Beauty Consultant

Victoria's boulevards are blessed with amazing foliage thanks to **Herb Warren**, the city's superintendent of parks from 1930 to 1970. Warren had the idea during the Depression to turn Victoria into a "city of gardens" to draw tourists. To make it blossom, he designed the hanging baskets of flowers that continue to appear on downtown lampposts every June, and began planting ornamental trees on public boulevards. Certainly most vivid are the approximately 3,000 **flowering cherry and plum trees** that burst with delicate petals every March. Nearly all were imported from Japan – in fact, the local Japanese community paid for more than 1,000 of them with prize money it won for its float in the 1937 Victoria Day parade. Arguably the best are the Kanzan cherries on Moss and Trutch Streets, or the Yoshino cherries on South Turner Street in James Bay, which holds a little festival when the trees are in bloom.

Gardening Tours

This city has many green thumbs, and often they first sprouted their gardening talents at the **Horticulture Centre of the Pacific** (505 Quayle Rd., 479-6162, hcp.bc.ca), a unique educational institution in Saanich. Starting in 1979, the HCP has grown to offer courses in everything from the history of topiary to landscape horticulture, taught in its demonstration gardens containing more than 10,000 varieties of plants. Visitors are welcome to tour the HCP's 36-hectare (90-acre) property, which includes a bird sanctuary, and conservation areas for rare native plants and wildflowers.

Times Colonist 10K
In 1990, the first race brought out 1,851 runners. Today, more than 12,000 participate, making it the second-largest 10-kilometre run in Canada.
April; 818-0956, tc10k.ca

Victoria Cycling Festival
Everything on two wheels, from fun rides to professional races. The Sooke Classic, 140 kilometres (87 miles) to Port Renfrew and back, has been won by such elite local riders as Roland Green and Alison Sydor. A spectators' favourite is the Bastion Square Grand Prix (see photo), 70 laps of a downtown block with plenty of thrills and spills.
June; 384-8223,
victoriacyclingfestival.com

The Garden that Love Built

The story of the **Abkhazi Garden** is as pretty as its flowers. It was started in 1946 by Peggy Pemberton Carter, who came to Victoria after spending over two years in a Japanese internment camp outside Shanghai. Soon after that she was reunited with Prince Nicholas Abkhazi, a member of the Georgian nobility she'd met in Paris in the 1920s, and who'd been a prisoner of war in Europe. They were married in Victoria, where they created their one-acre masterpiece — featuring native Garry oaks, ornamental evergreens, and alpine plants set into a dramatic piece of glaciated rock. Nicholas died in 1987, followed by Peggy in 1994, and the property was sold to a developer who planned to build townhomes on it. The Land Conservancy of BC came to the rescue and bought him out, and it's now paying off a mortgage to protect the garden as a heritage site. The garden, gift shop, and tea room are located at 1964 Fairfield Road (598-8096).

Victoria Dragon Boat Festival

Dragon boat races supposedly began in tribute to a beloved Chinese poet who drowned; fishermen furiously paddled out to save him, and beat drums to scare off carnivorous fish. Now the races are an exercise in teamwork, bringing crews from across the continent to the Inner Harbour.
August; 472-2628, victoriadragonboat.com

Victoria International Walking Festival

Tour the city in a way you can really appreciate it — on your feet! This fest woos pedestrians from everywhere to hike pre-planned routes, from short strolls beneath blossoming trees to cross-town marathons.
April; 1-877-488-9255, walkvictoria.ca

Above All Else

Victoria's Heritage Tree Society says the biggest tree in town is a **giant sequoia** that stands at the corner of Moss and Richardson Streets. The last time it was measured, the tree stood 45.7 metres (150 feet) tall, and its trunk was 193 cm (76 inches) across. The sequoia was given to British Columbia by the governor of California in 1886. Back then, several large trees were transplanted to Victoria (another giant sequoia stands in front of the legislature), but many were cut down after the estates they stood upon were subdivided into smaller lots. It's not hard to see why: if the big sequoia ever toppled, it would demolish any house in its way.

The Mystic Spring

One hundred and fifty years ago, the Songhees people had a large village at Cadboro Bay. One of their sacred places nearby was the valley known today as Mystic Vale, hidden in the southeast corner of the University of Victoria campus. According to their stories, this valley contained a spring of pure, cold water that had the power to enhance the fertility of young couples unable to bear children. Journalist D.W. Higgins elaborated on the legend in his 1904 book *The Mystic Spring and Other Tales of Western Life*: the spring formed a pool at the base of a maple tree, he said, and anyone who looked into the pool on a full moon would see their his or her future mate. And if the tree was ever cut down, the spring would dry up.

Not long after Fort Victoria was established, young people heard the story and travelled to see the spring. But the water had sinister depths. In 1862, Higgins wrote, a woman fainted after seeing "a low-browed, cunning face" in the pool. In 1868, an 18-year-old woman named Julia Booth was found dead nearby; a boy later testified at an inquest that he'd seen Miss Booth sobbing uncontrollably at the water's edge, and a note she left suggested suicide. Twenty years later, a settler chopped the maple into firewood. And just as the Songhees had warned, the spring disappeared.

Or did it? A creek trickles through Mystic Vale – its cold water actually provided basement refrigeration for a Cadboro Bay supermarket in the 1960s – but its source remains a mystery. Might it be the fabled spring? Enter Mystic Vale from Hobbs Road and see for yourself.

BREAKING THE THE WAVES
The **Ogden Point breakwater** isn't just used by divers and fishermen. Every year, some 500,000 people stroll its 2,500-foot walkway to the lighthouse and back for a view of the Strait of Juan de Fuca and arriving cruise ships. The breakwater was constructed of more than 8,000 granite blocks between 1913 and 1915 to protect the Inner Harbour and provide a berth for the installation of wartime machinery in local ships. The point itself is named after Peter Skene Ogden, a Hudson's Bay Company officer who never made it here, although he did spend time trapping fur-bearing animals in Utah, where there's a town with his name.

Photo: Angi Photo

SURF'S UP

The word is out: there's **surfing** on Highway 14. Loggers and hippies have been donning neoprene and riding boards at Jordan River and Sombrio Beach since the '60s. Jesse Oke-Johnson, who grew up with his clan in a squatter's shack at Sombrio, was widely considered the best surfer in Canada until he drowned in a car that rolled off the Port Renfrew pier in 2000. (The family was booted off Sombrio in the late '90s to make way for the Juan de Fuca hiking trail.) Today surfers come from all over the Pacific Northwest to these beaches for the long, uniform waves — annoying the locals, who wish the place had remained a secret. The surfing's only worthwhile on certain days in the wintertime though, so call Cathy at Shakies Drive-Inn *(250-646-2184)* right on the beach at Jordan River, and she'll tell you the conditions.

The Water Underground

Hidden beneath the capital region are 24 **aquifers** — vast subterranean pools of water, filled with rain that's seeped down through our fractured geology. Wells to these aquifers provide water for many homes in the Highlands, along with farms in Sooke, Metchosin, and remote parts of Saanich that aren't connected to the regional supply from Sooke Lake. In some parts of town, these pools go untapped, with soggy consequences. The University of Victoria sits atop a 7.3-square-kilometre aquifer that often overflows in late winter and floods yards in the Uplands.

In a few places where trapped water is under geological pressure, it re-emerges as **springs**.(Some say the spring water comes from the Olympic Mountains, forced under the Strait of Juan de Fuca by the pressure of the Olympic glaciers, but that's just a myth.) In the 1880s, settler Michael Finnerty bottled and sold water from his Spring Bank Farm (today's UVic campus), claiming it had curative powers. Spring Ridge (Fernwood), of course, had functioning springs, which likely feed the backyard wells in the district today. Another spring is on a private lot just south of the Langham Court Theatre. From 1913 to 1948, it was tapped by the Crystal Springs soda company, which had a bottling works at 1244 Richardson Street. The building has been replaced by an apartment block, but the spring out back still runs.

All Wet?

Victorians moan about **rainfall**, but we actually suffer far less of it than our neighbours. Vancouver's annual precipitation is around 1,200 millimetres (47 inches), and Seattle gets 900 millimetres (36 inches), but thanks to the rain shadow of the Olympic mountains, only 750 millimetres (28 inches) falls in Victoria. (Sequim, Washington, a town directly behind the Olympics, gets only 16 inches annually.) The rains also vary a great deal in the capital region itself. The Sooke Hills get 1,300 millimetres annually while only 600 fall in Oak Bay, so named because its lands were once dry, grassy meadows studded with Garry oak trees.

Lost Streams

Conservationists have done tremendous work reopening or "daylighting" several creeks in the city that were largely paved over after World War II. One is **Bowker Creek**, which had a population of coho salmon (proven by a Native midden found next to Oak Bay's public works yard) until it was culverted (see photo) to prevent flooding of the residential area north of the Royal Jubilee Hospital. Many parts of the creek have since been reclaimed, and are now popular with mallard ducks. Other streams will never be so lucky. **Harris Lake**, which once sat just east of Vic High, drained down the north-facing slope of today's Fernwood district and then ran west to Rock Bay along today's Bay Street. Engineers later incorporated the watercourse into the sewers emptying into the bay at the west end of Queens Avenue. A century ago, a **peat marsh** existed where View and Vancouver Streets meet. (That's why the intersection is sinking.) It drained into a ravine that ran parallel to Johnson Street, and out to the harbour where the blue bridge is today. (The lower floor of Market Square and the basements of many Johnson Street businesses used to be the bottom of the ravine.) Another swamp once lay just east of the Cook Street Village, draining in two directions: one stream ran east to Ross Bay, reaching the ocean next to the cemetery, and the other ran west to James Bay, the site of the Empress Hotel. Natives canoeing from the north used this stream-and-swamp route as a shortcut to Victoria's harbour in stormy weather.

LET'S GET NAKED

One advantage of an intricate shoreline is that it provides places where one can tan in the buff. **Nude sunbathers** seeking privacy head to the sand west of Witty's Lagoon (take the steps at the end of Witty Beach Road), and the north end of Saanich's Sayward Beach (head down from the lot on Parker Avenue). Those seeking clothing-optional company peel to View Royal's Prior Lake (look for the parked cars on Highland Road), where naturists congregate on the dock like barking seals. It can get crowded, so bring an air mattress. For the real skinny, see *members.shaw.ca/co-bc*.

Row, Row, Row Your Boat

Paddling was the principal mode of transportation in this region for millennia. Now it seems to be one of our primary forms of recreation. Olympic-calibre jocks and school crews practice at the **Victoria City Rowing Club** (5100 Pat Bay Hwy., *vcrc.bc.ca*) on Elk Lake, which offers learn-to-row programs, and rents single sculls on

SWIMMING HOLES

Victoria doesn't need outdoor pools. It has lakes that are warm enough to swim in all summer, and only minutes from town. (Good thing, too, because the ocean's always hypothermically cold.) Judging by the crowds, everyone knows about Saanich's Elk Lake and its Hamsterly Beach, and View Royal's Thetis Lake, which has islands and dive-able cliffs.

For a more secluded swim, try Metchosin's woodsy Matheson Lake, (access off Rocky Point Road) with a small beach and a 3.4-km (2.1-mile) trail around the water. Up the Saanich peninsula, look for Durrance Lake (park your car at the far end of Durrance Close, off Willis Point Road). If its sandy shore is busy, just around the corner on Ross-Durrance Road is secluded Pease Lake, which remains as rustic and pristine as the day it was formed.

weekends. A century ago, huge rowing regattas were major events on the Gorge waterway, and they're making a comeback with the new **Gorge Rowing and Paddling Centre** *(#115-2940 Jutland Rd., 380-4669, gorgekayaking.com)* in the Selkirk Water development. Rowing, dragon boat, and outrigger teams use the centre (with access to gym facilities, and a pub), but it also has recreational rowing lessons, and rents single sculls and kayaks.

If you're more into sightseeing than strenuous exercise, a sea kayak is the vessel you need. One of the best kayak shops anywhere is **Ocean River Sports** *(1824 Store St., 381-4233, oceanriver.com)*, which also gives lessons and rents boats from its dock out back. From there, beginners can paddle up the Gorge to Portage Inlet, although the "reversing falls" under the Tillicum bridge can be tricky. More experienced kayakers can tackle the many superb day trips around the region, such as Chatham and Discovery Islands off Oak Bay, the shoreline of East Sooke Park, and prominent rocks near Sidney such as D'Arcy, Mandarte, Rum, and Reay islands. For details, get Aileen Stalker and Andrew Nolan's *Sea Kayak Paddling Through History: Vancouver and Victoria* or Mary Ann Snowden's *Sea Kayak the Gulf Islands*. If you want to go with a group, try the **Victoria Canoe and Kayak Club** *(355 Gorge Rd. West, 361-4238, vckc.ca)*.

Survival Suit

Take a dip in the ocean here, and you won't be shocked to learn that the University of Victoria has been a pioneer in cold-water research. In the 1970s, if anyone died in local waters, they were simply victims of "drowning." But UVic profs John Hayward, John Eckerson, and Martin Collis thought hypothermia was the cause, and they conducted experiments with volunteers immersed in frigid water to learn how the body loses heat. From their groundbreaking research, they developed the **Mustang UVic Thermofloat lifejacket**, containing a thermal hood and a flap to insulate the groin. The Thermofloat won numerous design awards, and became standard equipment in the boating industry.

Going Deeper

British Columbia is consistently rated by readers of *Scuba Diving* magazine as the best place to dive north of the Mexican border, and many prime sites are right around Victoria. Most convenient is the **Ogden Point breakwater**, where armoured crabs, rockfish, and friendly wolf eels reside; the Ogden Point Dive Centre *(199 Dallas Rd., 380-9119, divevictoria.com)* rents gear so you can literally step out of the shop and into the sea. More fine sites are on the **Saanich Inlet**, including Senanus Island, populated with rare white cloud sponges; explore them with Rockfish Divers *(884-4174, rockfishdivers.com)*. Several shipwrecks are parked near Sidney, such as the freighter *G.B. Church* and the HMCS *Mackenzie*, a Canadian destroyer. Both were sunk in the 1990s by the **Artificial Reef Society of BC** *(artificialreef.bc.ca)*, which recently submerged an old Boeing 737 near Chemainus. Without question, though, the most spectacular diving is at **Race Rocks** (see page 26). Its walls are a jungle of sponges, anenomes, and nudibranches, and octopi and sea lions hang out to dine. For details see *Diver's Guide: Vancouver Island South*, a book by Greg Dombowsky, who's at *dive.bc.ca*.

RVYC and a Bottle of Rum

The history of the **Royal Victoria Yacht Club** is tied up with booze. During prohibition in the 1920s, many club members used their boats to haul cases of Scotch across the straits to the United States, and one of the largest bootlegging outfits around was run by RVYC commodore Harry Barnes, whose yawl *Minena* was so well-known to authorities that it was subject to seizure if it entered American waters. (This prevented Barnes from competing in many of the club's long-distance races.) During a 1925 regatta hosted by the club, Ernie Adams of Victoria broke the open outboard world record in his powerboat *Miss Victoria II*, a ship designed with a V-shaped hull favoured by rumrunners.

SEA LIFE ON LAND

Even if you don't dive, you can get a glimpse of Victoria's oceanic diversity at **Undersea Gardens** *(490 Belleville St., 382-5717, pacificunderseagardens.com)*, the spaceship-like tourist attraction afloat in the Inner Harbour. Its underwater theatre is the only place you'll see an octopus, a cabezon (see photo), or Muppet-like wolf eel without getting wet. The **Marine Ecology Centre** in Sidney *(Port Sidney Marina, 9835 Seaport Pl., 655-1555, mareco.org)* also has numerous aquariums, touch tanks, and live video from the nearby ocean floor.

The Big Stink

SECRET VIEWPOINTS
The best bird's-eye view of downtown Victoria is at **Vista 18**, the bar and restaurant atop the Chateau Victoria Hotel *(749 Burdett Ave.)*. The bar lights reflect in the windows after dark, so try it during the day. For a no-frills overlook of the harbour and Old Town brickwork, take the elevator from the street to the top of the **parkade at 575 Yates**. If you're east of downtown, turn off Fairfield Road and up Masters Road to **Moss Rock Park**, where you can get fine views of Government House and the Ross Bay cemetery. If in Esquimalt, turn off Old Esquimalt Road at Cairn Street and then hike up the paved walkway to **Highrock Park**, where you'll enjoy panoramas of the naval base, Portage Inlet, and Sooke Hills.

Victorians are an environmentally green bunch, but if you want to see them flush red, mention that every day the city pumps 129 million litres (34 million gallons) of **raw sewage** into the Strait of Juan de Fuca. The city's been piping out its poop at Clover Point since 1894, but in the 1970s it started to become an international scandal, as towns across the water in Washington State cleaned up and demanded Victoria do the same. The issue came to a head in 1992, when capital region taxpayers were asked to approve a treatment facility costing $379 million or more; 57 percent voted against it, prompting Americans to cancel conferences and announce tourist boycotts. To end the outrage, in 1993 Victoria politicians agreed to abide by a 20-year schedule to build a facility. They've dawdled over the location and financing for it ever since.

Recently the issue has resurfaced thanks to "**Mr. Floatie**" (see photo), an activist mascot who goes around town cheerfully asking everyone to "join the movement" for a treatment facility. Embarassed, Victoria politicians are spluttering again that they will find money for the project. Some scientists say it's not worth forcing every citizen to pay hundreds more in annual property taxes: the city has reduced much of the toxic gunk that was going into sewers (by regulating photo labs, for example), and the 100,000 cubic metres of water that floods through the Strait of Juan de Fuca every second (a rate equal to that of the Amazon River) disperses the organic matter without significant harm to sea life. But environmentalists point out that the effluent still contains heavy metals, runoff fertilizer, and other poisons – making local shellfish inedible, and turning up in the bodies of the region's struggling orca whales.

Walking It Off

Victoria brags that it is "Canada's most walkable city," and it's probably true: more than 10 percent of our residents use old-fashioned shoe leather to get to work. But there are also plenty of wonderful strolls to take your mind off the office. In town, the most picturesque ambles are up Government Street and through James Bay to Beacon Hill Park, or the **Westsong Walkway,** which starts from the Delta Ocean Pointe Resort and follows the north shore of the harbour to the West Bay marina (where you can catch a harbour ferry back to the Empress). In Oak Bay, wander up **Willows Beach** (look for the eagle's nest near Bowker Avenue) along the shore to Cattle Point and the bird- and butterfly-filled Uplands Park. For more routes, find the *Walk Downtown Victoria* map at the Tourism Info Centre, or Rosemary Neering's delightful *New Victoria Walking Guide.* If you need motivation, local groups such as the Garden City Wanderers and Juan de Fuca Pathfinders are affiliated with **Volkssport,** an international federation of walking enthusiasts. See *volkssportingbc.ca* for contact info.

A-mazing

Photo: Susan Norman

When goofy attractions like the Glass Castle disappeared, fun-loving Victorians were lost – and now they're found wandering the **Galey Corn Farm Maze** *(4150 Blenkinsop Rd., 477-5713, galeyfarms.com),* a three-hectare summer attraction with a petting farm, a ghost town, and half-scale models of a Sphinx and pyramid. For meditative meanderings, look for a **labyrinth,** a spiritual tool designed to quiet a busy mind. (A maze is designed to confuse; a labyrinth consists of one long and winding path, representing the journey of the soul.) The south yard of Christ Church Cathedral *(951 Quadra St.)* has one, built of concentric rings of stones laid by work crews from William Head prison. Two more are set into the lawns next to James Bay's New Horizons Centre *(234 Menzies St.)* and St. Andrew's Anglican Church in Sidney *(9691 4th Ave.).*

DISTANT PEAKS

Some of Victoria's best scenery isn't even in Canada. Across the Strait of Juan de Fuca stand Washington State's **Olympic Mountains,** named in 1778 by an English captain who thought them so beautiful that Greek gods dwelled there. The gods must wear Gore-tex: the Olympics are the wettest place in the lower 48 states, getting 3,600 millimetres (142 inches) of precipitation annually. The highest point, Mount Olympus, stands 2,428 metres (7,965 feet) tall and is surrounded by eight glaciers. If you look east on clear days, you'll see snow-capped **Mount Baker,** a 3,285-metre (10,778-foot) volcano 50 kilometres east of Bellingham, Washington. Baker erupted five times between 1820 and 1870, and experienced a minor burp in 1975. It still emits plumes of steam, heated by the molten rock of the subducted Juan de Fuca plate.

CACHING IN

Like everyone else on the planet, Victorians are spaced out on **geocaching**, the scavenger-hunt game using global-positioning system (GPS) receivers to locate hidden containers with little prizes. There are more than 3,200 caches stashed around town. For their co-ordinates and chat, see *bcgeocaching.com* and *vigps.com*.

CLIMBING THE WALLS

Those born without a natural fear of heights are often found **rock climbing** at Esquimalt's Fleming Beach, at the end of Lampson Street. Rain or shine, they also get vertical at the **CragX Climbing Gym** (*341 John St., 383-4628, urbancliffculture.com*), which rents shoes and harnesses and offers training for all levels of climbers.

Take a Hike

For adventures involving boots and backpacks, the dedicated members of the **Outdoor Club of Victoria** (*ocv.ca*) organize hikes every weekend all year, rain or shine. You can also put together your own excursion by consulting *Hiking Trails I: Victoria and Vicinity* (see *hikingtrailsbooks.com*) or the handy Club Tread website (*clubtread.org*), which describes and rates local hikes. Favourite day treks include the 10.8-km (6.7-mile) waterfront of **East Sooke Park**, and the 25 km (15.5 miles) of trails through **Gowlland Tod Provincial Park**. For longer overnight journeys, some take the 49-km (30.5-mile) **Juan de Fuca Marine Trail** from China Beach to the tide pools of Botanical Beach near Port Renfrew – although it's muddier than the famous West Coast Trail, and many of its highlights are accessible from Highway 14. (If you park near the Sombrio River, you can walk down to a suspension bridge and, just to the west of it, caves where sea lions congregate.) Truly unknown, however, is the 80-km (50-mile) **Kludahk Trail**, which follows the San Juan Ridge all the way from Leechtown to Port Renfrew through alpine meadows, and is the only place near Victoria with enough snow for backcountry ski touring in winter. A map exists, but it's as hard to find as the trail itself (insiders screamed when someone posted the map on the Club Tread site), and you'll need the permission of the secretive Kludahk Outdoors Club to use the cabins en route.

Stray Bullets

If you hike the coast west of Sooke, you might want to pack a Kevlar vest. The navy's **Whiskey Hotel firing range** occupies an offshore stretch of the Strait of Juan de Fuca between Sheringham and Sombrio points and occasionally bullets have strayed into civilian territory. In 1995, surfers complained that helicopters were strafing logs 50 metres from the curl at Jordan River, inadvertently recreating a scene from *Apocalypse Now*. In 1998, hikers on the Juan de Fuca Marine Trail had to run when a visiting American ship tested its guns on floating targets, and shot up the beach instead.

getting high

Don't laugh, but Victoria has mountains. What they lack in elevation, they make up for in mythology.

Mount Douglas

Pioneers knew this 227-metre (745-foot) ice-age survivor as "Cedar Hill," because its trees were cut into the stakes that became the walls of Fort Victoria. A surveyor officially named the peak in 1859 after James Douglas, founder of the fort and then-governor of BC. (Only a peak greater than 1,000 feet can be properly called a "mountain," but the surveyor tactfully said he didn't want to "lower" the governor by naming it Douglas Hill.) Since then Mount Doug's become known as the best place to get a panoramic view of the city and the surrounding seas (see photo), and there are several pleasant trails climbing to its summit. (You can also drive up on Churchill Road, a 1938 make-work project.) Look for the entrance to a failed 1870 copper mine at the intersection of Harrop and Whittaker trails. The subject of Emily Carr's *Cedar*, one of her last and greatest paintings, is the grove of trees just south of the parking lot off Cordova Bay Road.

Mount Finlayson

The Saanich natives Natives call this 419-metre (1374-foot) peak WQENNELE'L, or "looking up." Easy to see why: its west face is practically vertical. Terrified hikers have been rescued from these cliffs after straying

BE PREPARED

If Victoria experiences an earthquake like the 6.9 number that hit Kobe, Japan in 1995, it would destroy buildings, topple hydro poles, and fracture gas, water, and sewer lines. Emergency services would be overwhelmed just caring for the 20 percent of the population that are senior citizens. So self-reliance is crucial: along with food and first-aid supplies, a household earthquake kit should have four litres of water per person per day, prescription medications, thick-soled shoes for walking on broken glass, and cash. (Visa will not be accepted at the apocalypse.) To get ready, visit **Custom First-Aid Systems** *(2047 Oak Bay Ave., 595-0744, customfirstaid.com)*, which sells pre-packaged kits, along with food rations, hand-crank radios and flashlights, and pepper spray.

off the invigorating path up the southern slope from Goldstream Provincial Park. But stick to the well-marked route, take sensible footwear (the rocks are slippery when wet), and you're in for great views of the Saanich Inlet. The climb is also popular with trail runners, who recently did it 22 times in 30 hours – the equivalent of scaling Mount Everest from sea level – to raise money for the BC Schizophrenia Society.

Mount Newton

L'AU,WEL,NEW or "place of refuge" to the Saanich people, because their ancestors survived a great flood by tying their canoes to an arbutus tree atop this mountain, and their women and children hid upon it during times of war. (The Saanich refuse to cut or burn arbutus today, out of respect.) Currently the 305-metre (1001-foot) peak is in John Dean Provincial Park, named after the outspoken realtor, traveler, and naturalist who donated it and the surrounding lands to the province in 1931. Dean refused to put a road in ("more vandals travelled by car than on foot," he explained) but the government has since built one, and desecrated the summit with a huge radar dome for the nearby airport. Nevertheless, it's a fine place to stroll through one of the few patches of old-growth Douglas-fir forest left in Victoria.

Mount Tolmie

This 125-metre (410-foot) Garry oak-covered hill near the University of Victoria got its exaggerated title as early as 1846, and has been prone to ballyhoo ever since. In the 1890s, a realtor built a giant wooden toboggan slide on its slopes to draw thrill-seeking clients. That venture burned down, but a rival successfully developed lots around the peak by offering carriage service from his downtown office. Starting in 1923, Mount Tolmie was known for the sunrise services held every Easter by the evangelical Rev. Dr. Clem Davies. As many as 8,000 attended his amplified sermons on the mount, and in 1928 the faithful erected an 18-foot red neon cross that glowed over the city at night. The services ended during World War II, when the military claimed the hill and built the observation platform that's there today, a nice place for stargazing and birdwatching.

THE SKY IS FALLING

Building or expanding a house in Victoria often requires hiring one of the city's six **blasting companies** to dynamite some rock. Sometimes they enjoy their work a bit too much, however. In 2005, residents of fast-growing Langford complained that flying boulders blasted off construction sites damaged cars in the Home Depot parking lot, and hit several houses. In one case, a two-kilo stone crashed through the ceiling of a child's bedroom.

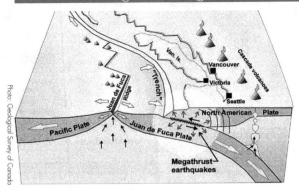

Photo: Geological Survey of Canada

Just off Vancouver Island, a gigantic slab of rock known as the Juan de Fuca plate inches slowly eastward and disappears beneath the even-larger North American plate, upon which our island sits. But here's the sticky part: the plates are locked, and the North American plate is buckling. (Victoria, which sits atop the fold, is actually rising several millimeters per year.) One day, it will snap loose – and the resulting **earthquake** may rival one in 1700 which wiped out Native villages and created a tsunami so big that it tossed whales into the forest.

Victoria already gets plenty of earthquakes. The Pacific Geoscience Centre *(pgc.nrcan.gc.ca)* in Sidney records more than 200 small quakes in this region every year. But geophysicists say that when the big one hits, Victoria will suffer more than other cities: there's a 37 percent likelihood in the next century of a quake big enough to destroy buildings in Victoria, versus only 22 percent in Vancouver. This probability already affects daily life here: millions have been spent quakeproofing local schools, and if an old building downtown sits empty, it's likely because the owner can't afford a seismic upgrade to bring it up to code. The same rules do not apply to houses, however, and it's anybody's guess how many will be levelled by major tremors – although you can get an idea from the Victoria earthquake maps published by the BC Geological Survey at *em.gov.bc.ca*. The risk of "amplification" is particularly bad on former marshland in the Cook Street Village, behind Fairfield Plaza, and around Swan and Blenkinsop Lakes and Rithet's Bog. According to the maps, the steep slopes of the Marigold neighbourhood and Cadboro Bay Village may also be vulnerable to slides. Did your realtor mention that?

Geological Field Notes

- Most of Vancouver Island is a formation of volcanic rock, granite, and limestone known as Wrangellia, which rammed into North America 100 million years ago. Victoria's western communities are geologically distinct, however: about 55 million years ago the mineral-rich sedimentary rock of the Pacific Rim Terrane collided with southern Vancouver Island, and 13 million years later the volcanic sea-floor rock of the Crescent Terrane attached itself, creating the southernmost tip of the island. These terranes are separated by the **Leech River Fault**, which extends from Sombrio Beach to Esquimalt Lagoon. The fault line, largely traced by Loss Creek, is so prominent that it's visible from space.

- **Gold** from the Pacific Rim Terrane still washes out in the Sooke River and Loss Creek. Miners continue to pan for gold on Loss Creek today.

- The Construction Aggregates **gravel pit** in Colwood was created by massive runoff when the last ice age receded 13,000 years ago. (Langford Lake is another glacial

leftover.) Opened in 1920, the pit was one of the largest in Canada, but is steadily being filled in by the Royal Bay development. The pit mainly supplies gravel to construction sites, but it has also shipped sand to Hawaii to replace eroded beaches. It's also the subject of an Emily Carr painting at the Art Gallery of Greater Victoria.

• Dallas Road has its own mineral: **Dallasite**, consisting of green and black chips of volcanic rock set in white quartz. Though found all over eastern Vancouver Island, it got its name because it was first noticed on Victoria's waterfront.

• The **Victoria Lapidary and Mineral Society** (islandnet.com/~vlms) puts on a rock and gem show every March. The **Rockhound Shop** (777 Cloverdale Ave., 475-2080, rockhoundshop.com), sells jewellery-making tools, metal detectors, and gold-panning equipment. For hands-on geology, visit **Mineral World** (9891 Seaport Pl., 655-4367, scratchpatch.com) in Sidney.

Victoria underwent a scientific revolution in 1913, when the Canadian and British governments commissioned two state-of-the art research facilities to be built in the city. One was the **Dominion Astrophysical Observatory** (see photo), constructed atop 223-metre (732-foot) Little Saanich Mountain. Dr. John Stanley Plaskett designed a 1.8-metre (72-inch) telescope and spectrograph to study the motion of stars. Horse teams dragged the lens elements to the peak, and when the telescope was completed in 1918 it was the largest in the world. (Six months later, it was dwarfed by a 200-inch scope on California's Mount Palomar.) Today the 45-ton telescope is the largest anywhere open for public viewing, and visitors can learn about its work next door at the **Centre of the Universe** (5071 West Saanich Rd., 363-8262, hia-iha.nrc-cnrc.gc.ca). The observatory also is adjoined by the prestigious **Herzberg Institute of Astrophysics**, whose astronomers have recently discovered new moons around Jupiter, Saturn, Neptune, and Uranus, and were the first to "weigh" a black hole (using infrared light emitted 13 billion years ago) that's three billion times the mass of the sun.

The other facility from that era is the **Gonzales Observatory**, atop Victoria's Denison Road. Local meterologist Francis Napier Denison designed and developed this weather station to provide crucial forecasts for the many ships delivering goods to and from the Pacific Northwest; he was so dedicated to his work that he and his wife lived in the observatory for more than 20 years. The building is closed to the public today, but its grounds are still open and used for research. Several years ago, UVic scientists tested the air column here for subatomic particles because the windswept hill enjoys some of the purest air on the Pacific Ocean, along with some spectacular views.

A decade ago, a few good restaurants in Victoria struggled to stay afloat amid seas of gravy and British pub grub. Today, farms raising heirloom and organic produce and meats have turned southern Vancouver Island into "Canada's Provence," and fresh, fantastic food is all over town – although tourists enjoy little of it around the Inner Harbour. Here's where to find it.

Breakfast Comes Eclectic

For many years, the king of downtown breakfasts has been **The Blue Fox** *(919 Fort St., 380-1683)*, famous for its eggs Benedict platters and French toast. Lately, however, some of the crowds have moved to the adorable **Shine Café**, *(1548 Fort St., 595-2133)*, and the fun-loving **Floyd's Diner** *(866 Yates St., 381-5114)* for its trucker-portion egg-and-potato breakfasts in numerous variations. With "The Mahoney" (named after the gambling-addict Flord's movie *Owning Mahoney*), you get whatever the kitchen prepares, and the waiter flips you double-or-nothing for the price of it. All these places are busy on weekends, so be prepared to line up.

If you prefer to savour your first meal of the day, **Mo:Lé** *(554 Pandora Ave., 385-6653)* is a hip brunch spot, doing up dishes like chanterelle and back bacon scrambled eggs, and organic spelt pancakes. **Lady Marmalade** *(608 Johnson St., 381-2872)* nearby serves stylish all-day breakfasts, including cheddar-and-spinach waffles with bacon and roast tomatoes. If only a buffet will quell your appetites, **The Black Olive** *(739 Pandora Ave., 384-6060, theblackolive.ca)* lays out a Euro-style smorgasbord on Sundays, with bennies, salads, a whole baked salmon, omelettes on demand, and more for only $12.

CHANGES TO THE MENU

Some people follow chefs' moves as closely as sportswriters monitor the NHL draft. If you're one of the former, look in many delis and restaurant foyers for *EAT* **magazine** *(eatmagazine.ca)*, a free Victoria-based publication that's become the equivalent of *The Hockey News* for BC's exploding food and beverage scene ("F&B" to insiders), providing all the latest dope on local cuisine.

There are numerous alternatives to the ubiquitous Starbucks. For location, nothing beats **Paradiso di Stelle** *(10 Bastion Square, 920-7266)*; sipping an espresso at its harbour-facing outdoor tables is the closest thing around to experiencing an Italian *piazza*, and it does grilled *panini* and fine *gelati* too. Organic coffee fiends and Chinatown characters congregate at **Bean Around the World** *(533 Fisgard St., 386-7115)*, although once they find a seat they never leave; for an alternative (and killer hot chocolate), try the **Solstice Café** *(529 Pandora Ave., 475-0477, solsticecafe.ca)* nearby. Away from downtown, serious devotees of the bean seek out **Caffé Fantastico** *(965 Kings Rd., 385-2326;* second location in the Cook Street Village), which has a rep for some of the best coffee in the Pacific Northwest, and Sam Jones defends his ranking as one of the continent's finest baristas at **2% Jazz Espresso Bar** *(2621A Douglas St., 384-5282, 2percentjazz.com)*, swirling his *spuma* like Emily Carr used her oils.

The English practice of taking afternoon tea is attributed to a 19th-century duchess who wanted to overcome the "sinking feeling" she felt late in the day – likely induced by hypoglycemia because the custom was to eat nothing between breakfast and a late dinner. Historians say the duchess's habit caught on during the industrial revolution because employers realized the break helped workers toil for longer hours. Whatever the reason, afternoon tea remains a tradition in today's Victoria. To experience it, try the following:

The Blethering Place

A stalwart restaurant in Oak Bay where you're infinitely more likely to meet a former RAF pilot than you ever will at The Empress. Afternoon tea is $15. This is also the best place for traditional dinners of roast beef and Yorkshire pudding, pork with crackling, and other heart-stopping classics. Open daily, but call ahead to make sure tour groups haven't filled the tables. *2250 Oak Bay Ave., 598-1413, thebletheringplace.com*

The Empress Hotel

A classic, and everyone knows it – in summer, demand for afternoon tea at The Empress is so great that they're often still serving it at 8 p.m. For $50 per person (alcohol not included), you get live music, silver pots of tea served on the Empress's own pattern of china (based

LUNCH ONLY

Some fine restaurants don't work nights. Foodies lunch weekdays at **Daidoco** *(22-633 Courtney St., 388-7383)*, hidden in Nootka Court near the Empress, for Japanese *sozai* (small plates) of fresh local seafood and organic produce (e.g., octopus salad, or handmade cakes stuffed with strawberries). Another hidden gem is **Cucina** *(#10, 532-1/2 Fisgard; no phone)*, in a set of former tenements converted into live-work studios in Chinatown's Dragon Alley: Cordon Bleu-trained Mirjana serves up new Adriatic-themed dishes every day in her condo kitchen. Also Mediterranean but out near UVic is **Olive Olio's** *(3840 Cadboro Bay Rd., 477-6618)* in a streamlined former gas station, worth a stop for great soups and salads.

on a service presented to the hotel by King George VI during his 1939 visit), strawberries with cream, finger sandwiches, and award-winning pastries. Five seatings after 12 p.m., more when a cruise ship is in town. Reserve at least two weeks ahead.
721 Government St., 384-8111, fairmont.com/empress

Four Mile House

This Tudor mansion built in 1858 was once an inn, and then a cabaret and brothel for Esquimalt's sailors. Today it's a cozy pub and restaurant, serving tea daily with huge platters of goodies for only $13. If you hear a spoon tapping against a cup and no one's there, that's the ghost of a woman who died in the house while her husband was away on a sea voyage.
199 Old Island Hwy., 479-2514, fourmilehouse.com

James Bay Tea Room & Restaurant

Just behind the Parliament Buildings, a quaint house full of royal family portraits that has been serving tea since 1983. The usual finger sandwiches, scones, and tea are only $11, and the menu includes such Anglo staples as kippers or Welsh rarebit on toast. Open daily.
332 Menzies St, 382-8282,
jamesbaytearoomandrestaurant.com

Point Ellice House

An interesting alternative to the Empress: take a harbour ferry up to this mansion, built in the 1860s for the O'Reilly family, and packed with over 15,000 items of their curious household Victoriana (e.g., a kerosene-heated curling iron). Volunteers from the Capital Mental Health Association serve tea 11 a.m.-3 p.m. daily, May to October; it's $20, which includes a tour of the building.
2616 Pleasant St., 380-6506

White Heather Tea Room

The best tea in town, foodwise, although the traffic outside dampens the mood. Agnes Campbell does wonderful baking, and the various-sized teas (from $11 to the $36 "Big Muckle" tea for two) include many surprises, such as cheese scones with chicken-apple filling or a Stilton-and-port pâté. Closed Sunday and Monday.
1885 Oak Bay Ave., 595-8020

THINK GLOBALLY, EAT LOCALLY

As you can tell from this chapter, Victorians enjoy an extraordinary variety of locally grown food. But the bounty is threatened. Forty percent of the region's farmers are near retirement, and hungry developers are making unbeatable offers for their properties (even when they're part of our mountainous province's Agricultural Land Reserve, or ALR) and paving it over for suburbs, blind to the fact that California lettuce will cost $20 a head if oil hits $200. What to do? Buy local even if it seems to cost more, says **Farm Folk/City Folk** *(ffcf.bc.ca)*, a BC advocacy group for greater "food security." Lobby politicians to protect the ALR. And support the cause at **Feast of Fields** *(feastoffields.com)*, a tasty fundraiser that brings together the region's conscientious chefs for a giant cookout on a local farm every September.

critics' choice

Food writers often praise these restaurants as the best in the city. Bring the plastic to find out if they're right: entrées at many of these places push $30.

Brasserie L'Ecole

Chef and co-owner Sean Brennan prepares French bistro fare with style: cured pork chops on creamed spinach and lentils, or a sensational steak *frites*. As the name suggests, the place offers an education in European beers, but all wines are available by the glass if your table buys two or more. Closed Sundays and Mondays.
1715 Government St., 475-6260, lecole.ca

Café Brio

One of Victoria's first truly good restaurants, and still going strong. Greg Hays and Silvia Marcolini are congenial hosts, welcoming devoted regulars into their warm gallery for French- and Italian-influenced dishes like *confit* of Cowichan Bay duck leg with braised chard, and grilled Sooke trout with gnocchi.
944 Fort St., 383-0009, cafe-brio.com

Camille's

Chef and owner David Mincey is dedicated to local cuisine: a typical tasting menu will include items such as Port Renfrew chanterelle soup with wild stinging nettle pesto and Cowichan Valley free-run chicken stuffed with pine mushrooms, all served in the haunted basement of downtown's former Law Chambers.
45 Bastion Sq., 381-3433, camillesrestaurant.com

Paprika Bistro

George Szasz, a son of the family that ran Vancouver's famous Szasz's on South Granville deli, hews to Hungarian tradition in Oak Bay with an upscale menu heavy on delicious, decadent meat (e.g., lamb three ways with house-made sausage).
2524 Estevan Ave., 592-7424, paprika-bistro.com

TASTY TOURISM

Southern Vancouver Island's best farms and wineries are so well hidden that even locals have a hard time finding them. Avoid fiddling with a map — and watching out for cops after sampling that pinot gris — by taking a regional tour instead. **Travel With Taste** *(385-1527, travelwithtaste.com)* does private one-day tours of Cowichan or Saanich peninsula farms and vineyards, with transportation, wine tastings, and a three-course lunch included, for about $250 per person; longer tours are possible, too. Their guides include Elizabeth Levinson, who literally wrote the book *(An Edible Journey)* on the region's cuisine. **Crush Wine Tours** *(888-5748, crushwinetours.com)* advertises shorter day tours of the same areas for around $80.

Temple

A former Freemasons' lodge transformed into a cool, Zen space with a translucent bar (DJs on weekend evenings) and smart cooking that mixes with the seasons (roast oysters, organic beef carpaccio). A good place to be seen drinking a cocktail, though it's stingy with wine by the glass.
525 Fort St., 383-2313, thetemple.ca

Zambri's

Rustic yet inventive Italian cuisine, in the unlikely location of a downtown strip mall. At lunch and dinner (except on Mondays), Peter Zambri whips up dishes like penne with sausage, ricotta, and crushed amaretto biscuits on top, or braised pork shoulder with polenta.
911 Yates St., 360-1171, zambris.ca

DIRECT TO PLATE

For a complete culinary experience north of the Malahat, nothing tops dining right at the place that grew your food. Book ahead for renowned chef Mara Jernigan's six-course Sunday lunches at **Fairburn Farm** *(3310 Jackson Rd. in Duncan, 250-746-4637, fairburnfarm.bc.ca)*, home to North America's only water-buffalo dairy. Tour the orchards around **Merridale Ciderworks** *(1230 Merridale Rd. in Cobble Hill, 250-743-4293, merridalecider.com)* and then dine on the deck of its La Pommeraie bistro. Or visit the vineyards of **Zanatta Winery** *(5039 Marshall Rd. in Duncan, 250-748-2338, zanatta.ca)*, the oldest in the region, then sip its superb sparkling cayuga in Vinoteca, a 1903 farmhouse that's now a rustic onsite restaurant.

destination dining

These legendary establishments are worth a trip from town, if you can afford to make it.

AL FRESCO

For fine waterfront dining, avoid **Milestones'** crowded tables on the Inner Harbour causeway and stroll north of the Johnson Street Bridge to the **Canoe Brewpub** *(450 Swift St., 361-1940, canoebrewpub.com)*, which has a southwest-facing patio overlooking the harbour, or the **Queen Mother Waterside Café** *(407 Swift St., 598-4712, qmwaterside.ca)* next door, a sister to the venerable Toronto diner, serving "global comfort food" of Laotian stir-frysfries with salads and burgers. (The tempura-fried calamari's more addictive than crack.) Away from the water and the traffic, there's a hidden patio in back of **Ferris' Oyster Bar and Grill** *(536 Yates St., 360-1824)* and on the roof of the **Strathcona Hotel** *(919 Douglas St., 383-7137)*, which keeps the BBQs fired and beer taps running all summer long, fueling the players at the world's only rooftop beach-volleyball courts.

The Aerie

Austrian businesswoman Maria Schuster bought 30 hectares atop the Malahat in 1984 and has developed it into one of the world's premiere resorts (so says *Travel+Leisure* magazine), with dining to match. Expect French flavour with seasonal seafood, game, and vegetables from 60 local farms, and prices as elevated as the views. The most intriguing feature is the fall mushroom hunt, when guests join a Benedictine monk on a forest trek, and then enjoy a three-course lunch using the fungi they've found. Thirty minutes from the city on Highway 1, less if you use the helicopter landing pad.
600 Ebedora Ln., 743-7115, aerie.bc.ca

Deep Cove Chalet

The region's finest French restaurant since Pierre and Bev Koffel established it in 1974, in a rambling former tea house that once stood at the end of BC Electric's Interurban line. In 2003, the Koffels nearly went the way of the streetcar: literally hours before the building was to be demolished, a friend bought it and gave them a long-term lease, preserving the only place around Victoria to get a proper soufflé.
11190 Chalet Rd., 656-3541, deepcovechalet.com

Sooke Harbour House

For more than 25 years, celebrities and gourmands have ventured to this remote inn to sample the most adventurous dining on the coast. Owner Sinclair Philip is a champion of "bioregional" cuisine, sourcing unusual local items that chef Edward Tuson turns into dishes as eclectic as the art on the inn's walls. The "gastronomic adventure" menu is guaranteed to have items you've never seen, like gooseneck barnacles in lobster broth with seaweed oil. The wine cellar is insured for $500,000. Past guests include Tim Allen, Mikhail Baryshnikov, Cindy Crawford, Robert DeNiro, French president Valéry Giscard d'Estaing, David Duchovny (he proposed to wife Téa Leoni here), Jodie Foster, Richard Gere, Jane Goodall, Robert Plant, Bonnie Raitt, Alan Rickman, and Wesley Snipes.
1528 Whiffen Spit Rd., 642-3421, sookeharbourhouse.com

the United Nations of food

Practically every culture has culinary ambassadors in Victoria. These restaurants do their homelands especially proud.

Cajun

If you hanker for crab cakes, jambalaya, and gumbo made with alligator meat, **Blue's Bayou** *(899 Marchant Rd., 544-1194)* is the most authentic Louisiana grill for thousands of miles around. The entire restaurant sits on a pier sticking into Brentwood Bay, and much of it is on an open deck, so bring your sunglasses.

Chinese

Several Victoria restaurants offer infinitely superior alternatives to fluorescent sauces and MSG. Those in the know line up (especially on weekends) for the lunchtime dim sum at **Don Mee** *(538 Fisgard St., 383-1032)*, when waitresses parade dishes fresh from the kitchen on carts (see photo) past tables of ravenous diners. Point

to what you want and they'll add it to your bill. (Don't pass up the sticky rice wrapped in lotus leaf.) If you've never done dim sum, try it here for a real Pacific Rim experience. Locals also flock to **J&J Wonton Noodle House** *(1012 Fort St., 383-0680)* to see Joseph Wong's team of chefs "wok" their magic. The specials are always a fine bet, as is anything containing their crispy roasted garlic. Closed Sundays and Mondays. Joseph's brother-in-law runs **John's Noodle Village** *(823 Bay St., 978-9328)*, which is

KID-FRIENDLY

Looking for a place to take your young family downtown? Even the pickiest kids will approve of **Café Mexico** *(1425 Store St., 386-1425)*, or the **Old Spaghetti Factory** franchise *(703 Douglas St., 381-8444)* near the Inner Harbour. Veggie parents can take their sprouts to the **Green Cuisine** buffet (page 114), which has a play corner, or **rebar** (page 114), which runs its in-house kids' toys through the dishwasher after every use.

just as good as **J&J** but without the crowds. For superbly spicy Chinese, try **Szechuan** *(853 Caledonia Ave., 384-0224)*, where you're also likely to hear interesting conversations carried over from the cop shop across the street.

First Nations

Smoked salmon, Dungeness crab with sea asparagus, johnnycake with local blackberries, and other modern versions of indigenous cuisine will claim your appetite at the **Riverwalk Café** in the Quw'utsun' Cultural and Conference Centre in Duncan *(200 Cowichan Way, 877-746-8119 or 250-746-8119, quwutsun.ca)*.

French

For white-tablecloth elegance without snooty pretensions, you can't do better than **Chez Michel** *(1871 Oak Bay Ave., 598-2015)*. All the classics – *foie gras*, onion soup, Coquilles St. Jacques, filet mignon with Bernaise – are prepared and served with care and good humour. Closed Mondays.

German

For more than 30 years, schnitzel, sauerbraten, and schnapps have been the order of the day at downtown's **Rathskeller** *(1205 Quadra St., 386-9348)*. It's so authentic it's got fresh hot pretzels, and live oom-pah-pah accordion Friday and Saturday nights.

Greek

For more than 20 years, Victorians have grabbed chicken souvlaki or gyros from **Eugene's** *(1280 Broad St., 381-5456)*. For more formal Greek cuisine, set sail to **San Remo** *(2709 Quadra St., 384-5255)*. Proud owner Paul Psyllakis splashes oil from his own olive groves back in Crete on every dish at **The Black Olive** *(739 Pandora Ave., 384-6060, theblackolive.ca)*, including his legendary roast lamb.

Indian

Da Tandoor *(1010 Fort St., 384-6333)* is a perennial Victoria fave, serving up rich butter chicken and other Mogul dishes from northern India. **Spicejammer** *(852 Fort St 480-1055)* adds African

I SCREAM, YOU SCREAM

In the summertime, everyone who visits Beacon Hill Park has to get a soft ice-cream cone from the **Beacon Drive-In** *(126 Douglas St., 385-7521)*, in business since 1959. (Despite the name, it's not really a drive-in: you have to walk up to order at the window.) For real Italian gelati, try **Paradiso di Stelle** (page 102), **La Collina** (page 112), or **Ottavio** *(2272 Oak Bay Ave., 592-4080, ottaviovictoria.com)*. But the best ice cream around isn't sold at a stand at all; instead, head to a supermarket and look for **Shady Creek Ice Cream** in the freezers. The company once won an Ethics in Action award for its use of local organic ingredients, and its flavours – lemon-thyme, lavender, dandelion – are a sweet reminder of the Garden City at any time of year.

flavours in such dishes as fried cassava or kuku paka, a coconut-chicken curry from Zanzibar.

Italian

If you want to don the black pinstripe and swirl a big Barolo, **Il Terrazzo** *(in the alley behind 555 Johnson St., 361-0028, ilterrazzo.com)*, is a romantic space with rich pastas, lamb and veal. For casual Italian, everyone loves **Pagliacci's** *(1011 Broad St., 386-1662)*, founded in 1979 by the ebullient Howie Siegel. In keeping with the movie-themed pasta dishes (Howie also owns the movie house Roxy Cine-gog), numerous stars have dined at Pag's, including Winona Ryder (she stayed in the limo and had the food brought to her), Mel Gibson (drank every night, loved the lasagna), and Ian McKellen (reputedly smoked pot with the kitchen staff). Bob Dylan ordered the tortellini with bacon and cream for takeout.

Jamaican

Everyting's irie at the **Jamaican Jerk House** *(607 Pandora St., 383-5344)*, including its goat curry, salt fish with ackee, and vegetarian options. The best deal is the $10 jerk chicken buffet on Friday evenings, followed by live reggae bands.

Jewish

Matzo ball soup, lox and bagels, gefilte fish, and knishes are some of the ever-changing offerings at the **Jewish Community Centre** *(3636 Shelbourne St., 477-7185)*, open for lunch only, Tuesday to Friday.

Getting Baked

A wise man who moved away said the three things he missed most about Victoria were bookstores, brewpubs, and bakeries. These places turn out the town's best breads and pastries.

Boland's
Oak Bay's second-oldest surviving business (after Oak Bay Hardware), a household bakery started in 1964 in the front half of a residential house. A new set of owners lives in back, but they pledge to keep baking mince tarts and apple strudel for the neighbourhood.
677 St. Patrick St., 598-5614

Bond Bond's
The only artisanal bakery right in the downtown core, serving up crusty

loaves for white-collar aficionados to take home after work. Try the olive, anise, and lavender baguette.
1010 Blanshard St., 388-5377

Breadstuffs
An incredible selection of pies, including blackberry-apricot, rhubarb-ginger, and plum, plus reputable hazelnut-toffee bars and shortbread.
1191 Verdier Ave. (Brentwood Bay), 652-5162

Cascadia Bakery
A bakery spin-off of the rebar restaurant, providing Chinatown with hearty breads and pies made with organic whole-grain flour. Excellent coffee and *panini* to enjoy in-house too, although getting a seat is tricky at lunchtime.
1812 Government St., 380-6606, rebarmodernfood.com

Dutch Bakery
Victoria's longest-running bakery, opened in 1956 by the Schaddelee clan from Rotterdam, with recipes that have hardly changed since then. They've sold more than two million vanilla slices, consisting of custard between sheets of puff pastry. The coffee shop in back is practically a museum, where you can get a feel for what downtown was like 50 years ago — and meet the old-timers who remember it.
718 Fort St., 385-1012

Korean

For a taste of home, ESL students make a pilgrimage to the stylish **Guru** *(1015 Fort St., 384-5337)* downtown for its vast menu and authentic dishes (the mushroom grill and bulgogi are standouts) served on sizzling hotplates.

Mexican

Adriana Ramirez is from the Baja peninsula, so it's no surprise that there's superb fish at **Adriana's Cocina Mexicana** *(1527 Amelia St., 388-0800, adrianascocina.com)*, situated on a downtown side street that is a museum of the city's early brick Italianate homes. Adriana's prawns, snapper, and ceviche are excellent, as is her chicken molé. Several generations of the Diaz family work at **Los Taquitos** *(in an industrial park at 2512 Bridge St., 384-9092)*, cooking up traditional dishes from various regions of Mexico. They make their own salsa and chorizo, and run the only corn tortilla factory in Victoria; many patrons buy an extra bag of tortillas to take home.

Thai

There's much more than *pad thai* at **Sookai Thai** *(893 Fort St., 383-9945)*. Try the superb *tom yum goong* (citrusy prawn and mushroom soup) and *chor muang*, violet-coloured flower dumplings stuffed with minced chicken. Many vegetarian options too; open for lunch, closed Sundays.

Vietnamese

Thuy Nguyen came to Canada in 1992 with her elderly mother and little more than the clothes on her back. She saved money from cleaning jobs to create **Saigon Nights**, a beloved restaurant that served up family recipes next to the Odeon cinema for more than a decade. After a 15-month sabbatical, she's reopened nearby *(915 Fort St., 384-2971)*, to the delight of her many fans.

food from the deep

Fish and Chips

A summer isn't complete without a visit to **Barb's Place** *(310 St. Lawrence, 384-6515, open March to October)* on Fisherman's Wharf. Former bus driver Barb Pedersen opened her fish shack in 1984, and since then it's become a landmark, earning mentions in a Harlequin romance and the *New York Times*. All fish is as you like it: grilled, steamed, or deep-fried. Away from the water, cast a line to **Fairfield Fish and Chips** *(1275 Fairfield Rd., 380-6880)*, which hews to tradition by wrapping takeout in newsprint. They also grill superb beef burgers. In Oak Bay, try **Willows Galley** *(2559 Estevan Ave., 598-2711, closed Mondays and Tuesdays)*, a neighbourhood institution since 1920 that looks like the cabin of a Cal 29 and is just as crowded. Get your meal to go and take it to Willows Beach a few blocks away. North of the Malahat, seek out the **Rock Bay Café** *(1759 Cowichan Bay Rd., 746-1550)*, a diner overlooking the docks in picturesque Cowichan Bay that serves gigantic two-piece fish-and-chip dinners.

Best Sushi

Obviously, a city on the Pacific has some great sushi. **Kaz** *(#100-619 Store St., 386-9121)* near Chinatown was recently voted best in Victoria by a panel of *Times Colonist* experts; try the exotic rainbow roll, stuffed with several varieties of fish. The **Marina Restaurant** *(1327 Beach Dr., 598-8555, marinarestaurant.com)* has

Italian Bakery

Since 1978, this Pozzolo family institution has been the place to get such seasonal yeast-free breads as *panettone*. Next door on Quadra they run La Piola, a deli and restaurant serving up risottos, pastas, and hand-tossed thin-crust pizzas made with organic ingredients they grow themselves.
3197 Quadra St., 388-4557; 103-2360 Beacon Ave. (Sidney), 656-7263

La Collina

Victoria's appetite for European baking has been proven by this business, grown to four locations since 1996. Superb biscotti, and such exotic breads as Gorgonzola with walnuts. (Call ahead for availability.) The Cedar Hill outlet serves pizzas in the evenings and bistro dinners on weekends.
3115 Cedar Hill Rd., 751 Vanalman Ave., 1286 McKenzie Ave., and 101-2376 Bevan Ave. (Sidney), 727-6577, lacollina.ca

Little Vienna Bakery

An oasis amid the Wonder Bread sold elsewhere in Sooke. Raspberry tarts, *schnecke* (snail) cinnamon buns, and other European delicacies, plus sandwiches and a deli counter.
#6-6726 Westcoast Rd. (Sooke), 642-6833

Mount Royal Bagel Factory

Fed up with supermarket "bagels" that were just buns with holes, two former Montreal musicians established this bakery in 1992 to create the real thing. The plain and sesame are the most authentic bagels in town, although they also do multigrain and dessert-quality cinnamon ones that cater to Island tastes.

6-1115 North Park St., 380-3588

Patisserie Daniel

As befits the name, excellent French baking and a cozy place to enjoy a bowl of *café au lait*. Daniel Vokey's muffins are the best in town (try the sour cherry). Great savoury quiches and tarts at lunch.

768 Fort St., 361-4243

Pure Vanilla

Fabulous fruit tarts and decadent baby cakes (try the lemon-lavender) that you can eat in the café, along with soup and sandwiches. Like the neighbouring real estate, it ain't cheap: an eight-inch "24 Karat Cake," covered with dark chocolate *ganache* and sprinkled with gold dust, costs $40.

2590 Cadboro Bay Rd., 592-2896

outstanding fish, but its sushi bar is tucked in back; if you sit at the regular tableclothed seats (with views of Mount Baker) and order from the sushi menu, you can have your *kaki* and eat it too. If there are vegetarians in your party, try downtown's **Futaba** *(1420 Quadra St., 381-6141)*, which has fishless entrees and *norimaki* made with brown rice, along with all the standards. For atmosphere, nothing tops **Sushi on the Sea** *(6669 Horne Rd., 642-6669, sushionthesea.com)*, aboard an oceangoing trawler at a wharf in Sooke. Open Friday and Saturday evenings or by reservation, its specialties include a hemp roll made with hearts of cannabis plants, cucumber, and asparagus. You can't get more west coast than that.

Fancy Fish

Victoria's sharpest fish restaurant is **Lure** in the Delta Victoria Ocean Pointe Resort *(45 Songhees Rd., 360-5873)* next to the Johnson Street Bridge. Be prepared to splurge to enjoy entrées like apple-cider poached halibut with pork belly, although you'll have great views of the harbour. Catch more water views and fine fish at the **Blue Crab Bar & Grill** in the Coast Harbourside Hotel *(146 Kingston St., 480-1999, bluecrab.ca)*.

Which Fish?

If you pay attention to the news, you know that our appetites are decimating the world's fish stocks. That's why the BC chapter of the Sierra Club has published a **Citizen's Guide to Seafood** *(sierraclub.ca/bc)* listing what's safe to eat and what isn't. Halibut, sablefish, Pacific octopus, albacore tuna and Dungeness crab are "OK for now," but avoid monkfish, bluefin tuna (the *toro* of sushi), Chilean sea bass, tiger prawns, and fake crab. Another no-no is farmed salmon, which researchers claim are destroying wild stocks. Until recently there was no protection for the dozens of species lumped together as "rockfish" (also sold as "local snapper"), so give them a break too.

Welcome to Planet Vegan

Audrey Alsterberg opened **rebar** *(50 Bastion Square, 361-9223, rebarmodernfood.com)* as a health-boosting juice stand in 1989, and it's since evolved to become one of the most successful vegetarian restaurants in Canada, famous for its Monk's Curry and shittake potstickers. (Divine their secrets in Alsterberg's bestselling cookbook of the same name.). More down-to-earth types seek out **Green Cuisine** *(#5-560 Johnson St., 385-1809, greencuisine.com)* on the lower level of Market Square for its one hundred percent vegan, hot and cold, pay-by-weight buffet. Open 10 a.m. to 8 p.m., it's the nerve centre for Victoria's eco-fringe, where you're likely to overhear conversations ranging from forestry policy to witchcraft.

Life's a Slice

Downtown, **The Joint** *(1219 Wharf St., 389-2226, eatatthejoint.com)* serves more wholesome pizza than most: all doughs and many of its ingredients are organic, and it caters to vegetarians with soy cheeses and non-meat pepperoni. **Ali Baba** *(1011 Blanshard St., 385-6666)* has been serving up great slabs since 1986, although their space has all the atmosphere of a Romanian bus station; more comfortable is **The Brickyard** *(784 Yates St., 995-2722)*, a convenient stop for a slice and a pint of local beer before or after a movie. For home delivery, try the beloved family-owned **Romeo's Place** *(603 Gorge Rd. East, 383-2121, more locations at romeosplace.com)*, which has a thin-crust special of chicken filet, capicollo, and mushrooms, or **Hothouse Pizza** *(110-180 Wilson St., 383-6700; 3-4071 Shelbourne St., 472-3663)*, the better half of the Cain-and-Abel split between the two Greek brothers who once ran the popular Villages chain.

The Roost Farm Bakery

Hamish Crawford and Bonnie Yarish raise ostriches, pheasants, and sheep on their farm near the airport, but what really sets them apart is the wonderful baking they do with red spring wheat they grow themselves, producing the only truly local bread in Victoria.
9100 East Saanich Rd., 655-0075

Sally Bun

Todd and Cindy Ryan create Victoria's equivalent of the Caramilk secret: fluffy buns stuffed with delicious fillings. The ham-and-egg is a great quick breakfast, and the curry vegetable or (highly addictive) lox and cream cheese go well with soup for lunch. Secluded patio out back.
1030 Fort St., 384-1899

True Grain Bread

The finest baking north of the Malahat. Authentic croissants (rare in these parts) and *pain au chocolat*, along with numerous varieties of organic bread. Closed Mondays and Tuesdays.
1725 Cowichan Bay Rd., 250-746-7664

Wild Fire

Ever-changing graffitied walls identify downtown's funkiest bakery. Wild Fire stone-mills organic grains and bakes them in a wood-burning oven on the premises, producing the city's chewiest baguettes. (Wild Fire gets it: the *raison d'être* of the baguette is its crust.) Also has organic coffee and pastries to munch on while regarding the eclectic and erratic passersby.

1517 Quadra St., 381-3473

Willie's Bakery

After fleeing the Franco-Prussian war, Saxon baker Louis Wille set up in this downtown storefront in 1887, and more than a century later, the owners of the Il Terrazzo restaurant next door re-established the space as a fine bakery in his honour. ("Willie" is a misnomer, but no one pronounced old Louis' surname properly anyway.) Big draws are breakfasts made with organic free-range eggs, and the sunny brick patio.

537 Johnson St., 381-8414

For more than 20 years, hungry Victorians have faithfully queued for big breakfasts at **John's Place** *(723 Pandora Ave., 389-0711, johnsplace.ca)*, a clattery downtown establishment; waffles and French toast are the morning staples; handmade burgers and gigantic pies at lunch. For a blast from the past, visit the copper-topped coffee shop of **Paul's Motor Inn** *(1900 Douglas St., 382-9231)*. Enterprising hotelier Paul Arsens opened this modernist diner in 1956, employing all sorts of publicity gimmicks – a groundbreaking ceremony with giant cutlery (see photo), the world's then-largest plastic sign – and fans still squeeze into its booths for a grilled cheese. Since 1963, truckers and school kids in Sooke have beelined to **Mom's Café** *(2036 Shields Rd., 642-3314)* for its jukebox and all-day eggs and burgers.

Literature & the Arts

Victorians are a bohemian lot – per capita, more people in this city identify themselves as artists on tax returns than anywhere else in Canada, and Victoria's audiences are second only to Ottawa's in the amount they spend on cultural goods. Here's a sketch of what Victoria creates, attends, and reads.

Emily's Last Laugh

To what can one attribute the ever-growing interest in **Emily Carr**? Certainly it's her reputation as one of North America's best 20th-century painters, ranking her alongside Frida Kahlo and Georgia O'Keeffe. Or her prescient environmentalism and appreciation of First Nations culture, decades before they became mainstream. But perhaps it's the arc of her biography, from early misunderstanding to late-blooming triumph, which captivates every struggling artist.

Born in 1871 on a farm backing onto the then-wilds of Beacon Hill Park, she learned her independence quickly: both of her parents were dead by the time she was 16, and she used her inheritance to study art in San Francisco and London. In 1907, she began travelling along the BC coast and sketching Aboriginal villages, and over the next six years created from these sketches more than 200 paintings in the bold, vivid style of French Impressionists. But when she exhibited this work in Vancouver in 1913, none of it sold, and when she offered it to the BC government, it was rejected – plunging her into a depression that kept her from painting for more than a decade. (Carr had suffered a nervous breakdown before in 1903, and spent 18 months in an English sanatorium undergoing shock therapy.) She became known around Victoria as a grumbling eccentric, raising sheepdogs, wheeling her pet monkey Woo around in a baby carriage, and running a boarding house, the "House of All Sorts" at 646 Simcoe. (She decorated its top-floor studio with two immense totemic eagles, which are still there today.) But by 1927, the Canadian art world was opening up to the grand abstracted landscapes of the Group of Seven, and when Group founder Lawren Harris saw Carr's work, he wrote letters of effusive praise, encouraging her to head back to the woods. Inspired by Walt Whitman's poetic transcendentalism, she painted with ever-bolder strokes, striving to capture the radiant, shimmering energy of the wilderness, rendering such local landmarks onto her canvases as Esquimalt Lagoon, Goldstream, and the cedars of Mount Douglas Park. After a heart attack in 1937, she stayed home and wrote, and her first memoir, *Klee Wyck* ("the laughing one," a nickname the Haida people gave her), won a Governor General's Award for literature. She wrote four more books before she died in 1945 at a nursing home at 270 Government Street (now the James Bay Inn), only a block from where she was born.

Today, visitors from around the world come to Victoria to learn more about Emily Carr — and though many of her later oil paintings ended up at the Vancouver Art Gallery, a selection of her art and letters are permanently displayed at the Art Gallery of Greater Victoria. Those seeking a more personal encounter troop through her family home at 207 Government Street (383-5843, emilycarr.com). Her grave is also the most visited site in the Ross Bay Cemetery (it's just on the other side of the hedge opposite Arnold Avenue), especially on March 2, the anniversary of her death. For several years, there's been talk of creating a statue of her, which has not yet been realized. But perhaps that's just as well. Along with her art, the monuments she most wanted the world to see are the "tabernacle woods" of BC that inspired her.

Offbeat Galleries

Alcheringa

The city's best showcase for contemporary Aboriginal art features work from Canada, Papua New Guinea, Micronesia, and Australia. Especially strong for hand-carved masks and statues.
665 Fort St., 383-8224, alcheringa-gallery.com

Community Arts Council Gallery

If any space lives up to Emily Carr's unfulfilled dream of a democratic civic gallery where the works of humble artisans rub frames with more-professional peers, it's the CACG. (Imagine coughing up a hairball as you pronounce it the "Cack.") This city-run gallery is an eye-pleasing escape from the bustle of downtown.
#6G-1001 Douglas St., 381-2787

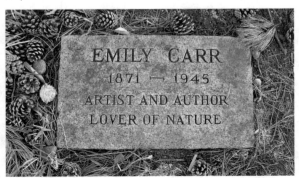

EMILY CARR
1871 — 1945
ARTIST AND AUTHOR
LOVER OF NATURE

Group of Eleven

If a jealous rival had dropped arsenic into the appies at an early meeting of **the Limners**, (see photo) Victoria's visual arts scene would've been set back half a century. When they first gathered in 1971 at the suggestion of elder states-brush **Maxwell Bates**, the 11 founding Limners (who took their name from the wandering portraitists and sign-painters of the Middle Ages) were already established artists, merely seeking the camaraderie and convenience of meeting and exhibiting as a group. They didn't plan to overthrow the establishment – but they shook it up nonetheless, teaching thousands of students, and creating an entirely new audience for contemporary art in Victoria.

Notable names signed to the guestbook for that formative meeting include: **Myfanwy Pavelić**, who painted actress Katharine Hepburn and former prime minister Pierre Trudeau, and was the first Canadian to have work exhibited in the National Portrait Gallery in London; poet, professor, collagist, and witch **Robin Skelton** and his calligrapher wife Sylvia; **Herbert Siebner**, who kick-started modernism in Victoria with his expressionistic oil paintings and lithographs; sculptor **Elza Mayhew**, whose monolithic bronze castings stand beside Ottawa's Rideau Canal and Charlottetown's Confederation Centre (and whose senile dementia was brought on by styrene poisoning from making her moulds); and **Karl Spreitz**, photographer and filmmaker. Later members include fabric artist **Carole Sabiston** and ceramicist **Walter Dexter**, both of whom won the prestigious Saidye Bronfman Award, and internationally acclaimed printmaker **Pat Martin Bates**. The group continues to accept a few new members (after much debate) and surviving Limners held an exhibition in 2005. The best place to see their classic work, however, is at the University of Victoria: one of Siebner's graffito murals resides next to the entrance of UVic's cinema, Mayhew's *Coast Spirit* obelisk stands in front of the McPherson Library, and many of Pavelić's paintings are kept by the Maltwood Gallery and visible online at *maltwood.uvic.ca*.

Deluge

The operators of the former Rogue Art space atop the Eaton (now Bay) Centre have reconvened in an old fire hall. Often the work is by the city's best alternative artists and affordably priced. Deluge has a busy social calendar too, making it a smart place to meet downtown.
636 Yates St., 385-3327

Fifty Fifty Arts Collective

An artist-run centre that presents shows by graffiti artists, fashion designers, cartoonists, and more, plus a Shock Corridor cinema series. The hours are difficult to predict, so visit the online schedule first.
2516 Douglas St., thefiftyfifty@hotmail.com

Legacy Art Gallery and Café
Over the decades, patrons have donated more than 15,000 works of art to the University of Victoria, comprising everything from Ming vases to paintings by Jack Shadbolt and Richard Atilla Lukacs. Rotating shows from these collections go on display at this new gallery, in a former bank bequeathed to the university by developer Michael Williams – finally giving UVic a real downtown presence. But when will it get off its duff and build a downtown?
630 Yates St., 381-7670

Though they're on practically every street corner downtown (ok, an exaggeration), **totem poles** aren't indigenous to Victoria. The local Songhees natives created wooden figures for the walls of their ceremonial dance houses, but true totem poles originated farther north among such peoples as the Haida and the Kwakwaka'wakw, who carved images of their legendary beings and tribal crests into single logs of red cedar, and then erected them to commemorate their peoples' origins and achievements.

Starting in the 1870s, hundreds of totem poles were bought or stolen from coastal villages and shipped to museums around the world. British Columbians were so concerned that the province's cultural heritage was vanishing that in 1886 they petitioned the government to create the BC Museum of Natural History and Anthropology (today's **Royal BC Museum**) and acquire its own collection of Native artifacts. The museum relocated several historic totem poles to **Thunderbird Park** at the corner of Douglas and Belleville streets, but moved them indoors in the 1950s (many stand preserved in a glass room on the museum's northeast corner) and hired **Mungo Martin**, one of the last surviving Kwakwaka'wakw master carvers, to make replacements. He and his assistants created nearly all the replica poles in Thunderbird Park.

One of Mungo Martin's original works stands in **Beacon Hill Park** near Dallas Road. This huge pole depicts a legend of his clan, about an ancestor who awoke to see a gigantic pillar of live, chattering animals rising out of the beach, followed by a man announcing that these creatures were the crests of his people. (Contrary to cliché, the "low man on the totem pole" isn't the least important: the largest figure is most significant, and it's often at the base.) When this 39-metre pole was erected in 1956, it was the tallest in the world, although the record is currently held by one in Alert Bay on the northern tip of Vancouver Island.

Many other local poles were the product of a 1958 "Route of the Totems" contest. First place went to the one in front of the Swartz Bay ferry terminal coffee shop, depicting a grizzly bear holding a killer whale, created by **Henry Hunt**, who became the museum's chief carver after Mungo Martin died in 1962. Henry Hunt also created the most-photographed pole in the city, at the northwest corner of Government and Belleville, of a frog, a bear holding a copper (a plate representing wealth), and a dancer. In front of the museum, you'll find a curious pole carved in 1979 by his son Richard Hunt, of

the supernatural bird Kolus, a chief holding a copper, and a bear holding a man (see photo). The man is based on a friend of the carver who'd had a childhood accident with an axe. Look closely and you'll see that part of one of his fingers is missing.

Ministry of Casual Living

Is it a gallery, an arm of government, or a grow-op? That's one of many questions raised by this former Fernwood retail space, converted by two UVic grad students in 2002. It's rarely open, but its *faux*-bureaucratic sign is just realistic enough to draw curious passersby to see the current display in the window.

1442 Haultain St.,
ministryofcasualliving.ca

The Trials of Public Art

Much of the artwork created in Victoria comes and goes with nary a peep from many citizens – instead, locals are more likely to save their invective for the city's latest piece of public art. Frequently paid for by developers in need of rezoning, numerous pieces of **street-level sculpture** around town have caused letters-to-editors pages to be filled with angry critiques.

You'd think that eco-themed art would please Gore-tex-clad Victorians, but guess again: one of the most hated pieces in town is **Illarion Gallant's** *Bowker Accord*, a barren metal tree and bubbling pond in front of the medical building at 1990 Fort Street. Though it's supposed to commemorate the creek buried under the pavement, its principal effect has been to depress every outpatient who passes by. (Perhaps having learned from this, Gallant's latest commission is to create a bouquet of sunny six-metre flowers to stand outside the Victoria airport.) Another environmental contradiction is *Millennium Peace*, a 2,500-kg marble slab near Clover Point donated by sculptor (and former Dutch Bakery cake decorator) Maarten Schaddelee: its carvings of frolicking dolphins are innocent enough, but its eco-friendly message is overpowered by the fact that it's right next to the station that pumps the city's sewage into the ocean.

Like most people, Victorians want the meanings of public art to be utterly transparent: a brass sailor shouldn't look like anything other than a brass sailor. Perhaps that's why the city's most-heated debates recently have been focused on the mystifying work of veteran installationist and UVic professor **Mowry Baden**. In 2002, *Monday Magazine* readers judged his piece in front of the condo tower at 605 Douglas Street – a set of rust-coloured mattresses and a sheet-metal banner declaring *Night is for Sleeping, Day is for Resting* – to be the city's worst

Open Space

Founded as an artist-run cultural centre in 1971, Open Space continues to host the city's most innovative events and exhibitions – experimental theatre, avant-skronk jazz, head-scratching conceptual installations, guerrilla film screenings, and performance art "happenings" that seem straight out of Chelsea. *510 Fort St., 383-8833, openspace.ca*

Xchanges Gallery

Tucked away on a residential street in Vic West, this artist-run gallery and hive of studios puts on an eclectic series of programs, from drop-in drawing classes to triple-X erotic art shows. Regularly open weekend afternoons. *420 William St., 382-0442, xchangesgallery.org*

eyesore. (If you parse Baden's massive Zen koan as revealing the secret motto of bored government employees who walk past it to work, you'll understand why they hate it so much.) Surpassing himself, soon afterward Baden got city approval and $120,000 to create his weighty *Pavillion, Rock, Shell* (see photo on previous page), provoking hate mail that continued long after it was installed in front of the Save-On Foods Memorial Arena in 2005. Perhaps hockey fans will eventually realize that Baden's glacial-boulder-and-steel-chambered curiosity is the only refuge on the arena's austere, pre-fab plaza — but even if they don't, the 3,000-kilogram sculpture will be nearly impossible to move.

HIDDEN TREASURES

It might seem odd to describe Victoria's major civic gallery as "unknown," but many locals still can't find the **Art Gallery of Greater Victoria**'s Rockland hideaway. Too bad: this former banker's mansion (plus a modern wing) holds exhibitions of world-class contemporary art, and stages new shows of the 16,000 items in its collection, including works by Picasso, Dürer, Goya, and Monet, along with one of the best troves of Asian art in Canada. (The courtyard also houses the only original Shinto shrine outside Japan.) The gallery's most valuable canvas is a scene of Venice by Canaletto worth $3 million — although there's debate about whether he actually painted it. Several years ago restorers brought its colours back to life by swabbing them with Q-tips soaked in their own spit. *1040 Moss St., 384-4101, aggv.bc.ca*

Spray-Can Salon

A decade ago, the warehouse district around the Esquimalt railway tracks was plagued by vandalism and fights. In 2001, a police-affiliated non-profit group decided to channel the violent energy of the neighbourhood kids into something more constructive, and created the **Trackside Art Gallery** *(800 Hereward St., rocksolid.bc.ca)*, purportedly the world's largest outdoor gallery for youth. Once a year, they hold an art contest and reprint the best work as illuminated billboards; now there are several dozen of them above the tracks, plus constantly changing displays of ground-level graffiti.

Photo: British Columbia Archives F02852

Mystery Theatres

Victoria, birthplace of Surrealism. Tourism brokers have been slow to print this claim on brochures, but it's true: long before the surrealist photography of Paris shutterbug Man Ray, **Hannah Maynard** was using multiple exposures and collage techniques to produce unsettling new styles of portraiture right here in little ol' Victoria.

After emigrating from England with her husband, Maynard opened a photography studio at 733 Johnson Street in 1862. Her first experiments were her "Gems of British Columbia," *Sgt. Pepper*-like montages of children's faces she'd photographed during the year. Subsequent Gems incorporated the previous years' portraits, until her final versions squeezed 20,000 cherubs into a frame. Maynard also took police mug shots and bragged that she'd photographed every person in town.

But in the mid-1880s, after her two daughters died of typhoid, Maynard became fascinated by spiritualism and communication with the dead, and began creating multiple exposures in which repeated images of herself appeared in morbidly playful tableaux. In one, she leans from a picture frame to pour tea on her unsuspecting triple image (see photo); in another, multiple Maynards pose beside a pedestal holding up her grandson's severed torso, surrounded by images of her dead daughters. And you thought *your* grandma was creepy.

Pricy rents and vigilant fire inspectors have always made it difficult for small and medium-sized theatre groups to find legit performance space in downtown Victoria. Here's an overview of local thespians and the odd places you'll find them acting up.

The Belfry
Where: a former Baptist church
In the '70s, it was a shelter for transient youth and a performance space for the likes of Lawrence Ferlinghetti and the Kronos Quartet. Today, after energetic fundraising and many renovations, it's the city's showcase for top-notch Canadian and international drama.
1291 Gladstone Ave., 385-6815, belfry.bc.ca

Kaleidoscope Theatre
Where: various
After more than 30 years producing professional drama for kids and adults, Kaleidoscope continues to put on its original shows in various local schools.
383-8124, kaleidoscope.bc.ca

Naturally Talented

As you'd expect in a place blessed with environmental wonders, the Victoria area is home to two of the world's finest nature artists. **Robert Bateman** quit teaching art and geography in Ontario in 1976 to paint full-time, moved to Salt Spring Island, and has since become Canada's most successful wildlife painter, commanding $75,000 and more for his acrylic renderings of wolves, cougars, and whales. (His style, which could be branded "Greenpeace realism" for its portrayals of animals at their noblest moments, was inspired by Andrew Wyeth's attention to detail.) An outspoken environmentalist (he recently denounced a North Saanich marina's expansion into a bird sanctuary), his donated works have raised millions for local and international wildlife causes; they're also exhibited at Sidney's **Peninsula Gallery** *(100-2506 Beacon Ave., 655-1722, pengal.com)*.

Fenwick Lansdowne was born in Hong Kong and spent much of his childhood at the Queen Alexandra Solarium at Mill Bay (he contracted polio as an infant), where he was fascinated by overwintering seabirds and songbirds of the surrounding forest. Largely self-taught, when he was still a teen, his counsellor at Victoria High School got his bird paintings to a curator of the Royal Ontario Museum, resulting in a ROM show and a *Maclean's* magazine cover story. His numerous books, such as the two-volume *Birds of the West Coast*, remain bestsellers, and his work's often shown at **Winchester Galleries** *(2260 Oak Bay Ave., 595-2777, winchestergalleriesltd.com)*.

Langham Court Theatre

Where: a converted barn and carriage house

Since 1929, this ever-changing stable of amateur and student actors has staged more than 500 shows, making it western Canada's oldest community theatre.

805 Langham Ct., 384-2142, langhamcourttheatre.bc.ca

Photo: Tim Matheson

Phoenix Theatre

Where: university campus

One of Canada's top theatre schools produces a full season of plays, often employing huge casts and elaborate stagecraft (swimming pools, hockey rinks) that can only be realized with dozens of students and an institutional budget.

University of Victoria, 721-8000, phoenixtheatres.ca

Ghostly Apparitions

When he died in 2003, **Hans Fear, a.k.a. "Ghost,"** was the most venerated street artist in Victoria. Afflicted with schizophrenia, Fear drew constantly, churning out dozens of sketches a day and spraying his cartoony renderings – influenced by sources as diverse as Japanamation and Gustave Doré – on walls all over town. You can still see examples of his work on the side of Mount Royal Bagel at 6-1115 North Park Street (see photo), and the insurance offices at 1580 Cook Street. Musicians hold a concert in his memory every February to raise money for schizophrenic patients with artistic ambitions.

historic houses

McPherson Playhouse

This handsome theatre at the corner of Government and Pandora opened in May 1914 as part of the growing empire of Alexander Pantages – a cook in a Victoria café back in 1900 who later got rich (rumour said) by sweeping up gold dust from saloon floors in the Klondike. For over a decade, the building was part of Pantages' chain of vaudeville houses across America: Al Jolson played in it, as did boxer Gentleman Jim Corbett, who told tales of his days in the ring. Pantages' business was killed off by the movies, and the theatre underwent numerous name changes until its owner Thomas Shanks McPherson died and willed the building to the City of Victoria. It reopened in 1965 (after a thorough modernist renovation) with a solo performance by *The Bride of Frankenstein's* Elsa Lanchester.

Photo: Barbara Pendrick

Puente Theatre

Where: a house in Fairfield

Named after the Spanish word for "bridge," this society provides a window into Victoria's immigrant communities by producing plays from Latin America, Africa, the Caribbean, and Asia, holding workshops (techniques of the theatre of the oppressed) and staging readings – often in the tiny and well-hidden La Run theatre.

592-4367, puentetheatre.ca

Theatre SKAM

Where: Where not?

While these theatrical innovators – who never met a loading dock, public park, or Plymouth Volaré they couldn't turn into a stage space – have gone on to bigger things and cities, they still return for an annual "Summer Kamp" of dramatic derring-do in unexpected venues.

386-SKAM, skam.ca

Royal Theatre

When the 1,400-seat Royal Theatre at 805 Broughton Street opened in 1913, it was one of the grandest theatres on the west coast, built of over a million bricks and 400 tons of steel shipped from the east. Perhaps too grand for little Victoria: after losing money for decades, in 1946 it became a movie house (Famous Players threatened to tear it down in 1969) until 1982, when it was taken over by the McPherson Foundation. Some $3 million was spent in the late 1980s adding lobbies on either side to buttress the building, and recently it's undergone a $2-million exterior restoration, repairing (among other things) its terracotta gargoyles (see photo) – although overhauling its cramped seating, orchestra pit, and staging will cost 10 times that much. Past performers include Will Rogers, Fred Allen, Jimmy Durante, John and Ethel Barrymore, Bing Crosby, Bob Hope, Charles Laughton, Katharine Hepburn (in *As You Like It*), Paul Robeson (in *Othello*), Sarah Bernhardt, Jascha Heifetz, Ignace Jan Paderewski, Mikhail Baryshnikov, Rudolph Nureyev, Vincent Price, Shirley MacLaine, Tom Jones, Harry Belafonte, Bob Newhart, Stompin' Tom Connors, Ray Charles, Nana Mouskouri, Marcel Marceau, Victor Borge, Rich Little, and Honor ("Pussy Galore") Blackman.

William Head on Stage

Where: a prison

Since 1981, William Head Institution has run the only theatre in Canada where the actors are more captive than the audiences. One inmate/thespian tried to escape from the penitentiary in the stage coffin from a production of *Dracula*. Curious audiences should be that eager to get in to catch this unique dramatic experience.

6000 William Head Rd., 391-7000

Victoria Conservatory of Music

The conservatory was originally conceived in 1964 as a training camp to provide more string players for Victoria's symphony. After labouring in several locations (including Craigdarroch Castle), in 1998 it took over an asymmetrically gothic United church at 907 Pandora Avenue, which has since proven a fine home. The rose-windowed sanctuary (its semi-circular design was supposed to bring clergy and congregation together), now called the Alix Goolden Hall, is the best place in town to hear a recital. Famous conservatory grads include singers Richard Margison, Benjamin Butterfield, and Barbara Livingston, and pianists Jon Kimura Parker and May-Ling Kwok.

literary Victoria

To get a real sense of Victoria's unknown dimensions, there's no better source than local literature.

First Nations Victoria

The tales and legends of the Saanich people are now being written down – and interpreted with 21st-century consciousness – by **Philip Kevin Paul**, a boxer-turned-poet and son of the late Tsartlip chief Philip Paul. In "ĆIȺȺĆU," a poem in his prize-winning first collection, *Taking The Names Down From The Hill*, he considers an old Saanich word when he sees a "No Hunting" sign on land where his ancestors tracked animals:

Maybe everything has gone as planned,
by some plan, but I still want to know
why no one said a word when someone
fenced off the Place of Deer, and what
the Old People ate when the spring came
and they weren't allowed to hunt.
Just one word.
ĆIȺȺĆU, the name of the spring hunt.
ĆIȺȺĆU, name of the sick deer and
the tide that leaves salt to cure them.
ĆIȺȺĆU, the one word waiting
behind a salal blind to erupt
from its own eternity of silence
and run down the hill.

(Reprinted with permission from Nightwood Editions.)

Debutante Victoria

The '50s were as pinched as a Dungeness crab – at least, that's how they're portrayed by **M.A.C. Farrant** in *My Turquoise Years*, her memoir of absentee parents and Cordova Bay beach, back when it was considered far from town:

The beach here was littered in summer with pale families
spread out on wool blankets having their lunches –
bottles of Coke or Orange Crush and floppy white
bread sandwiches. People out for the day, chancing the
tides and the weather, city people. . . . These were kids

Fantastic Festivals

Victoria's best annual art, music, and theatre events. (For multicultural and civic events, see Living.)

The Belfry's Festival Series
A quick study of the best of Canadian contemporary theatre: short runs of experimental plays that have recently wowed audiences across the country. *March; 385-6815, belfry.bc.ca*

Fringe Theatre Festival
Brechtian songspiels, Ukrainian mime, *One-Man Star Wars* – anything goes at this uninhibited, unjuried extravaganza of experimental dance, drama, and comedy, featuring new local shows and seasoned performers touring from fringe festivals across Canada. *End of August; 383-2663, intrepidtheatre.com*

who were shamefully white or blotchy red with sunburn. Their fathers, wearing white undershirts and rolled-up pants that exposed their gnarly feet, slept after lunch with newspapers spread over their faces. Their mothers wore cotton housedresses – never shorts or bathing suits – and spent the entire beach time hollering at their kids to stay close to shore. We pitied them all.

(Reprinted with permission from Greystone Books.)

Bluesy Victoria

There's more to Victoria musically than bagpipes and punk guitars. **Charles Tidler**, the playwright with the raucous laugh and Henry Miller sensibility, finds jazz and blues jumping out everywhere, in his 2001 monologue *Red Mango*:

Friday Night, I stand at the doors of the Glad Tidings Church on Quadra Street and look in. The gospel singers The Blind Boys of Alabama are whooping it up in front of five hundred people. An electrifying musical union of flesh and spirit, they wail, shout, cry and jump for Jesus. Shouting is the mother of the blues. Wild, wild, wild Clarence Fountain can jump as high as heaven, holding a note to the end of time. This blind old man with ten gold rings on his ten fingers is a human trinity of flesh, art, and belief. Five hundred men, women and children jump with Clarence, jump up and down and howl with joy. Howling with joy is an antidote to doubt, to pain, to the terror of existence.

(Reprinted with permission from Anvil Press.)

Rustic Victoria

Victoria may be the only city with residents who haul hay in the morning and teach at the university in the afternoon. The best of our dungareed philosophers is **Tom Henry**: now editor of *Small Farm* magazine, during the 1990s he charmed CBC Radio listeners with his ruminations on mud rooms, "jobsite evangelists," and other phenomena of rural Victoriana. In his collection *Dogless in Metchosin*, he explains "estate cars," the unlicensed, dilapidated vehicles locals use for errands on their property:

Smoke is as common to estate cars as fleas and bad

JazzFest International

Major stars stop by Victoria on their summer tours: past performers have included Dave Brubeck, Cesaria Evora, and Charlie Haden. Inventive DJs (Bonobo, Kid Koala) and world-music artists (Calexico, Rachid Taha) are often part of the line-up too. *End of June; 388-4423, vicjazz.bc.ca*

Moss Street Paint-In

More than 70 painters, sculptors, performance artists, and musicians line Fairfield's Moss Street all the way to the waterfront, displaying their latest work and often producing more right on the spot. A unique event that really shows off Victoria's creative, civilized personality. *July; 384-4171, aggv.bc.ca*

breath are to dogs. This is because their engines are worn and out of tune. The smoke isn't always your #1 Pennzoil either, as owners tend to dump whatever goop is on hand into the engine. Like bar oil for the chain saw. That comes out of an old engine as a sour pink mist. Run into a nasty haze on a country road and there's a good chance an estate car is nearby.

(Reprinted with permission from Harbour Publishing.)

Twelve-Step Victoria

Vancouverites and Torontonians live longer than Victorians — because we have higher rates of alcoholism and depression. Both these forces manifest themselves in **Patrick Lane**'s *There is a Season*, his searing 2004 memoir about booze, death, and the healing power of his Saanich garden:

This morning I was cleaning ivy away from the side of the compost bin and found two empty vodka bottles tucked behind the vines. Vodka still pooled at the bottom of the bottles, a translucent liquid jewel behind the glass, a thimbleful, no more. I thought of the day I must have lifted the bottles and drained them, held them to my lips until the last vodka slipped down the glass. A thimbleful left, a narrow swallow, a lip, a tongue away behind the glass walls, the metal cap.

(Reprinted with permission of the author.)

Delinquent Victoria

The Garden City is rooted upon dark matter. Lately this fact has come to light in volumes about the murder of Reena Virk (see page 213), but even in the flower-power 1960s, Victoria was overgrown with crime. **Britt Hagarty**, a local drummer and junkie who did time in the former Fisgard Street police station, recaptured its ambiance in his 1979 novel *Prisoner of Desire*:

The Victoria city jail is a depressing place, noisy, dirty, filled with stumblebum winos, sullen pock-marked Indians, pimply-faced juvenile delinquent joyriders, junkies going through withdrawal, anyone who's been arrested but hasn't yet been transferred to Wilkinson Road Jail where most people await trial on Vancouver Island. Dinner is supplied by a local Chinese restaurant

Symphony Splash

Victorians love free events, and this one's a doozy: up to 40,000 people spread out on the Parliament Buildings lawn (or take to canoes and kayaks) to hear the Victoria Symphony perform on an Inner Harbour barge. The cannons of the *1812 Overture* traditionally finish the show.
First Sunday of August; 385-9771, symphonysplash.ca

UNO

There's no theatre more minimal than this festival of solo performance, featuring monologuists, comedians, and dancers selected from across North America.
End of May; 383-2663, intrepidtheatre.com

Victoria Blues Bash

Touring blues legends (Buckwheat Zydeco, Duke Robillard) rip it up at Ship Point on the waterfront and other venues around town.
Labour Day weekend; 388-4423, vicjazz.bc.ca

Unique Sounds

Victoria has numerous ensembles, but these strike a distinctive chord.

Gettin' Higher Choir

The Victoria Choral Society may be the oldest classical choir in town, but certainly the largest is this 300-plus, non-auditioned choir that welcomes all to rediscover the joy of singing in harmony.
386-3184, shivon.com

Jazz Vespers

On the third Sunday of every month, Rev. Ken Gray of Colwood's Church of the Advent serves the Lord and his passion for jazz simultaneously, with improv prayer services featuring some of the city's best musicians.
510 Mount View Ave., 474-3031, colwoodanglican.ca

whose cook ought to be imprisoned himself for the suffering he's imposed on the local prisoners. There are no sheets on the hard bunks, and most cells usually have only one solitary flea-bitten blanket. There are seldom any interesting books lying around and the lights go out early, about nine-thirty, so it wasn't much fun for an insomniac like myself.

(Reprinted with permission from Talonbooks.)

Urban Victoria

View Towers, the 1972-built monstrosity at the corner of View and Quadra, is downtown's largest apartment block – and a frequent stop for cops on the beat. It's also the inspiration for *Zed*, **Elizabeth McClung**'s 2005 debut novel, about a 12-year-old girl trying to survive in a building thick with junkies, sex offenders, and sociopaths.

The Tower, an unpainted concrete tenement block twenty storeys high with basements and sub-basements below. At the end of the hall ran concrete stairs, unpainted and unventilated, winding back and forth, up and down. They were cob-webbed, grimed, half-lit, urine-scented, and suspiciously sticky. Still, a majority of the tenants used them, unless they were suicidal enough, or drunk, or stoned or oblivious enough to take the elevators. Not that anyone had died ... yet. But both elevators did have a tendency to groan a little.

(Reprinted with permission from Arsenal Pulp Press.)

Oriental Victoria

Victoria's old Chinatown was never rendered into fiction by anyone who actually lived there, but it has been beautifully portrayed by locally raised poet and novelist **Marilyn Bowering**. In *To All Appearances a Lady*, she tells a historical ghost story that sweeps across the Pacific from 19th-century Asia to the leper colonies and opium dens of colonial Victoria, in the voice of a half-Chinese ship's pilot haunted by his 100-year-old stepmother:

Boardwalks and dusty streets. Peddlers loading up with goods. Notice boards, advertisements, businessmen sweeping their premises. And a grid of Chinatown streets in the early morning light. The whiskey sellers in the ravine at Johnson Street rolled barrels of tangleleg into carts, and Indians set out in canoes from the canvas settlement across the harbour to meet the shipments. . . . The sun rose over Pandora, Cormorant, and Fisgard streets: streets banded north-south by Douglas, Government, and Store; streets fronted by poulterers, shippers, provisioners, and interpenetrated by the multitudinous alleys that ran, like so many cracks in stone, through the heart of this network of commerce. A maze where tenement piled on tenement like so much waste.

(Reprinted with permission from Random House Canada.)

Sexy Victoria

Local authors don't spend all their time between the covers; they're also exploring the places to get off in the Garden City. The always-adventurous Susan Musgrave, for example, once confessed that she lost her virginity on the lawns of UVic — in the exact spot where its law school was later erected. But the most sensual spot for literary lovin' seems to be the beachfront below Dallas Road, its reputation cemented by **Linda Rogers** and her *Woman at Mile Zero* (1990), the cover of which features the poet lounging on the shoreline rocks in a sea-soaked dress:

Last night, the sea was wild on Dallas Road. It hit the restraining wall with the angry slap of a mother when she and her child share the same strangely sexual fear of death, when he perversely dangles himself from a tenth story window or runs in front of a car. Or my hand on your cheek when we are too far apart for kissing. Or yours on mine. I saw you on the wall. We danced together in the waves and headlights. Maybe we were trying to push each other off.

(Reprinted with permission from Oolichan Books.)

Moodswing Orchestra

Therapy that swings: a society based out of the psychiatric wing of the Royal Jubilee Hospital brings together people with mental illnesses in various groups that play blues, country, and big-band tunes. *2328 Trent St., 592-5114, pacificcoast.net/~fom*

Palm Court Orchestra

Nothing evokes the feeling of 1930s British high society more than this venerable Cowichan Bay-based group, which has performed light-hearted (Cole Porter, Gilbert and Sullivan) tunes with teacup-and-wicker authenticity since 1987. *(250) 748-9964, palmcourtorchestra.com*

Soft Openings

Opera has been staged in Victoria since at least 1885, and numerous international stars (Ernestine Schumann-Heink, Dame Kiri Te Kanawa) have performed here to enthusiastic audiences. Since 1979, local buffs have been keen subscribers to productions of **Pacific Opera Victoria** *(pov.bc.ca)*, which has staged an extraordinary number of world premieres considering the city's geography and size. Star tenor Ben Heppner had one of his first roles in a POV production, and tenor Richard Margison and director Robert Carsen did their first shows here before going on to global fame – although they don't mention it on their resumés, because saying you debuted in Victoria doesn't impress at the Met.

Kino Experimental

Most Victorians don't know it, but their city has a place in the history of cinematic art. The king of American experimental film, **Stan Brakhage**, made several of his most important "metaphorical film poems" here in the 1990s, inspired by his wife Marilyn, who grew up in Oak Bay. His "Vancouver Island Trilogy" includes *A Child's Garden* and *the Serious Sea* (see photo), a 70-minute imagining of Marilyn's childhood, filmed at her family home on McNeill Avenue, and the *Mammals of Victoria*, in which storm-tossed waters at Cattle Point evoke the turbulence of her adolescence. Brakhage spent the last years of his life in Victoria before he died in 2003, and yet his trilogy's never been shown here. Another cinematic artist is **Rick Raxlen**, who has cranked out dozens of amusing postmodern films in his cramped Fort Street studio, many incorporating his own hand-painted animations, found materials (old ska records, *Mutt and Jeff* cartoons), and Dadaist texts. His work has exhibited at such venues as New York's Museum of Modern Art, but Victorians are most likely to see it on his website, *raxpix.com*.

BASSES LOADED

No less than *Time* magazine declared Victoria's own **Gary Karr** the "world's leading solo bassist." That's not news to aspiring classical performers, as students lug their bulky instruments from the four corners of the globe to attend his summer Karr Kamp at the University of Victoria. Karr recently retired from an international performing career to concentrate on recording and teaching, so the only way to hear him create his sonorous sounds live is to visit the city when he joins his happy "Kampers" for their annual "Basses Loaded" recital at the end of July.

garykarr.com

postcards from the edge

Literary giants drop in to Victoria all the time. Occasionally, they pen a few words about the place.

Rudyard Kipling

Even a PR flack on Paxil couldn't reproduce the gush of superlatives that the author of *The Jungle Book* poured upon Victoria after his first visit in 1889. In a letter to his family, he scribbled a panegyric to the Garden City that's been cribbed by civic boosters ever since: *To realize Victoria you must take all that the eye admires most in Bournemouth, Torquay, the Isle of Wight, the Happy Valley at Hong Kong, the Doon, Sorrento, and Camps Bay; add reminiscences of the Thousand Islands, and arrange the whole round the Bay of Naples, with some Himalayas for the background.*

Less publicized, however, is an imperialist speech he delivered to the local Canada Club on a return visit in 1907: *The time is coming when you will have to choose between the desired reinforcements of your own stock and blood, and the undesired races to whom you are strangers, whose speech you do not understand, and from whose instincts and traditions you are separated by thousands of years.*

Raymond Chandler

The hardboiled author of *The Big Sleep* and other detective novels was born in Chicago but became a naturalized British citizen during his boyhood in England. So when the US joined World War I in 1917, the adventure-seeking Chandler was ineligible for the American forces, so he enlisted in the Canadian forces instead. He spent three months in Victoria — which he considered drearily provincial — doing his basic training with the Gordon Highlanders, and went off to fight in France. He never returned here, although 30 years later he recalled his visit in a letter to a Canadian journalist: *If I called Victoria dull [in a previous letter], it was in my time dullish as an English town would be on a Sunday, everything shut up, churchy atmosphere and so on. I did not mean to call the people dull. Knew some very nice*

G-G a-Go-Go

An extraordinary number of recipients of Canada's greatest literary prizes, the Governor-General's Awards, are or have been Victoria residents. They include:

Poetry

• P.K. Page for *The Metal and the Flower* (1954)

• Patrick Lane for *Poems New and Selected* (1978)

• Stephen Scobie for *McAlmon's Chinese Opera* (1980)

• Phyllis Webb for *The Vision Tree* (1982)

• Don McKay for *Night Field* (1991), and *Another Gravity* (2000)

• Lorna Crozier for *Inventing The Hawk* (1992)

• Jan Zwicky for *Songs for Relinquishing the Earth* (1999)

• Tim Lilburn for *Kill-site* (2003)

ones. The only semi-local reference in his writing appears in *Playback*, an unproduced screenplay about a Canadian cop who thwarts American villains. One scene features the changing of the guard in front of the BC legislature, which Chandler airlifted from Victoria to Vancouver.

F r a n z   B o a s

The father of North American anthropology got his start in Victoria. Early in 1886, he saw Nuxalk dancers from Bella Coola perform in Berlin, and several months later stepped off a steamship here, resolving to make his name (and fortune) by collecting Native artifacts for museums. Luckily for him, Victoria at the time was a magnet for "endless Indians of various tribes" (he wrote), and he combed their encampments, making contacts and seeking out storytellers. ("I am as well known here in Victoria as a mongrel dog. I look up all kinds of people without modesty or hesitation.") From the city he made numerous trips up and down the coast, gathering more than 250 myths – including the Songhees legend of a rope that extends up to the stars from Knockan Hill (north of Portage Inlet), visible only to men who remain pure. Boas may have been less than pure himself, motivationally speaking, but he was certainly ahead of his time in recognizing the variety of BC's native cultures, and the importance of their legends.

S a u l   B e l l o w

During the spring of 1982, the Nobel-winning author was a guest lecturer in the University of Victoria's English department, a position he took so he could retreat to a rented house on Swan Lake. But Bellow's visit was anything but quiet: he was relentlessly pursued by Barnett Singer, a UVic sessional who'd been fixated on the writer since the '70s and became his tour guide, showing Bellow around town and taking him to dinner at Pagliacci's. In his spare time, Bellow wrote the title story of his 1984 collection *Him With His Foot In His Mouth*, about an American musicologist hiding in BC to to evade legal problems; though it contains no overt references to Victoria, conversations Bellow had here ended up in the text. *"Nothing bad ever happens,"* one local said over dinner. *"Do you mean that every gas chamber has a silver lining?"* Bellow replied, spinning a line later used by his protagonist – and providing a timeless put-down to Victoria's sunny disposition.

Booktown-by-the-Sea

Sidney was once only known as home to sleepy retirees and disgruntled youth. But several years ago bookseller Clive Tanner had the idea to rebrand the peninsular municipality as a "booktown," and rallied Sidney's bookshops (many of them owned by family members) to the cause. The anchor is the all-purpose **Tanner's Books** *(2436 Beacon Ave., 656-2345)*, but look for military manuscripts at **The Book Cellar**, kids' lit at the **Children's Bookshop**, nautical volumes at **Compass Rose**, craft and cookbooks at **Country Life Books**, antiquaria at the **Haunted Bookshop**, and whodunits at the **Mystery Bookshop**, all on or near Beacon Avenue and online at *sidneybooktown.ca*.

Words Aloud

Local and visiting writers read Friday nights at **Planet Earth Poetry**, organized by poet and private detective Wendy Morton at the Black Stilt Café *(103-1633 Hillside Ave., 370-2077, http://planetearthpoetryat blackstilt.blogspot.com)*. Running for over a decade, this reading series has also published an anthology of its best work. Open mic to start, followed by scribes with new books. Another longstanding society of wordsmiths is the **Victoria Storytellers' Guild** *(1831 Fern St., 386-7802, victoriastorytellers.org)*, which meets the third Monday of every month, and organizes storytelling workshops and festivals.

The Good Book

In addition to a downtown location of the Chapters chain, Victoria has bookshops catering to every whim.

Bolen Books

Expect to get shelf-shocked wandering the 20,000 square feet of this independent bookstore in Hillside Centre, open daily until 10 p.m. Bolen also holds author readings and signings practically every week, so check out their online events flyer. *1644 Hillside Ave., 595-4232, bolenbooks.com*

Chronicles of Crime

A shop as sleek as a well-oiled .45. Former UVic prof Frances Thorsen sells new and used crime and mystery books, fiction and non-fiction, plus film-noir videos. Local crime writers read here, too. *1057 Fort St., 721-2665*

bookbiz

Two local companies have capitalized in a big way on the demand for the written word:

abebooks.com

Back in 1996, a government computer programmer and friends in the second-hand book trade created a website to match sellers and buyers of old volumes. Today, Victoria-based Advanced Book Exchange (abebooks.com) is the world's largest distributor of used and rare books, connecting more than two million readers daily with 13,000 sellers in North America and Europe. Ironically, the site's been so successful that several local used bookshops have recently closed, complaining that their former walk-in customers are now doing all their browsing online.

Trafford Publishing

If you've got a book in you, Trafford (383-6864, trafford.com) will play midwife to your words. Started in 1995, this Victoria company has become the planet's leading "on-demand" book publisher, charging authors a fee to digitally lay out and store their manuscripts, and printing only as many copies as are ordered. Trafford has published more than 9,000 titles and releases 300 more every month, consisting of everything from fitness manuals to a telepath's interviews with whales – although their all-time bestseller is a kids' guide to mutual funds, appropriately named *When I Grow Up I'm Going to Be a Millionaire.*

Dark Horse Books

If you're into transgressions of time, space, and social convention, explore this shop for SF, new age, occult, metaphysical, film, performing arts, queer, and radical literature.
623 Johnson St., 386-8736

The Grafton Bookshop

An English-style antiquarian bookseller, stocked with the cream of the collections of Oak Bay's literate residents. First editions often turn up here: not long ago a *Lord of the Rings* trilogy was on sale for $7,000.
2238 Oak Bay Ave., 370-1455

Ivy's Bookshop

Since 1964, the place to browse in Oak Bay for new and classic titles. It's also the site of a famous poetry punch-up: after being dismissed from the university's English department, visiting poet-in-residence Robert Sward decked literary lion and UVic prof Robin Skelton at an Ivy's reading in 1969.
2184 Oak Bay Ave., 598-2713

The World at His Doorstep

Victoria's been home to many legendary journalists (Pierre Berton, for example, attended Victoria College), but the dean of them all was **Bruce Hutchison**. Starting at the *Victoria Times* as a sportswriter at age 16, he eventually became its editor, a columnist for the *Christian Science Monitor*, and editor of the *Vancouver Sun* – all while remaining firmly planted at a house he built himself at 810 Rogers Avenue in Saanich. A loyal Victorian and master of telecommuting before the word was invented, Hutchison was also a confidant of several prime ministers, and penned numerous award-winning books about Canadian politics. He died in 1992, and his legions of fans are hoping to turn his house into a historic site, although its farmland (the subject of his *A Life in the Country*) is doomed to be swallowed up by suburbia.

Hidden Library

Victoria's grandest temple to the written word is at the back of the Parliament Buildings. In the **Legislature Library**, added to the main structure in 1915, you'll find a vast marble atrium, a woody reading room with gorgeous carvings (see photo), and the BC Newspaper Index (listing headlines from 1901 to 1990) in handy card-catalogue form. It's only open to the public when the legislature's not sitting, so call 387-6510 for hours.

Langford Book Exchange

A former tea salesman started this bookshop in 1961 just as he was going blind. Now it's one of the oldest businesses in Langford, and the family saga is carried on by his granddaughter.
106-721 Station Ave., 478-0914

Munro's Books

A central location, gorgeous interior, and bibliophilic staff — owner Jim Munro was once married to CanLit icon Alice Munro — make this former bank the top downtown stop for book-hounds. The basement used to be a pistol range, where bank clerks practiced fending off thieves; according to legend the place is still haunted by the ghost of a teller who got caught with her hand in the till and hung herself in the vault.
1108 Government St., 382-2464, munrosbooks.com

Famous Papers

Some extraordinary bibliophiles have lived in Victoria, and when they've passed on, their papers have often ended up in the special collections of **UVic's McPherson Library** *(721-8275, gateway.uvic.ca/spcoll/sc.html)*. Its archives include handwritten drafts of poetry by Sylvia Plath and Ted Hughes; original manuscripts by Rudyard Kipling, Ezra Pound, Henry Miller, and Lawrence Durrell; one of only two diaries kept by *I, Claudius* author Robert Graves; as many as 100,000 letters to English poet John Betjeman from such luminaries as Evelyn Waugh and W.H. Auden; documents signed by US presidents Thomas Jefferson, James Madison, and Andrew Jackson; more than 100 World War II-era comic books of Canadian super-heroine Nelvana of the Northern Lights; a self-portrait by Charlie Chaplin; a 750-year-old encyclopedia; and letters signed by Albert Einstein, Napoleon, and Admiral Horatio Nelson – whose handwriting was bad at the time because he'd just had his arm shot off.

Odd Bookmarks

Victorians are voracious readers, spending $57 million annually on books, magazines, and newspapers. But sometimes we get . . . distracted. As humourist May Brown discovered a few years ago, an astonishing variety of things have been left in books and returned to Victoria's libraries, including tax notices, doctor's prescriptions, a $500 cash rent payment, letter openers, knitting needles, socks, nail files, combs, bandages, dental floss, savings bonds, needle-nose pliers, a bra, and a butter knife with butter still on it. The most curious object is a 1959 hunting and angling permit made out to singer Bing Crosby, a frequent visitor to the Island. Speculation is that the permit, found in a printing company envelope, was discarded because of a typo in Crosby's given name, Lillis, incorrectly spelled as "Lillias."

Shopping

Any bozo can buy a T-shirt on Government Street – but you're smarter than that. Authentic souvenirs of Victoria abound, along with vintage clothing, cheap CDs, and exotic foodstuffs, if you know where to look.

Sheep Chic

For centuries, the Coast Salish peoples wove blankets and cloaks from plant fibres, mountain-goat hair obtained by trade, and the fur of Pomeranian-type dogs they raised. But after the English established sheep farms in the Island's Cowichan region in the 1850s, Native women learned to knit from the settlers' wives, and applied their traditional weaving techniques and patterns to English fishermen's sweaters. **Cowichan sweaters** became the garb of choice for anyone working in BC's outdoors: the shawl collar protected against the chill, the raw wool retained much of its water-repelling lanolin, and the workmanship was so durable that it lasted for generations. By the 1950s, they were the height of rustic fashion, given to royalty and US presidents – and an economic necessity for Native families shut out of BC's industrial boom. Today, the sweaters are enjoying a comeback, especially among Europeans, so much so that Cowichan designs are being ripped off by brand-name manufacturers. (Tip: fakes have seams along their sides.) But First Nations grandmothers still knit the real thing, for sale at the **Cowichan Trading Company** (1328 Government St., 383-0321), or the **Quw'utsun' Centre** in Duncan (200 Cowichan Way, 746-8119, quwutsun.ca).

Niche Furniture

Not all Vancouver Island trees are shipped abroad as raw logs and pulp: a few stay here, and get turned into beautiful tables and chairs instead. For nearly 20 years, **Camosun College's fine furniture program** has offered woodwork courses, and several of its graduates have started businesses that are literally homegrown. Look for the creations of Joseph Gelinas and Sandra Carr (*gelinascarr.com*), or Evan Sandler (*liveedgedesign. com*), who salvages driftwood or scrap left behind by logging companies and refashions it into high-end pieces that end up in posh resorts like Tofino's Wickaninnish Inn. Check out Sandler's creations at the **Pickle Ridge Furniture Gallery** in the Whippletree Junction shopping centre, on the road to Duncan.
4705 Trans-Canada Highway, (250) 701-0168, pickleridge.com

Taunting Tees

If you dress for offense, you need the irreverent T-shirts of **Old Nick's Emporium**. As you'd expect of a boutique started by the drummer for local punk band Dayglo Abortions and employing tattoo artists for designs, no cow's too sacred for Old Nick's silkscreen slaughterhouse. One shirt parodies milk commercials with an image of Jesus asking, "Got Nails?" Some of their best work is local, such as a tribute to the Gordon Head neighbourhood *à la* Motörhead, or the mock-Lucky beer logo "Drunken Duncan," a shirt that's a hit with roughnecks north of the Malahat.
639 Johnson St., 382-6423, oldnicks.com

A PUZZLING FEAT

In 1996, University of Victoria grad David Manga started selling board games he'd designed out of own home. Today, his Outset Media is one of the fastest-growing companies in Canada. He's sold more than 100,000 copies of his **All-Canadian Trivia** game, and branched out to other amusements, some of which are locally specific, including a "Vancouver Island-opoly" game and jigsaw puzzles of paintings by Emily Carr and E.J. Hughes. Look for them in the National Geographic shop of the **Royal BC Museum**, at **Kaboodles Toys** (*1320 Government St., 383-0931*), **Bolen Books** (*111-1644 Hillside Ave., 595-4232*), or online at *outsetmedia.com*.

GET JADED

BC is the world's number one producer of nephrite — one of the two minerals commonly known as **jade**. Natives used it for axes and chisels, but trade in it really took off in the 19th century when Chinese labourers started collecting it from the BC interior and shipping it home — in the coffins of deceased relatives — to China. There, jade was prized as the "stone of heaven," and carved into bowls, vases, and figurines used in burial rites. Today, **Victoria Jade and Gems** sells modern figurines and jewellery made of nephrite (BC's official stone, by the way) along with items made of pink rhodonite from Salt Spring Island and the Cowichan Valley.
728 Douglas St., 361-4338

There's very little manufacturing left in downtown Victoria, but one factory that trudges on is **Viberg Boots**, a company that started making heavy-duty footwear in 1931, and now sells more than 8,000 handmade pairs a year to loggers, miners, hunters, bikers, and prison guards around the world. Though pricey, Vibergs are worth it: they're as tough as the solid brass used in their construction, and fans are so devoted that they'll spend more on shipping an old pair in for repairs than it would cost to buy new boots. Custom fittings are available in their shop, on the ground floor of the Hook Sin Tong building.
662 Herald St., 384-1231, workboot.com

Vibram® Lug
Sole & Heel

Let Your Freak Flag Fly

Starting your own country? The **Flag Shop** not only sells ensigns of recognized states, historic periods (USSR), and identities (gay pride, Rastafarianism), it also makes flags on request – including those with potential to upset the current political order. One such item is the Vancouver Island flag (see image), created just before the colony merged with BC in 1866; a historian discovered the flag and got the shop to recreate it, and today it's raised by proud Islanders who wish we'd let mainlanders twist in the wind 140 years ago. *822 Fort St., 382-3524, flagshop.com*

Up Your Kilt

Most of the "traditional" clan tartans were invented by crafty fabric merchants only a century ago, but that doesn't mean the kilt's not a practical bit of gear. Steve Ashton, a former US Marine and helicopter pilot who flew in Vietnam and Iraq, has updated the Scots dress at **Freedom Kilts** *(1311 Gladstone Ave., 386-KILT, freedomkilts.com)*, using durable cotton-poly blends, and adding pockets. Business is booming, he says, because lads are figuring out that kilts attract the lassies: "They show you got a pair." If you're looking for something more traditional, **Touch o' Tartan** *(30A Burnside Road W., 598-8961, touchotartan.ca)* does proper Highland kilts (rentals, too) and sells pipe and drum supplies. The **Edinburgh Tartan Shop** *(inside Stormtech at 921 Government St., 953-7790)* is principally a tourist trap, but it's a place to pick up Scottish-themed scarves, sweaters, ties, and blankets, if that's what you're on about.

Stylin'

Believe it or not, Victoria's becoming a fashion mecca. Numerous independent boutiques strut around lower Johnson Street ("LoJo" to the hip), showing off wares you won't find at any mall.

Bliss
"Fresh fashion," mainly by LA designers. A select few styles means there's as much as 50% new stock on the racks every week. Affiliated with Calibre, a Euro-oriented men's store at 561 Johnson.
543 Johnson St., 386-0479

Complex
Victoria's centre for urban street style, with CDs of local hip-hop artists, designer ball caps, exclusive lines of running shoes you won't find at Footlocker, and German spray paint for the discriminating graffitist.
612 Johnson St., 480-0522, complexonline.com

Flight 167
One-of-a-kind clothing, jewellery and art, all by local designers.
167-560 Johnson St., 361-1678

Heart's Content

Pearl Jung moved to Victoria from Newfoundland in the 1980s, but she stays in touch with her rough-and-tumble roots. Along with British mod wear, motorcycle jackets, and Doc Martens, she sells hand-knit Newfie sweaters that'll keep you warm on the waterfront. Try on a pair of boots while sitting in the old auditorium chairs with built-in hat racks underneath.
18 Fan Tan Alley, 380-1234

Rebel Rebel

A fixture on the local fashion scene, this store offers its own Weiso line of one-of-a-kind "reconstructed" clothing (a trend being faked by big labels) for both men and women — and international lines as well, including Rock & Republic (whose designers include "Posh" Beckham.
585 Johnson St., 380-0906, rebelrebelfashion.com

Perhaps it's a lack of head offices or an obsession with comfort, but Victorians generally dress like slobs — despite big-city aspirations, this is one place where Gore-Tex is practically considered formal wear. If you need some serious attire, though, there are a few stores to try.

Women should seek out **Hughes** *(564 Yates St., 381-4405, hughesclothing.com)*, located in the old Majestic Theatre, showcasing elegant business clothing by French, Italian, and Canadian designers; menswear and shoes as well. **Nushin** *(606 Trounce Alley, 381-2131; 2250 Oak Bay Ave., 595-2223, nushin.com)* deals in Versace, Msiamo, and other chic import lines, fresh from fashion-show runways. **Sunday's Snowflakes** *(1000 Douglas St., 381-4461, sundaysnowflakes.com)* carries business and casual wear by Canadian designers such as Parkhurst and Linda Lundström. For designer wear at a discount, look for **Dots** *(724 Fort St., 383-2683)* or **Verve** *(2013 Government St., 385-8378)*, which is co-owned by Hughes and sells off their leftovers.

Since 1923, Victoria men have gone to **British Importers** *(960 Yates St., 386-1496, britishimporters.com)* for power suits, although recently they've moved to the Harris Green neighbourhood and started selling jeans and women's clothing, which says something about who wears the pants in this town. **D.G. Bremner and Company** *(106-2360 Beacon Ave., Sidney, 654-0534)* sells colourful shirts by Georg Roth of Germany, plus trousers and other accessories. **Outlooks** *(554 Yates St., 384-2848, outlooksformen.ca)* is *the* downtown shop for the younger sharp-dressed man. Stylish proprietor Dale Olson carries everything from suits to shoes, for a complete straight-guy makeover. And **W & J Wilson** *(1221 Government St., 383-7177)*, located in a former Western Union telegraph office, is a good place to get a nice sweater for dad. Their Oak Bay store *(1210 Newport Ave., 592-2821)* caters mainly to older ladies with style and cash.

vintage duds

Victoria is the used-clothes capital of Canada. Thanks to our elderly residents, a high turnover of government employees, and a general inclination toward pinching pennies, Salvation Army ("Sally Ann") thrift stores here do more business per square foot than anywhere else in the country. Here are some of the other places that specialize in second-hand couture:

Flavour

Old-school logos on sweatshop-free American Apparel T-shirts and cool second-hand accessories including sunglasses, sneakers, jackets, purses, and hats. Also sells wares by local designers, and used video games.
581 Johnson St., 380-3528

Roberta's Hats

Berets, boaters, bowlers, cloches, porkpies, Castro-style military caps — Roberta Glennon's been selling them all since 1992, using the work of predominantly Canadian milliners. Susan Sarandon, Jewel, Nelly Furtado, and Diana Krall have all bought hats here, as has Billy Joel, who picked up several fedoras to wear onstage at Carnegie Hall.
1318 Government St., 384-2778

Side Show

Proprietor Suzanne does masterful alterations of vintage clothing on a sewing machine in the corner of this basement store, as well as whipping up latex and vinyl wear for drag and fetish shows. She also stocks the work of local designers, and assembles the work of wannabe Gaultiers as well.
559 Johnson St., 920-7469

Smoking Lily

As Daffy Duck once said: this dressing room's so small, you have to go outside just to change your mind. But this 44-square-foot boutique (possibly the tiniest in Canada) conceals a booming enterprise. Since 1995, Julie Higginson and Trish Tacoma have been adorning shirts, scarves, handbags, and more with quirky patterns you won't find anywhere else, such as medical instruments, circuit boards, helicopters, and insects. (A pair of their Pierre Trudeau undies is in the Royal Ontario Museum.) Now, 14 employees are cooking up new designs in their atelier around the corner. Watch for a sale of returns and leftovers every February.
569 Johnson St., 384-5459, smokinglily.com

House of Savoy

Vintage men's and women's clothes and shoes, sold on consignment. Big collection of wedding dresses. (see photo, previous page)
1869 Oak Bay Ave., 598-3555

HunterGatherer

True vintage women's wear from the '40s and '50s, with pearl necklaces and other jewellery to help you dress up like your gran. Open afternoons Wednesday to Sunday.
102A-3 Fan Tan Alley (entrance on Pandora), 386-4546

The Patch

A cavernous space with clothes for the kids: baggy pants, satin baseball jackets, and midriff-baring tops. Brand-name (Gap, Guess) recycled clothing and lots of jewellery too.
719 Yates St., 384-7070

Retro Wear

Irony's the theme of this boutique stocked with '70s and '80s gear, including "As Seen on TV" K-Tel appliances, lunchboxes, and heat-transfer decals for T-shirts. Also rents wigs and costumes.
202-610 Johnson St., 384-9327

Value Village

The last word in second-hand bargains. The Victoria branch of this chain reportedly does the highest sales volume of all its 200 outlets across North America. The most famous find here was a box of original animation cels from *Snow White and the Seven Dwarfs* that later sold for $50,000. Today, such treasures are more likely to end up on eBay, but you can still get amazing deals on used clothing — such as Parisian all-wool suits for $7 — if you're willing to look through acres of donated junk.
1810 Store St., 380-9422

Given the number of erotic shops for a city of its size, it seems Victorians ain't lackin' in the lovin' department. **Garden of Eden** *(106B-1483 Douglas St., 385-3523)* was the first adult boutique in BC when it opened to great controversy in 1975, and it still carries a wide (thick?) assortment of toys, vibrators, videos, books, mags, games, and lotions along with thongs, corsets, thigh-high vinyl boots, and other sexy fashions. **Kiss and Tell** *(531 Herald St., 380-6995)* is a far more soothing and upscale erotica mart, with Canadian-made domination gear, aromatic soaps and oils, and an extensive line of Ben Wa products and prosthetics. **Love Den Romantic Accessories** *(109-735 Goldstream Ave., 383-1269, loveden.ca)* serves the kinks of the Westshore, offering books, movies, body products, and silky lingerie you can try on in a change room equipped with a mirrored stage, brass pole, and a comfortable chair for viewing pleasure. The **Romance Shop** *(2018 Douglas St., 380-0069, theromanceshop.org)* claims to have Vancouver Island's largest selection of sex toys, all sold by "Ms. Romance," who's given hundreds of free sex-ed seminars in private homes since 1994. Just like Victorians of old, we may appear strait-laced — but behind the curtains, there's a lot of spanking going on.

Still Life

In business since 1984, and the anchor of Johnson Street's ever-expanding fashion row. A smart selection of Canadian and international designers, with Ben Sherman shirts, Kitchen Orange dresses, and Nudie and Diesel jeans.
551 Johnson St., 386-5655

Whitebird

The ultimate basement hangout, stocked with everything a hipster needs. Club wear, DJ mixing equipment, wax for the turntable, and a lounge with a full kitchen (open for lunch, 11 a.m.-3 p.m. daily) serving up curries, wraps, smoothies, and a killer espresso shake.
768 Yates St., 380-7040, www.white-bird.com

Food, Glorious Food

These ethnic and specialty delis have items you won't find at Safeway.

Ambrosio Market and Deli

Jodi and John Ambrosio DeMederios (who also own Ploughshare) offer fine imported meats, cheeses, oils, and pastas, but their real service is providing local, pesticide-free produce, and European meats, cheeses, and pastas that nearby supermarkets don't stock.
101-1075 Pendergast (Cook Street Village), 995-8733
1503 Wilmot Place (Oak Bay), 592-7225

B & V Market

This could pass for any corner store, but past the display of girlie magazines in front are hard-to-find bulk Indian spices and condiments, along with frozen chapatis, naan, and Caribbean spices and Jamaican patties as well.
3198 Quadra St., 380-1455

for conscientious consumers

"Eco-chic" is a significant trend in Victoria, judging by the number of stores selling organic attire. **Fiber Options** *(587 Johnson St. and 642 Yates St., 721-3263)* was one of the first on the scene, and has been nominated for business ethics awards for selling comfortable, casual hemp wear. The clothes at **Hemp and Company** *(547 Johnson St., 383-4367)*, an upmarket Kootenays-based chain, are Canadian-made, and are smart enough that they could pass for Gap. **Granola Groovy Eco Store** *(1005 Broad St., 477-0146, granolagroovy.com)* prides itself on dealing in sweatshop-free and fairly traded goods, including clothes and organic cotton bedding. **Not Just Pretty** *(1036 Fort St., 414-0414, notjustpretty.com)* sells organic cotton clothing by local designers, and skin-care products too. And not to be outdone, the Lululemon yogis have opened **Oqoqo** *(120-560 Johnson St., 380-6310)*, specializing in organic cotton and soy wear. Scoff if you like, but regular cotton farming uses colossal dustings of pesticide — and those who don't care are going to wear it. Here are two other eco-friendly shops:

Soap Exchange
  Some of the most toxic chemicals in your environment are under your kitchen sink. Reduce the burden on the Earth and your family by picking up biodegradable dishwashing soap, laundry powder, and other cleaning products, all in refillable containers sized from personal to industrial use. Everything they sell is produced in Canada, and without animal testing, so your conscience can be as clean as your sheets.
1393A Hillside Ave., 475-0033, victoriasoapexchange.com

Ten Thousand Villages
  This international chain run by Mennonites sells fair-trade San Miguel coffee, Bangladeshi shoulder bags, Indonesian flutes, Pakistani footballs, Salvadorian wooden children's toys, and many other items produced by not-for-profit organizations in developing countries.
330-777 Royal Oak Dr. (Broadmead), 727-7281, tenthousandvillages.com
1976 Oak Bay Ave., 598-8183
102-2360 Beacon Ave. (Sidney), 655-0832

Victorians born today have a life expectancy of 80.9 years – higher than the average of every developed country except Japan. Perhaps it's because of all the health food stores. **Lifestyle Markets** is a local empire with three suburban locations *(1180-2950 Douglas St., 384-3388; 343 Cook St., 381-5450; 9769 Fifth St. in Sidney, 656-2326, lifestylemarkets.com)*, all stocked with organic produce, natural groceries, and huge selections of nutritional supplements and vitamins; they also have great delis with salads, baked goods, and fresh-squeezed juices. If you're downtown, **Seed of Life** *(1316 Government St., 382-4343)* is a groovy '70s-era shop with lots of bulk food, and, nearby, **The Vitamin Shop** *(1212 Broad St., 383-1212, canadianvitaminshop.com)* and **Self-Heal Herbal Centre** *(1106 Blanshard St., 383-1913)* can provide further nutritional aid. In Saanich, there's **Planet Organic** *(109-3995 Quadra St., 727-9888, planetorganic.ca)*, part of a national chain, which also holds numerous seminars, workshops, and cooking classes.

Blair Mart (a.k.a. Mediterranean and Middle Eastern Foods)

An oasis on a derelict stretch of Pandora, with crates of nuts and olives, flatbreads, canned goods, real Turkish delight, plus a take-out counter with baklava and other pastries, all sold by a kindly doctor from Dubai. Open daily until 10 p.m.
924 Pandora Ave., 721-1626

Burnside Food Market

Direct from India: ghee, mustard oils, vegetables, soft drinks, and snacks unique to the subcontinent, along with hair products made with coconut oil and the all-purpose curative Noni Juice. Open daily until 9 p.m. For a complete experience, rent a Bollywood musical at India Video next door.
658 Burnside Rd. W., 479-4228

Charelli's

The best of local and import foods all under one roof: La Collina breads, tapenades, and ready-to-go soups, sandwiches, and appetizers.
2863 Foul Bay Rd., 598-4794

Cook 'n' Pan Polish Delikatessen

Krakus pickles, herring in cream sauce, sesame snaps, and other Eastern European favourites. Busy at lunch, serving excellent borscht, handmade perogies, bigos (sauerkraut stew), and cabbage rolls.
1725 Cook St., 385-5509

Fisgard Market

There are several intriguing Chinatown markets, but this one's the best. Inexpensive Asian produce and frozen dim sum favourites (e.g., sticky rice in lotus leaf), plus packages of salted duck eggs, banana blossoms in brine, and other things you won't know how to cook. Also sells dishware and bamboo steamers to get you started.
550 Fisgard St., 383-6969

meet you at the meat market

If God didn't want us to eat animals, why did She make them taste so good? To tempt you, of course, at these butcher shops.

Cowichan Bay Farm

Lyle and Fiona Young lovingly raise chickens and ducks on pasture (instead of antibiotic-laced commercial feed), then kill and sell them whole at an on-farm store, open daylight hours year-round. The Youngs raise beef and lamb too, but demand is so great that you have to place orders a year in advance.
1560 Cowichan Bay Rd., 250-746-7884, cowichanbayfarm.com

Choux Choux

An authentic French *charcuterie*, with housemade pâtés and terrines (try the organic pheasant and walnut), all the fixings for cassoulet, merguez sausages for your couscous, and a wide range of imported cheeses.
830 Fort St., 382-7572

Galloping Goose Sausage Shop

A United Nations of encased delicacies is produced by this Metchosin meatgrinder: andouille, boerewors, bratwurst, chorizo, Greek loukaniko, Swedish potato, Ukrainian garlic, and seasonal specialties like Autumn Herb flavoured with apple, onion, and caraway. Also at select grocery stores, and the Moss Street and Metchosin markets.

4484 Lindholm Rd., Metchosin, 474-5788, islandnet.com/~sausage

Osman Halal

Osman Raghe, peace be upon him, slices up organic lamb, goat, and chicken, following Islamic halal rules – as with kosher meat, the carcass is completely drained of blood before butchering – for Victoria's 4,000 Muslim residents. Soups, samosas, and curries available for lunch.

2618 Quadra St., 381-2295

Ronald Orr and Sons

An authentic Scots butcher shop, with the brogues to prove it. The Orr clan moved here in the '70s and have been serving up Ayrshire bacons and hams, puddings, pies, haggis, and great sausages ever since. Remember: if it's not Scottish, it's low-fat, high-fibre crrrap.

6-7103 West Saanich Rd., Brentwood Bay, 652-3751

Slater's Meats

A proper English butcher shop, with chops, roasts, hams, a large selection of cheeses, and imported mustards and jellies.

2577 Cadboro Bay Rd., 592-0823

Starke's Deli and Sausage Factory

An old-style English deli, famous for its house-made sausages and hearty lunchtime sandwiches, including a baron of beef for $6.

3-10055 McDonald Park, Sidney, 656-4399 (messages only)

The Village Butcher

Scotch eggs, black pudding, and haggis for Tweed Curtain traditionalists, and hormone-free beef, local lamb, and free-range pork for clean-living newcomers. Closed Sundays and Mondays.

#208-2250 Oak Bay Ave., 598-1115, thevillagebutcher.com

Fujiya Japanese Market / Sakura Japanese Products

Along with sushi-to-go, these stores sell sushi-grade fish and other accoutrements to make your maki at home. Plus soba noodles, miso paste, and Pocky sticks.

Fujiya: *3624 Shelbourne Ave., 598-3711*

Sakura: *1213 Quadra St., 388-3636*

Italian Food Imports

The effusive Segato brothers make a lunchtime offer you can't refuse: big sandwiches from ingredients in their deli case such as the "Soprano," a grilled panini with capicollo, provolone, and spinach. Their shelves groan with dried pastas and family-sized containers of oils and marinated vegetables.

1114 Blanshard St., 385-7923

Maria's Deli and European Imports

In business for nearly three decades, providing Gordon Head with meats, sausages, cheeses, pastas, drinks, tuna packed in olive oil, and other Mediterranean items.

4080 Shelbourne St., 477-7823

Ottavio

The greatest selection of cheese in all Victoria: more than 100 varieties, including raw-milk types impossible to find elsewhere. Also has bread and pastries from the Italian Bakery (owned by the same family) and superb gelati made with organic milk and fruit, best savoured on their sunny terrace.
2272 Oak Bay Ave., 592-4080, ottaviovictoria.com

Ploughshare Farm Market and European Imports

Chickens wander about, adding further authenticity to this shop near Beaver Lake. Carries pesticide-free produce, free-range turkeys and chickens (not the ones out front!), and unusual items such as squid-ink pasta.
4649 W. Saanich Rd., 479-2322

William Strong and family have been selling their daily catch at **The Fish Store** on Fisherman's Wharf *(12 Erie St., 383-6462)* for more than 30 years. Along with the ever-popular salmon and halibut, they also have more exotic items like loin of albacore tuna and sea urchin. **Finest at Sea** just across the park *(27 Erie St., 383-7700, fasseafood.com)* has nine ships on the oceans; after decades of selling to Asia, the owner wanted to make his fresh, wild fish available locally as well, and now offers it at a retail outlet below his office. If you're downtown, sail to **Neptune Seafood Galley** *(813 Fort St., 383-5621)*, which has smoked salmon in cedar gift boxes at prices cheaper than tourist shops. In Sidney, cast a line to the **Satellite Fish Company**, right on the dock *(2550 Beacon Ave., 656-2642)*, where you'll find local salmon, halibut, lingcod, and live or cooked Dungeness crab. Pick a crab with a yellowish underbelly, indicating that it's mature and meatier.

Great Groceries

Victorians are rightly proud of **Thrifty Foods**. It started in 1977 with one store at Fairfield Plaza and has since grown to 20, making it the seventh-largest supermarket chain in Canada, and the largest private employer on Vancouver Island. Thrifty's community involvement and customer service easily trumps Safeway and other off-Island-based chains. But also check out **Market on Yates** (903 Yates St., 381-6000), started by Thrifty co-founder Ernie Skinner in 1999. MoY bakes truly artisanal bread on site (instead of in a factory), stocks free-range meats (and without foam packaging) in its butcher shop, carries a great variety of organic produce, and makes a point of putting local goods front and centre. Since it's downtown, it doesn't have acres of free parking, but that fits: MoY is urbane in every sense of the word.

Farm Fresh

Victorians are deeply blessed. In other cities, people drive through smog for hours just to find a farm selling fresh, local food. But here, working farms are only minutes away – and many of them open their gates on weekends, offering everything from ostrich meat to blueberries you can pick yourself. (For a list of what's in season where, see *islandfarmfresh.com*.) In addition, numerous farms have "honesty stands" (see photo) beside roads on the Saanich Peninsula and Salt Spring Island, selling fruit, eggs, and flowers.

Seven Valleys Fine Food and Deli

The Golestani family from Iran has Persian sweets, sheep's-milk feta, and hard-to-find Mediterranean items such as rosewater and almond oil. The store is named for the stages of the soul's journey, according to the Baha'i faith: search, love, knowledge, detachment, unification, bewilderment, and annihilation. Make sure you don't starve en route: grab some roasted peppers and hummus from the take-out buffet.
2506 Douglas St., 382-9998, sevenvalleys.biz

Wooden Shoe Dutch Groceries and Delicatessen

Over 50 varieties of salty licorice, horsemeat, jellied eel, shelves of Indonesian food hauled back from the colonies, ceramic tiles, cookware, lace, and, of course, wooden shoes (originally created to protect farmers' feet from mud and tool mishaps) for $99.
2576 Quadra St., 382-9042

To Market, to Market

A public market once stood where the Centennial Square fountain is today. Sadly, the building was demolished in 1959 — but the good news is that the same combination of entrepreneurship and community spirit is now spread around the region at dozens of smaller markets, from May to October. Downtown on Sundays there's the **Government Street Market**, where you can get palm readings, scrap-metal toys, didgeridoo serenades, and other oddities; there are hopes a food market will be revived in Centennial Square in 2006. Currently the **Moss Street Market**, Saturdays 10 a.m.-2 p.m. at Sir James Douglas School *(401 Moss St.)*, is the best food market in the city core, offering organic produce, cheese, and preserves from across the region — although the biggest line-ups are for mini-donuts, deep-fried on the spot. More rustically authentic are the **Peninsula Country Market**, Saturdays 9 a.m.-1 p.m. at the Saanich Fairgrounds *(1528 Stelly's Cross Rd.)* and the **Metchosin Farmers' Market**, Sundays 11-2 at the Metchosin Municipal Grounds *(4440 Happy Valley Rd.)*, where you'll rub elbows with farmers in their native habitat. The **Sidney Summer Market** takes over downtown Sidney on Thursday evenings, drawing huge crowds for food and live entertainment; it's the closest thing around to a Euro-style promenade. For a list of all the region's markets, see *bcfarmersmarket.org*.

THE IKEA EXPRESS

If you can't live without a *Lütefisk* shaving cup or *Bimbø* night table, a Pacific Coach Lines bus leaves every second Saturday morning from downtown Victoria direct to the IKEA outlet in Richmond, a Vancouver suburb, and returns that evening. Spend $250 or more and you get a discount of $35 (the price of the bus ticket). Call PCL at 385-4411 for reservations.

sweet stuff

Victoria is home to the world-renowned Rogers', among other chocolatiers, so we're well acquainted with all things chocolate.

Bernard Callebaut

This award-winning chocolatier from Calgary (where all his wares are made) has several franchises here. But if you really love his work, contact Melting Moments Chocolate Fountains (385-2462), a catering service that pumps 10 kilos of molten Callebaut through a huge cascading fountain, into which you dip fruit or cookies. We can't wait for them to offer a bathtub.
621 Broughton St., 380-1515, bernardcallebaut.com

Chocolat

Rogers' gets all the tourist traffic, but this chocolatier two blocks east is sweeter. Helene Pappas not only sells superb handcrafted Belgian chocolates – with several unusual flavours such as wasabi cream – she also has coffee and decadent desserts you can consume in the café.
703 Fort Street, 381-0131

English Sweet Shop

In business since 1910, with an old cast-iron Royal Mail drop-box in back to prove it. Jarloads of English sweets and toffees, plus all the bizarre UK grocery

favourites such as Bisto, mushy peas, and Spotted Dick pudding. Also does mail order to anywhere in the world.
738 Yates St., 382-3325, englishsweets.com

Fine Furnishings

As the local *Boulevard* magazine can attest, some Victorians live on the high end of the ever-growing income gap. Here's where they go to spend their money – when they're not in New York or London.

Alexandria

Nabil Gabriel Fayad has been designing and manufacturing elegant chairs, sofas, and lounge pieces in Victoria for 28 years, much of it built in back of his downtown store. Also sells wool rugs imported from Nepal.
560 Yates St., 381-5590, furniturebyalexandria.com

Charles Rupert

Historians Margaret Graham-Bell and Stuart Stark do a cracking business supplying heritage Arts and Crafts wallpapers, tiles, and tapestries to film companies and restorers of fine homes. Prince Charles' line of organic jams and Scottish toiletries are for sale as well.
107-401 Garbally Rd., 592-4916, charlesrupert.com

Lunn's Bakery and Chocolate Shop

A family business for three generations. Robert Lunn, the current chocolatier – trained in Europe – produces delicious handmade truffles made with local blackberries and salal, and *griottes* of Okanagan cherries soaked in cognac for two years before they're dipped in dark chocolate.

2455 Beacon Ave., Sidney, 656-1724

Rogers' Chocolates

A local institution since 1885, Charles Rogers started making his legendary dark chocolate Victoria Creams in the back of his grocery store (often wearing his bathrobe). Visiting sailors carried his wares around the world and his reputation spread. Tragically, his only son committed suicide, so Rogers and wife Leah poured their sorrows into their business. They often slept in the room upstairs instead of going home, and exhausted themselves so much that they'd regularly check themselves into a hospital to recover. The current owners remain true to Rogers' original recipes, and claim that more than a million of their chocolates get eaten every Christmas Day. (Dwight Eisenhower used to order them for White House guests.) If you want all the calories but half the price, the factory at 4253 Commerce Circle sells "imperfect" creams at a discount.

913 Government St., 384-7021, rogerschocolates.com

Chintz and Company

A renovated machine-works building, stuffed with 20,000 square feet of beds, sofas, tables, patio furniture, glassware, textiles (for the in-house customizing studio), and a Butchart Gardens' worth of artificial flowers.

1720 Store St., 381-2404, chintz.com

Design House

Stylish stuff for postmodernists with money. Specializes in sculpted chairs and tables by très hot designers such as Karim Rashid, Jasper Morrison, Antonio Citterio, and *Generation X* author Douglas Coupland.

616 Yates St., 383-3569, designhouse.ca

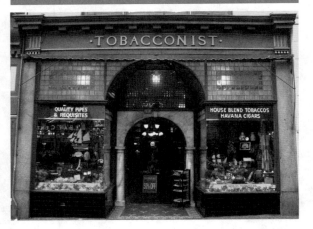

If you see a sign in a window that says "Cubans Here," there's no need to call Homeland Security – it's just another business offering a Havana stogie. Better than most is **Goodfellas** *(#1-1441 Store St. 385-2772, or 4291 Glanford Ave., 744-2772, goodfellascigarshop.com)*, run by the affable Lui Siletta, who also sells house blends of pipe tobacco and covers the cigar retailing in many of the city's pubs. But the real shrine to quality smoke is **Old Morris Tobacconists** *(1116 Government St., 382-4811, oldmorris.com)*, which has been selling cigars, tobacco, pipes, and walking sticks in its gorgeous mahogany and leaded-glass boutique since 1892. The gas-fueled electrolier (cigar lighter) made of Mexican onyx – only one of two in the world – was installed in 1910 and still burns today, even though the city's no-smoking bylaw prevents anyone from using it. Morris has long been a favourite of American celebrities: Mark Twain once smoked a cigar in the store, and it's since been patronized by Bob Hope, Bing Crosby, John Wayne, Dennis Hopper, and Kid Rock.

Gabriel Ross

Brand-name lines of designer furniture (Cattelan Italia, Herman Miller) for home or office, plus lighting, household accessories, and linens. Manufactures its own line of furniture as well.
589 Bay St., 384-2554, gabrielross.ca

Haute Cuisine

A big selection of European cookware, plus kitchen tools and utensils, bar equipment, pasta and ice-cream makers, and lots of cookbooks.
1210 Broad St., 388-9906

Muffet & Louisa

Muffet Billyard-Leake started selling quality kitchen, dining, bed and bath accessories more than 20 years ago in Sidney ("Louisa" apparently lives in Monte Carlo), and has been so successful that she's opened a downtown outlet that's as bright as a toothpaste commercial. She supports local charities too, so she's more deserving of your money than Wal-Mart.
1437 Store St., 382-3201, muffetandlouisa.com
2389 Beacon Ave., Sidney, 656-0011

Blasts From the Past

It's a miracle that people buy anything new in Victoria, considering the city's incredible variety of antique stores. The most popular ones located on Fort Street's "Antique Row," where the best include **Classic Silverware** *(826 Fort St., 383-6860)* for silver and linens, **Olde 'n' Gold** *(1011 Fort St., 361-1892)* for jewellery, **Shabby Tiques** *(1032 Fort St., 386-1177)* and its well-chosen selection of chintz, **The Old Vogue Shop** *(1034 Fort St., 380-7751)* for jewellery and funky '50s dishes and lamps, and **Vanity Fair** *(1044 Fort St., 380-7274, vanityfairantiques.com)*, the biggest and best antique mall in town, showing off the collectibles of more than 40 different dealers. Other good antique shops are farther afield. Just north of downtown, gaze upon **Water Glass Studios** *(1040 North Park St., 384-1515)* specializing in antique chandeliers and fixtures, tailored and priced for those repairing mansions, and **Elements Furnishing Finds** *(2-1115 North Park St., 382-3347)*, which is especially good for old Persian carpets. En route to Oak Bay, there's **Country Comforts** *(1967 Oak Bay Ave., 595-2966)* **Assorted Treasures** *(1969 Oak Bay Ave., 370-1926)* and **Crossroads Antiques** *(2000 Oak Bay Ave., 592-8000)*, which deal mainly in old furniture.

Everything Under One Roof

If you've got a list of errands, you'll probably be able to cross off most of them at **Capital Iron** *(1900 Store St., 385-9703, capitaliron.net)*, the best all-in-one store in Victoria. Housed in a former rice and flour mill, it has three floors of hardware, barbeques, lawn furniture, gardening equipment, and camping gear. But the real finds are downstairs: Capital Iron started in 1934 as a scrap- and ship-salvage business, and it continues that tradition with a basement full of old bells, anchors, swords, telegraph equipment, phones, radios, cash registers, and other industrial antiques, all for sale.

Out west, look for the **Sooke Trading Post** *(2076 Otter Point Rd., 642-3016)*, a sprawling second-hand "tingrotto" that's a good place to buy a used chainsaw.

Sydney Reynolds

Victoria's oldest china shop, remodelled in 1929 for the display of fine dining sets and unchanged since then. It carries Spode china, Burliegh earthenware, and Waterford crystal, just as it did the day it opened. Popular with famous guests of the Empress nearby: Bob Hope, Shirley Temple, and John Wayne all bought china here. *801 Government St., 383-3931, sydneyreynolds.com*

The Tuscan Kitchen

Beautiful Majolica pottery and other ceramics, plus a wide variety of European cookware and utensils, specialty oils, sauces, and Dean and DeLuca spices to help you enjoy *la dolce vita*. *653 View St., 386-8191, thetuscankitchen.com*

Funny Money

An extraordinary amount of extra income is made by Victoria businesses from American tourists who don't bother to convert US dollars until they get to the cash register. But that's not the only non-Canadian currency in these parts. Dozens of Victorians are part of **LETS (Local Exchange and Trading System)**, a monetary scheme that was invented on Vancouver Island in 1980, and is hugely popular in Britain. LETS members exchange goods or services and track the transactions (at *lets.victoria.bc.ca*), keeping capital in the community instead of having it skimmed off by distant shareholders. Homeopathy, gardening services, babysitting, tours, sporting goods, and even used vehicles are offered in the Victoria network, and LETS "green dollars" (credits) are accepted by vendors at the Moss Street Market.

Army Surplus

With Esquimalt the western home of Canada's naval fleet, there's no shortage of military goods in town. Some of it ends up at **Command Post of Militaria**, which sells military clothing and weaponry used by Canadian, British, US, and German forces from both world wars and beyond. The store also offers toy cars, advertising placards, and other antiques.
1306 Government St., 383-4421

Home and Garden Redux

ReStore

New and used tools, bathtubs, cabinets, flooring, paint, windows, and other building supplies, all donated by contractors and home-reno stores to the local chapter of Habitat for Humanity, a charity that's built more than 150,000 homes (including six in Victoria) for low income families around the world. *2100 Douglas St., 386-7867, habitatvictoria.com*

The Rave 'n' Iron

There are more than 30 practicing blacksmiths in Victoria, and some of their best work turns up in this Market Square boutique. Light fixtures, clocks, tables, art pieces, and more, all made of reclaimed and recycled steel. If you need a new gate for your mansion, they can fabricate that too.
101-560 Johnson St., 361-3644, theraveniron.com

Surroundings

The best-priced reconditioned furniture in town. Kristiane Baskerville and her assistants take old pieces too damaged to be resold as antiques, and remake them into beautiful new works: cupboards become bookcases, dining room sets are cut down to coffee tables. Some new accessories as well. Be sure to say hi to Bentley, the big cat.
249 Cook St., 380-0324

There are so many comic book and games stores along the 600-block of Johnson Street that it really should be called The Comic Strip. **Curious Comics** *(631 Johnson St., 384-1656, curious.bc.ca)* is a good source of Japanese *manga* and pop-culture collectibles such as posters, fridge magnets, bumper stickers, giant inflatable cans of Duff Beer, and Cheech and Chong action figures (Fibroweed van not included). If you're looking for a copy of *Amazing Spider-Man #135* or *Julius Knipl, Real Estate Photographer*, **Legends Comics** *(633 Johnson St., 388-3696)* is the most literate comic store in town, with a huge collection of vintage back issues. **Yellowjacket Comics and Games** *(649 Johnson St, 480-0049)* is good for action figures and the compulsive card game Magic, played in the shop several nights a week. **Games Workshop** *(625 Johnson St., 361-1499)* is a division of a UK chain specializing in figurine role-playing games such as *Warhammer 40,000.* **Tony's Trick and Joke Shop** *(688 Broughton St., 385-6807, magictrick.com)* is the best place downtown to buy a rubber chicken, a George Bush mask, or learn a trick or two from Tony Eng, who's performed for BC premiers and toured magic shows around the world. If you're in the market for a Pez dispenser or Einstein figurine, try **Zydeco** *(565 Johnson St., 389-1877, iloveduckies.com)*, which has all kinds of classic kitsch, including a huge variety of rubber ducks for bathtub or ocean experiments.

wired for sound

Q-Lectronic

A working gallery of refurbished electronic gear, including Dual turntables, reel-to-reel decks, and antique TVs (conveniently located kitty-corner from Sound Hounds). Q-Lectronic services vintage equipment too.
1545 Fort St., 595-5312

Sound Hounds

The source for high-end audio and home theatre equipment in Victoria, for those obsessed with proper "soundstage imagery" and "low colouration" so you can hear all the subtle tonal details of that new Foo Fighters album. Pricy, sure, but infinitely smarter service than you'll find at Future Shop.
1532 Pandora Ave., 595-4434, soundhounds.com

Westcoast Appliance

Many stores in town sell used appliances, but this is the best of them. Westcoast has a huge turnover, so fresh stock's coming in all the time, and they warranty their rebuilt appliances for one year. Ken Armstrong *(886-5910)*, who's based at the store, reconditions classic fridges and ovens that are as stylish (and energy-efficient) as a '57 Chevy.
#3-370 Gorge Rd. East, 382-0242

Eye Wares

Goo Goo Goggles

If you want to look like a Dutch architect, this is the place. William Van Gastel has sourced unique lines of European frames, and antique pieces from retiring optometrists. His shop is popular with film companies looking for character-defining eyeglasses.

761 Fort St., 381-7797

Maycock Optical

Power eyeware for professionals, and a wide selection for the rest of us. It opened for business downtown in 1949, and since then, it's expanded to locations at Lansdowne, Broadmead, and Sidney.

1018 Blanshard St., 384-4175, maycockoptical.com

On the Record

If you think recorded music should be free, try making some yourself. If you can't, then you should patronize these stores. **Ditch Records** *(635 Johnson, 386-5874)*, has the smartest new and used CDs and vinyl in town, and sells tickets for live gigs. DJs head to **Boomtown** *(105-561 Johnson St., 380-5090)* and **ISBOW**, a.k.a. It Sounds Better On Wax *(556B Pandora St., 414-7269)*. If buying or selling used CDs, **Lyle's Place** *(770 Yates St., 382-8422)* is your destination; Lyle's also has a huge selection of rock posters and T-shirts. **The Turntable** *(107-3 Fan Tan Alley, 382-5543)* has an amazingly comprehensive library of old vinyl. **Roger's Jukebox** *(1071 Fort St., 381-2526)* has vinyl too, including 13,000 old 45 singles, plus a huge selection of second-hand classical CDs, and old jukeboxes such as Shyler's Multiphone, a Seattle machine from the '30s that played songs over telephone lines. **A&B Sound**, located on the site of Victoria's first hospital *(641 Yates St., 385-1461)*, is an all-purpose electronics store, and stocks a better selection of CDs and DVDs than any mall. Save your shekels for their "super sales" on holiday weekends, when everything is 10 percent off or more. Tip: get there on Thursday when the sale starts, before that one copy of *Mingus Ah Um* disappears.

Media & Entertainment

It's hard to believe a little city thousands of miles from New York or LA could raise superstars, but it has. Victoria has been home to a Grammy-winning pop singer, an Oscar-nominated director, and legendary punk bands – not to mention some odd journalistic shenanigans.

Radio Interference

In 2001, strange reports started coming from the suburb of Colwood. VCRs and TV sets turned on and off spontaneously, residents said. Garage doors opened unexpectedly. Lawn sprinkler systems began spraying without warning. And one elderly couple's electric bed suddenly folded up – while they were still in it.

The residents blamed two FM **broadcasting towers** built the year before on Triangle Mountain, only 15 metres from some of their homes. They lobbied their municipal councillors, and when their stories made national news, the federal government got involved. One woman who lived near the towers even asked industry minister Allan Rock to come over to her house and lay in her brass bed, to feel for himself how it hummed from the radio waves. (Rock demurely refused.)

In his 2002 report, a federal consultant noted that radio towers had been on Triangle Mountain since the 1920s – in fact, it got its name because ships used it to triangulate positions. A tower was already there in the 1990s when houses went up around it, and buyers ignored it because they liked the mountain's views. The companies should have talked to residents before erecting the new towers, he concluded, but they hadn't done anything illegal. He didn't comment on the strange phenomena. The feds were satisfied. The towers stayed put.

Colwood councillor Ernie Robertson, who witnessed many of the odd happenings, says they continue to this day. The residents have given up trying to sue for removal of the towers (used by stations The Ocean, JACK-FM, and B107.3), but recently got revenge by blocking one of the companies' attempts to install cellular transmission equipment in the area. So if your cell phone goes wonky in Colwood, now you know why.

mondo media

The Mad Crapper

"Gee, this coffee tastes funny." In 1992, this was a common complaint in the newsroom of the *Times Colonist* newspaper – until some folks looked in the urn and discovered, to their horror, a floating turd. A manhunt for the crapper ensued, and over several weeks he left more calling cards in hallways and on chairs. No communiqué was issued, so the staff was left to wonder: Why? How? Did he do it on the spot? If he brought it in, did he freeze it to hide the smell? Suddenly the deposits stopped. Rumours blamed a maintenance guy fired for stealing fundraising-chocolate money – but the crapper was never caught, and to this day *T-C* employees wonder whether he's still in the building.

Holiday Viewing

During different holiday seasons, **Shaw Channel 11** replaces its community newsmagazine with a seasonal reality show. At Christmas, the audience is treated to an endless shot of a roaring fireplace, and during Easter, a bunch of adorable rabbits hopping around an enclosed pen. Shaw's yule log is already famous – several years ago, Jon Stewart's *Daily Show* did a report on an irate Victorian who injured himself one Christmas because his grandkids yelled "Fire! Fire!" when they saw the log on TV. But the rabbits create mischief too – the Shaw crew has to edit the tape because the bunnies are often caught humping on camera. Dog owners have also told the station that their mutts are so hypnotized by the wascally wabbits that they won't move until the TV is switched off.

Shot in Victoria

Reportedly the first movie filmed entirely in the Garden City was a comedy financed by the Canadian Pacific Railway in 1910 about two couples that swap partners (accidentally) aboard a CPR steamship. Since then, all sorts of moviemakers have passed through town. Here are a few of the notable features they've filmed here, and the stories that accompanied their visits.

The Crimson Paradise (released in 1933)

In 1927, the British government established a quota requiring one out of every five films shown in the Empire to be "British." Soon after, an English hustler named Kenneth J. Bishop landed in Victoria and tapped the star-struck ambitions of Kathleen

Humphreys (a granddaughter of coal baron Robert Dunsmuir) to create Commonwealth Productions, a company that would feed the quota. Humphreys invested $40,000 in this story of a disowned playboy who moves to Canada, becomes a lumberjack, and falls in love. Filmed at Craigdarroch Castle and the Cowichan River, it was Canada's first talking picture. For the premiere, the manager of Victoria's Capitol Theatre had an airplane drop 20,000 advertising leaflets over the city, and got all the local plutocracy to attend — but, as he admitted later, the film was "a real turkey. So lousy it was good." It played for three days, moved to Vancouver for a week's run, and then vanished forever.

The Anchorman

When news anchor **Hudson Mack** moved to the New VI station in 2004 after 19 years on the top-rated CH, the latter's supper-hour ratings dropped by 7,000 and those at the New VI (now Vancouver Island A-Channel) jumped by 9,500. Clearly, Hud is the face of the news to many Victorians. But what do they actually know about him? His full given name is Hudson Hamilton Mack — apparently because he was conceived in the back seat of a Hudson after it broke down in the Ontario steel town of Hamilton. He has a red 1966 Mustang once owned by his father, a legendary Calgary breakfast-show host. He owns CDs by the defunct local punk band Hudson Mack, but never saw them live. He's a devoted fan of the UK soap *Coronation Street*. Hud, who does extensive charity work, also defies the cliché of left-wing media bias: he's got a portrait of Ronald Reagan on his office wall, and recently travelled to DC to meet George W. Bush at a broadcasters' conference.

He Won't Be Undersold

Every city has its equivalent of Cal Worthington — a retailer who's become a local legend for his goofy TV commercials. In Victoria that's **Gordy Dodd**, who grew up in the Punjab region of northern India; he started Dodd's Furniture here in 1977, and in the years since has become one of the city's most beloved personalities, doing hilariously bad imitations of John Wayne, Austin Powers, The Incredible Hulk, and other pop icons in ads during the six o'clock news. (He also hosts a giant Thanksgiving dinner for the city's poor.) Dodd's output slowed after he underwent near-fatal heart surgery in 2004, but he's back commanding his showroom at 715 Finlayson, and fans eagerly wait to see what he'll come up with next. Check out his ads at *doddsfurniture.com*.

Higher Power

Victoria's first licenced radio station was created by God – or, at least, by God-like ambition. In 1922, the Reverend **Dr. Clem Davies**, a charismatic English-born preacher, was appointed the pastor of Centennial Methodist Church (now Centennial United) on Gorge Road. Davies knew the power religious radio stations had in the States, and he pushed his congregation to build one in the church basement – telling them, "We are going to broadcast over our own radio station, and you are going to pay for it, thank you very much." The 500-watt station, CFCL ("Centennial First, Centennial Last"), went on the air just in time for Davies' 1923 Easter Sunday address, marking the first broadcast of a church service in western Canada. Davies split from the church a year after that – he was sued for slander for calling an RCMP agent a drug addict – and later built followings in Vancouver and California. The station he started took a different path: it changed hands in 1926, went commercial, and in the 1940s became **CJVI**, a training ground for broadcasters who later became national TV personalities, such as the CBC's Ted Reynolds and CHEK's Ida Clarkson. Today, its frequency is used by Village 900, an AM station playing an ecumenical range of world music.

Secrets of the Atom

Photo: Rafy

Certainly the most famous filmmaker to ever come out of the Garden City is **Atom Egoyan**, the cerebral writer and director of 11 arty features, including *The Sweet Hereafter*, which was nominated for two Oscars (including best director), and won the Grand Prix at Cannes in 1997. Born in Cairo, Egoyan moved here with his artistic Armenian family (father Joe is a painter, mother Shushan is an interior designer, sister Eve is an accomplished pianist and composer) when he was two. Young Atom made his first film (an 8mm effort called *Lusts of an Eunuch*) while attending Mount Douglas Secondary School; after

Lucky Fugitives (1935)
After Commonwealth Productions went bankrupt, Bishop created a new company, Central Films, to make "quota quickies" for Columbia Pictures. In this one, a famous writer's evil identical twin escapes from prison, the writer gets handcuffed to a woman, and a romance develops while they're on the lam. The Crystal Garden pool becomes an ocean liner's swim tank and the fugitives jump from a train on the E&N line near Langford.

Special Inspector (a.k.a. Across the Border) and Convicted (1938)
Rita Hayworth's earliest starring roles came in two "quota quickies" shot in Victoria. In the first she plays an investigator trying to infiltrate a fur-smuggling ring; in the second (see photo) she's a rhumba dancer who fights to save her brother, accused of strangling his gold-digging girlfriend.

graduating, he created more films at the University of Toronto, where he studied international affairs and classical guitar. Eventually, one of his films got broadcast on the CBC, kicking off his brilliant career.

Egoyan's life has certainly informed his art: his 1991 film *The Adjuster* was inspired by a chance meeting after a fire destroyed his mother's interior design business on Fort Street. (The fire had been set by an arsonist who was angry about being alone on New Year's Eve.) So what are viewers to make of the kinky goings-on in his movies? It's tough to say; Egoyan simply could be articulating the muffled passions of Canadians, or there may be something more personal involved. As he told one interviewer about *Exotica*, his 1994 film about murder, smuggling, and voyeurism: "These are people who are doing things I would like to do sometimes." Egoyan lives in Toronto, but Victoria still informs his work; his slippery celebrity-murder mystery, *Where the Truth Lies* (2005), was partly influenced by mysterious incidents he witnessed as a teenager while working as a houseboy at the Empress Hotel.

Commandos Strike at Dawn (1942)

We shall fight them on the beaches — of Mill Bay, that is. The Saanich Inlet becomes a Norwegian fjord for this World War II propaganda piece starring Paul Muni (the star of the original *Scarface*) as a fisherman who leads a resistance against German occupiers. After missing the bus to the shoot one morning, several actors terrified guests at the Empress by striding through the lobby in Nazi uniforms. When the film was released here, kids were offered free admission if they helped the war effort by bringing a tin of fat to make glycerine for explosives.

Early Screens

In 1897, Victoria was the only city for a thousand miles where you could see a movie. (The first films screened at the Searchlight Theatre on Fort Street were newsreels of the Tsar's coronation and the Corbett-Fitzsimmons fight.) The first permanent movie house still standing is the **Avenue Theatre** (see photo), built in 1913 on Oak Bay Avenue at Foul Bay Road.

The Avenue once had a large arched entrance with a white marble ticket booth; despite such elegance, it was occupied by a mechanic's shop in 1922, and turned into apartments in 1943. Another cinema nearby was **The Oak Bay**, built in 1936. It closed 50 years later, but its sign still graces the 2100-block of Oak Bay Avenue.

Creature Features

The living dead aren't just wandering the Mayfair Shopping Centre – they're also stock characters for **Brian Clement**, Victoria's most prolific independent filmmaker. Since 1999, he's produced and directed five horror features, including *Meat Market* (flesh-eating zombies), *Meat Market 2* (zombies and Mexican wrestlers), *Binge and Purge* (cannibal supermodels dine on panhandlers and journalists), and *Exhumed* (samurai ghosts, grave-robbing doctors, post-apocalyptic gang war between vampires and werewolves). Although shot with volunteer casts at makeshift locations – police once got called to a garage to find a stuntman cutting up a fake corpse with a chainsaw – Clement's effects are remarkably good, winning prizes and helping him sell hundreds of DVDs at horror conventions.
frontlinefilms.net

DIY Moviemaking

If you've ever sat in front of a screen, saying, "I can do better than that," local societies can help turn your vision into reality. Some enroll in filmmaking courses at the **Canadian College of Business and Performing Arts** (*canadiancollege.ca*), but if you can't pony up $13,000 for the nine-month program, turn to **CineVic** (*2022 Douglas St., 389-1590, cinevic.ca*), an artist-run co-op with film equipment and a screening room for rent. CineVic also holds workshops and events showing members, films which you won't see anywhere else, because there's no public-access TV in Victoria. A society with a more artistic eye is **MediaNet** (*381-4428, media-net.bc.ca*), which meets monthly to watch and discuss experimental works.

Son of Lassie (1945)

Vancouver Island plays occupied Norway again in a drippy sequel to *Lassie Come Home*, starring Peter Lawford as an RAF navigator forced to parachute over enemy territory with his dog in his arms. In the film's climax, the two are reunited at the artillery installation at Esquimalt's Christopher Point. (Also in the scene is a huge cannon, loaned by the US Army, that could shoot all the way across the Strait of Juan de Fuca.) Airfield scenes were filmed at the Patricia Bay military airport.

Vixen! (1968)

Nymphomania, racism, incest, draft dodging, airplane hijacking, communism, and lewd dancing with a trout – every taboo gets broken in Russ Meyer's X-rated classic, partly shot in the Garden City (but mostly filmed in California). The opening credits feature scenes of the Empress, the Parliament Buildings, and the Inner Harbour.

bands on the run

An extraordinary number of acts that started in Victoria have ruled the charts – and they've penned tunes with things to say about their hometown, too.

Nelly Furtado

Claim to fame: A true superstar, she won a Grammy for the single "I'm Like a Bird," from her 2001 album *Whoa, Nelly!* – a CD that's sold seven million copies worldwide.

Little-known facts: First performed at the age of four at a local Portuguese festival. Honed her rapping skills by freestyling with friends (Swollen Members' Prevail and Moka Only) in front of the Eaton Centre and Johnny Zee's arcade, and later by jamming with Velvet on Sunday nights at Steamers.

Current residence: Toronto, with child.

Victoria song: "Saturdays," on her 2003 album *Folklore*, about working with her mother as a housekeeper at the Robin Hood Motel. "Explode" is about her dark days at Mount Douglas Secondary, a.k.a. "Mount Drug."

Five Easy Pieces (1970)

Many local landmarks figure in this angry-young-man masterpiece starring Jack Nicholson: Jack rides the Mill Bay ferry to visit his eccentric family's mansion (since demolished) overlooking the Saanich Inlet, breaks down before his stroke-ravaged father on the Dallas Road waterfront, and abandons Karen Black at a gas station on Highway 1 just north of Duncan. (For years, the defunct coffee shop next door claimed to be the site of the famous "chicken salad" scene, but it was actually filmed in Oregon.) Cinematographer Laszlo Kovacs recently told the *Times Colonist* movie critic Michael D. Reid that Victoria's low-arc sunlight and grey skies provided the perfect mood for the film.

Swollen Members and Moka Only

Claim to fame: Swollen Members won three best-rap Juno Awards for their albums *Balance* (1999), *Bad Dreams* (2001), and *Monsters in the Closet* (2002).

Little-known facts: Mad Child and Langford-raised Prevail and Moka Only formed the Members during a booze-fueled session at a Denny's. Their name refers to an extended posse or family. (Not an engorged organ, you pervert.) Prevail briefly dated Nelly Furtado. Moka's mom works at Victoria General Hospital.

Current residence: Vancouver.

Victoria song: Moka's "Walking Through Langford," on his 2001 solo album *Flood*. "Thetis, swimmin', Adidas, and women" are commemorated in a tribute to the Westshore suburb. There's but one L in the sky!

Hot Hot Heat

Claim to fame: The *New York Times* rated their "skewed, shifty" power-pop album *Make Up the Breakdown* as one of the best of 2002. Their single "Bandages" was banned by the BBC during the 2003 invasion of Iraq.

Little-known fact: Lead singer Steve Bays started performing in Grade 3 at Sir James Douglas Elementary by lip-synching Michael Jackson's "Bad."

Current residence: Vancouver.

Victoria song: "Get In or Get Out" on *Breakdown*, a rebuke to those who gripe about Victoria and don't move on.

Carolyn Mark

Claim to fame: Victoria's first lady of country heartache, with 11 albums to her credit, including a song-for-song remake of the *Nashville* soundtrack, and *Just Married*, a superb collection of duets.

Little-known facts: Grew up on a dairy farm in Sicamous, BC, in a family with Austrian musical roots; her cousin was the first female conductor of the Vienna Boys' Choir. Adores anthropomorphic figurines of vegetables, especially corn.

Current residence: Victoria, but constantly touring and playing venues as diverse as the South by Southwest Music Festival and New York's Knitting Factory.

Harry Tracy, Desperado (1982)

Victoria plays Portland, Oregon for a well-crafted western about the manhunt for the last member of Butch Cassidy's gang, starring Bruce Dern, singer Gordon Lightfoot, and Helen Shaver — who studied theatre at the University of Victoria in the '60s and lived in James Bay at 101 Menzies. The filmmakers covered the streets around Market Square with dirt and the city closed the Johnson Street bridge for several days, enraging local drivers.

Year of the Dragon (1985)

Fisgard Street masquerades as New York's Chinatown, a room in the Parliament Buildings serves as a police commissioner's office, and the Empress Hotel's sub-basement becomes a bean sprout factory where Mickey Rourke's detective finds a few corpses. After the shoot finished, the Empress staff was dismayed to find that the crew left behind a ton of rotting bean sprouts.

Bird on a Wire (1990)

Mel Gibson and Goldie Hawn accidentally rob a bank (the old Carnegie Library on Yates Street), steal a motorcycle in Market Square, drive through a hair salon in Bastion Square, and are chased by the cops up Fan Tan Alley. The *Laugh-In* girl and partner Kurt Russell later moved to Vancouver to support their hockey-playing son.

Little Women (1994)

Humboldt Street becomes Greenwich Village, Craigdarroch Castle plays a Boston ballroom, Royal Roads serves as a French chateau, and Cobble Hill is turned into a wonderland of cellulose snow in a fine remake of the Louisa May Alcott classic, starring Winona Ryder and Susan Sarandon. Gabriel Byrne set local hearts aflutter when he was seen dining alone at the Herald Street Caffé.

Victoria song: "After Bar Party at Our House," from her 2002 album *Terrible Hostess*, about a raucous bash at her Fernwood home.

Dayglo Abortions

Claim to fame: These iconoclastic drunk-punks got slapped with obscenity charges for their 1985 album *Feed Us a Fetus*. Charges against them were dropped, but the case against their distributor (ultimately acquitted by a jury) nearly bankrupted the band.

Little-known facts: Got their name when they won a case of Day-Glo spray paint in a "battle of the bands" contest on the same day that the newspapers were full of stories about an abortion-clinic bombing back east.

Current residence: Victoria, but still regularly tour Australia and Europe.

Victoria song: "Sea of Shit," from *Corporate Whores* (1997). A stinky blast at the city that refuses to treat its sewage. Plus it's the name of the junk-filled recording studio run by local punk promoter Scott Henderson.

NoMeansNo

Claim to fame: A seminal hardcore act, once described as "Motörhead after art school," that started here in 1981 and remains huge in Europe. As their "puck rock" alter egos the Hanson Brothers, they opened the 1998 NHL All-Star Game.

Little-known facts: Many. Wright brothers Rob (bass) and John (drums) refuse to make music videos, constantly recycle the same publicity photo of drooling blindfolded members, and play fast and loose with their biographies to throw reporters off the scent.

Current residence: Vancouver, as far as we know.

Victoria song: "Victoria," on 1994's *One Down and Two to Go*, a hilarious reworking of the Kinks' classic. Sample lyrics: *Newly weds, nearly deads / seas of green, skies of lead / constant rain on my head / stately homes for the rich / bowling green, cricket pitch / Victoria, what a bitch.* Gee guys, why'd you ever leave?

Long before cheap air travel or broadband, Island kids were pretty isolated. They had to entertain themselves – and that's why Victoria is thick with skilled musicians. Former radio promoter Glenn Parfitt has documented their history with the **Royal City Music Project** *(rcmpsite.com)*, a website profiling more than 350 bands from 1956 to 1985. As he points out, Victoria rockers went on to play in such famous groups as Heart, The Troggs, Ultravox, and Uriah Heep; Bob Rock, a Belmont Secondary grad, later produced number-one albums by Mötley Crüe and Metallica. (Others went on to different careers. Who knew that North Saanich MLA Murray Coell had a giant afro and played drums in a '70s outfit called New Day?) The project's also got a **hall of fame** at D'Arcy's Pub *(1127 Wharf St.)*, containing memorabilia of early Victoria bands such as The Pharoahs (see photo), a popular '50s surf-rock combo.

The island's vibrant punk scene is being commemorated by **All Your Ears Can Hear**, a project named after a ditty by the Infamous Scientists (whose members later became NoMeansNo) satirizing CKDA,

Excess Baggage (1997)

A witless comedy about a scheming rich girl (Alicia Silverstone) who fakes her own kidnapping and falls in love with a car thief played by Benicio del Toro. Locals complained when filming closed the Johnson Street Bridge for a week, to do a scene where the ransom money gets scattered over the Inner Harbour. Police later got called when bystanders tried passing the prop moolah at downtown businesses.

In the Company of Men (1997)

It wasn't exactly filmed here, but Neil Labute's acidic satire about two businessmen who seduce a deaf woman has Victoria connections. The tribal soundtrack was created by local composer Ken Williams (who has worked for Disney and the BBC) and pianist Karel Roessingh, the former mayor of the Highlands district. During Victoria's 1996 Christmas blizzard, director Labute was forced to spend several nights here trapped in a studio with the musicians, finishing the sound mix.

Scary Movie (2000)

Director Keenan Ivory Wayans uses Victoria High School (with an added fountain) for background scenery, and numerous locals for bit parts — including A-Channel reporter Howard Markson as Shannon Elizabeth's father — in this bad-taste spoof of slasher flicks. Wayans returned here to make *White Chicks* (2004), about which the less said is better.

Emile (2003)

Ian McKellen is a British professor trying to reconnect with his niece, *Crash*'s Deborah Kara Unger (a graduate of Oak Bay Secondary), in this meditative character drama. Victoria finally gets to play itself, in lovely scenes of the Inner Harbour, Clover Point, and St. Ann's Academy. One funny moment: Sir Ian sees the local paper and incredulously asks, "The *Colonist*?"

the local station that kept Prism and Trooper in endless rotation. There are plans for a two-CD set and book, starting with the 1977 shows by The Dishrags (an all-girl band often threatened by mack-jacketed yahoos), profiling groups like Squirrels in Bondage, Sludge Confrontations, and House of Commons (who squirted audiences with urine), and recalling such memorable gigs as the chaotic farewell concert by the communist surf band Red Tide, which nearly destroyed the Roxy Cine-Gog and sent panicked fans rushing for the exits. Many of these bands got started at Reynolds Secondary, which has its own music tribute site, **Reynolds Rocks!** *(the-tiki-hut.com/reynolds/).*

There are all sorts of weekly events where the city's musicians practice their chops. Among the best are the **Victoria Bluegrass Association** jamboree at the Orange Hall *(1620 Fernwood St., 388-4520, victoriabluegrass.ca)* every Tuesday night, and the **Victoria Folk Music Society** coffeehouse Sunday evenings at Norway House *(1110 Hillside Rd., 413-3213, victoriafolkmusic.ca)*, with an open stage and guest performers. But the real raspberry of Victoria jams is the Sunday-afternoon **Hootenanny** hosted by Miss Carolyn Mark at Logan's Pub *(1821 Cook St., 360-2711)*. Now running for over a decade, this singalong and piss-up draws dozens of country-fried punks; one memorable hoedown occurred during the blizzard of '96, when dancers from the Royal Winnipeg Ballet joined in, and had to be hauled away on sleds after last call.

The Blues Brother

If you're wandering along the Inner Harbour and suddenly hear a rollicking whoop-up of country blues, don't be too surprised when you discover it only takes one man to stir up all that joyous noise. **Dave Harris**, the bushy-haired Ohio-born granddaddy of local buskers, has been taking his music to the streets for more than 25 years, and can often be found with his kit – kick drum and hi-hat, guitars, fiddle, and rack-mounted harmonica – parked along the harbour causeway. Stop for a listen and Victoria's most conspicuously talented multi-instrumentalist will be happy to sell you one of his CDs of blues standards and snappy originals.

Spreading the Good News

"There are two world-class things in Victoria," opined one local jazz buff, "Butchart Gardens and **Louise Rose**." Audiences can thank the good Lord that this sweet-sounding Rose fell in love with the Garden City and decided to transplant herself here. Born in Norristown, Pennsylvania, she studied piano with Canadian jazz legend Oscar Peterson, and performed with Duke Ellington and other musical luminaries. While this ordained Baptist minister may have foregone a big-city jazz career when she settled in Victoria, that hasn't kept her music from moving the masses: still a regular on the festival circuit, Rose also leads the 100-strong Good News Choir, an all-ages, all-abilities community chorus always willing to throw open its songbook to new members (call *658-1946* for details).

X2: X-Men United (2003)
Wolverine (Hugh Jackman) and fellow superheroes battle it out with the evil Stryker's helicopter commando team in the halls of Hatley Castle (later recreated and shot up on a soundstage), serving as Professor Xavier's mutant training academy.

Window Theory (2004)
Corey Large, a graduate of St. Michael's University School, came back from Hollywood to shoot this comedy (from his own script) about a playboy who learns his best friend is marrying his high-school sweetheart. Despite *Maxim* girls and pornstar Ron Jeremy in the cast, the *Los Angeles Times* said the family-financed flick (Large's clan owns several Victoria businesses) was "lacking in charisma, sexiness, and decent jokes."

In the Land of Women (2006)

Teenage girls went crazy when *The O.C.*'s Adam Brody landed here to play a screenwriter who relocates to the Detroit suburbs (Oak Bay's Uplands) to care for his grandmother, and gets involved with a girl and her mother (Meg Ryan) next door. Other locations include Ten Mile Point, the Gorge Road Hospital, and Vic High.

Victoria also turns up in the pickpocket drama *Harry in Your Pocket* (1973), the chess-master intrigue *Knight Moves* (1992), the trashy *Intersection* (1994) starring Richard Gere, the creepy *Final Destination* (2000), and the 2003 disaster pic *The Core*, which spent $400,000 on a three-second stunt overturning a double-decker bus on Douglas Street. Watch for the forthcoming *X-Men: The Last Stand*, which got hundreds of locals to a casting call for "ugly and strange-looking" extras.

Whale Music

The Taj Mahal, Beijing's Temple of Heaven, the Garden City . . . okay, so Victoria isn't usually catalogued among the world's profound spiritual centres. But in 1970, when jazz star **Paul Horn** discovered Transcendental Meditation and became disillusioned with the LA scene (where he swung with Miles Davis and Tony Bennett), the Grammy-winning flutist chose Victoria to make his spiritual retreat, eventually building a house stuccoed with 20,000 oyster shells. Widely acknowledged as the "godfather of New Age music," Horn has recorded his ongoing *Inside* series in such sacred locales as Monument Valley and the Great Pyramid at Gizeh — although the meditative musician made his biggest splash locally when he brought his flute to Oak Bay's now-defunct Sealand aquarium and serenaded Haida, a killer whale in mourning for its mate, back to health.

Live Long and Poster

Some of the best graphic art you'll see in Victoria are posters for upcoming concerts, taped to the 58 downtown poles designated by the city for low-budget advertising. Several local shops crank out dozens of designs a year, among the best being **Malcontent Media** *(381-9518, malcontent-media.com)* and **Metropol** *(384-7653, imetropol.com)*. The latter has a substantial archive of old posters; visit their downtown studio and you'll find enough rockin' wallpaper to cover a dorm room. The most collectible posters around are by the legendary **Bob Masse**, who used Art Nouveau stylings to create psychedelic beauties for 1960s concerts by The Grateful Dead, Jefferson Airplane, and other west coast bands. Now living on Salt Spring Island, Masse is busier than ever, and often makes posters for big Victoria shows. Get them signed by the master himself via *bmasse.com*.

Aside from Jim Unger's *Herman*, the only strip worth reading in the *Times Colonist*'s comics pages is *The Coast*, created by that paper's fearless editorial cartoonist, **Adrian Raeside**. Though he was born in New Zealand and lives in Whistler, Raeside consistently nails local jokes about grow-ops, farmed salmon, water shortages, and the like – his work is practically a Rorschach test of the Victoria psyche. (See his portfolio at *raesidecartoon.com*.) The next generation is graphically represented by **Gareth Gaudin**, who's undertaken to create a cartoon a day until his death, drawing on local history and his shmoo-shaped Perogy Cat for his self-published *Magic Teeth* anthologies. Visit his Legends Comics shop *(633 Johnson St.)* or *magicteeth.ca*, tell him a good story, and you might end up in a future edition.

WE ARE AMUSED

Victoria's got a **Virtual Elvis**, and **Nearly Neil**, a Neil Diamond tribute act, but the reigning star of our celebrity impersonators is Carolyn Sadowska, who dons a tiara dozens of times a year to become **Queen Elizabeth II**. Sadowska, who once taught English in the Canadian North and restored aircraft for a museum, found her calling at an adult-ed course in improv comedy and first played Her Highness in 1984. Since then she's appeared in Spanish commercials and on Japanese TV, and regularly tours the United States to promote BC tourism. But she often creates the biggest fuss right here: driving to an event in her regalia, she'll shock other drivers, who wonder whether the royal has become the latest UK ex-pat to take up residence.
pinc.com/~queen

E-Media

Practically every Victoria cause and coffeehouse has a website. Some local sites provide more than just PR, however, and are essential complements to the mainstream media. For politics, gaze upon **Public Eye** (*publiceyeonline.com*), which legislature reporter Sean Holman seems to run on vim and vitriol alone, or Al Rycroft's **Peace, Earth and Justice News** (*pej.org*), which enjoys a considerable readership among Americans starved for progressive info. Environmentalists rely on Guy Dauncey's superb **EcoNews** (*earthfuture.com/econews*). The Island's folk and blues musicians turn to **Cosmic Debris** (*cvnet.net/cosmic*), while edgier artistes seek out **BrandX Media** (*brandxmedia.ca*) for its uninhibited discussions of 'zines, concerts, and CDs.

Agit Props

If you've got a problem with globalization, there's no better place to watch corporate pork get skewered than at the **Golden Piggy Awards**. Annually since 1997 (usually around April Fool's Day), Victoria's union members and activists pack the Roxy Cine-Gog for a Gong Show of greed, handing out prizes to CEOs and companies for the most outrageous performances of the past year. (The recipients are usually played by actors, but in 2005 a *Times Colonist* editorialist came in person to get an award for his rant against a national daycare plan.) The sing-alongs and skits are educational too, reminding audiences of wrongdoing that gets little media coverage, such as deadly Canadian-owned mines in Central America. Similar awards exist in Ontario and California, but let the record show: Victoria did it first.

Victoria promotes itself as a bit of Old England, but it's more like San Francisco in miniature. Whether you're into live jazz, philosophical debate, brewpub beer, all-night raves, or sadomasochism, there's plenty to do here after the sun goes down.

Cocktail Chic

Hidden away in Victoria's downtown hotels are several swellegant places where you can sip a Cosmopolitan in style. Classiest of all is the **Bengal Lounge**, the signature bar of the Empress Hotel *(721 Government St., 389-2727)*: originally a reading room when it was built in 1912, in the '60s it was converted into a Raj-themed space, and outfitted with potted palms, deep leather chairs, and a tiger skin above the fireplace. One local realtor did so much business in the lounge that he had a phone line installed at his regular table; John Wayne, who visited Vancouver Island on fishing trips in the '60s and '70s, often stopped in the Bengal after parking his minesweeper in the harbour. Another historically themed lounge that's hardly changed over the decades is the candlelit **Cook's Landing** in the Laurel Point Inn *(680 Montreal St., 386-8721)*: along with nautical bric-a-brac and a waterfront view of the Inner Harbour, it's got a padded baby grand suited for slurred requests of "Ebb Tide." Just behind the Empress in the Executive House Hotel is the plush, turf-green **Polo Lounge** adjoining Barkley's Steak House *(777 Douglas St., 382-7111)*, and downstairs lurks **Doubles Oyster Bar**, a dark and cozy place with a fireplace and discreet booths for private affairs. Across the street in the Chateau Victoria Hotel, you'll find the rooftop bar and restaurant **Vista 18** *(740 Burdett Ave., 382-9258)*. Once known as the Parrot House – the hotel was built on the site of a mansion owned by a wealthy spinster who gave her parrot a daily shot of brandy – this room enjoys the best bird's eye view of the city. Open 6:30 a.m. to midnight, it's also a great place to watch the sun come up after a night of carousing.

Harpo's in Memoriam

When *Monday Magazine* recently asked prominent Victorians what vanished feature of the city they missed most, many said **Harpo's**, the Bastion Square cabaret now occupied by the often-dark Upstairs Lounge. Between 1974 and 1995, an astonishing array of acts played Harpo's, including such jazz and blues legends as Bill Evans, Muddy Waters, and John Lee Hooker, and bands such as No Doubt, Stray Cats, and the Red Hot Chili Peppers. Its most famous incident, however, occurred in 1991, involving a then-unknown Eddie Vedder and the Seattle band that became **Pearl Jam**. A drunken Harpo's crowd, unwilling to acknowledge Vedder's self-proclaimed genius, enraged the singer so much that he tossed his mic stand at them – a tantrum later exaggerated into a star-making moment by Cameron Crowe in the pages of *Rolling Stone*. ("Unscrewing the 12-pound steel base of the microphone stand, Vedder sent it flying over their heads, like a lethal Frisbee," Crowe wrote. "They woke up. Vedder would never fully be the same.") There you have it: Victoria's to blame for launching the most overrated band of the '90s.

Party House

Many Victoria homes have served as punk concert halls, but the most famous of them is **The Rat's Nest**, the Burnside-Gorge area residence of Micky Christ drummer Gary Brainless. Since 1985, his basement studio has served as a stage for numerous great bands, including NoMeansNo, D.R.I., and Green Day (who also played Beacon Hill Park's Cameron Pavillion), and it rocks on to this day, especially during his legendary Halloween parties.

It's Alive

An appetite for visceral experience in an increasingly virtual culture? Whatever the reason, live music is resurgent in Victoria. For current listings, pick up the free *Monday Magazine* or visit *livevictoria.com*.

Hermann's Jazz Club
Victoria is home to many acclaimed jazz musicians — trombonist Ian McDougall, guitarist Marc Atkinson, violinist Anne Schaefer, and the multitalented Daniel Lapp, among others — and they often turn up at this intimate downtown room, owned for more than two decades by Hermann Nieweler. His own taste is for Dixieland, but anything goes here, especially at the longstanding Thursday-night jam sessions.
753 View St., 388-9166

pub crawl

Many years ago, drinkers directly suffered the effects of Greater Victoria's jurisdictional balkanization: in 1924, the City of Victoria voted to maintain prohibition but Esquimalt repealed it, and for three decades Victorians had to ride a streetcar or bus to the naval municipality to the west just to enjoy a mug in a beer parlour. Now there are pubs in all parts of town – and several have distinctive features to recommend them.

DOWNTOWN AND NEARBY

The Bent Mast

A creaky house built by a Hudson's Bay Company accountant at James Bay's "five corners" in 1884. Rumoured to have later been a brothel and home to the first flush toilets in town. The place to visit for real insight into James Bay's eccentricities.
512 Simcoe St., 383-6000

Christie's Carriage House

A Queen Anne mansion built in 1898 by Elbridge Christie, a carriage-maker. When he moved out in 1905, the building was carved into apartments and nearly demolished in the 1960s, but opened as a pub in 1986. Popular during hockey games, and nearly 30 beers on tap. One of the carriages parked out front is a 1905 Rockaway Coupe.
1739 Fort St., 598-5333

Garrick's Head

Men who were condemned to death in the courthouse on Bastion Square (now the Maritime Museum) were marched across to the original Garrick's Head bar for one last drink before they were hanged. The current pub, which opened in 1989, has a great deck for people-watching.
69 Bastion Sq., 384-6835

Logan's
Live music many nights a week, much of it country-punk and alternative, and ahead of the curve. Recent performers include Cat Power and Vic Chesnutt.
1821 Cook St., 360-2711, loganspub.com

Lucky
A brick-walled room with a long bar that wouldn't be out of place in Seattle, with DJs some evenings (the mod nights are a fave) and others showcasing hot indie artists on tour, such as The Arcade Fire, Three Inches of Blood, and Masta Ace.
517 Yates St., 382-5825, luckybar.ca

Steamers Pub
Pool tables, a sidewalk patio, and live music every night. Sundays are held down by the perpetual groove-machine Velvet, an ever-evolving combo of DJs and musicians.
570 Yates St., 381-4340, steamerspub.ca

Irish Times

A chateau-styled former Bank of Montreal (look for the gargoyles) designed by Francis Rattenbury and built in 1896, gorgeously restored and reopened as a pub in 2004. More than 20 varieties of draft beer flow from its brass taps, but they aren't cheap: the owner's gotta pay off those carpentry bills.
1200 Government St., 383-7775

South Bay Pub

Located in the Selkirk Water development that sucked many government offices out of downtown, the real draw of this modern pub is its sunny patio overlooking the rowers working up a sweat on the Gorge Inlet. Accessible by harbour ferry.
104-2940 Jutland Rd., 385-5643

Something's Brewing

If you like your beer fresh from the tank, you've come to the right place: Victoria boasts several great brewpubs.

Canoe Brewpub

This cavernous 1894 building once held the coal-powered generators for the city's streetlights. Now it contains brewing vats, a sports lounge, and a restaurant with excellent food, best sampled on the waterfront patio. Signature beer: the malty Red Canoe Lager.
450 Swift St., 361-1940, canoebrewpub.com

Hugo's

The hippest brewpub in town, on the ground floor of downtown's Magnolia Hotel. DJs, a dance floor, and in-house brew all draw a business-suited clientele. Signature beer: Super G Cream Ale, made with spicy ginseng.
625 Courtney St., 920-4846, hugoslounge.com

The Penny Farthing

A big-wheeled bicycle that once rode at the front of the annual Oak Bay Tea Party parade gave the name to this civilized establishment (the bike now sits in the rafters), a modern version of an English pub with private snugs, fireplaces instead of TV sets, and a roast beef carvery on Sunday nights.
2228 Oak Bay Ave., 370-9008,
pennyfarthingpub.com

The Fin and Gill

Pub classics like fish and chips and microbrews on tap at Esquimalt's West Bay Marina, an easy ride on the harbour ferries from downtown. Military personnel enjoy a 10% discount. Check out the nautically themed houses (see page 37) nearby too.
453 Head St., 381-1400, finandgill.ca

Tudor House

Built more than a century ago as a nursing home, it was turned into living quarters for Esquimalt navy personnel around World War I, and became a civilian watering hole by 1937. It called itself a "hotel" – though it was nothing of the kind – to get a beer-parlour licence. Now it's Esquimalt's principal sports bar.
533 Admirals Rd., 382-5625

Spinnakers

Canada's first in-house brewpub opened in 1984 and its taps are still flowing strong. There's an emphasis on local cuisine in the main-floor restaurant, and the upstairs pub's covered deck overlooking Lime Bay is the best place in the city to drink during rainy weather. Signature beer: brew guru Michael Jackson once rated Mitchell's Extra Special Bitter one of the best beers in North America, but also try the latest specialty brew; Spinnakers once made an ale using hops smuggled into a microgravity lab on the space shuttle *Discovery*.
308 Catherine St., 386-2739,
spinnakers.com

Brentwood Bay Lodge Pub

Even if you can't afford to stay in this cool new waterfront hotel and spa, you can probably scrape together enough for a pint of local draft in its pub, which shares a kitchen with the award-winning (and pricier) Arbutus Grill next door.
849 Verdier Ave., 544-5102

Maude Hunter's

In the first decades of the 20th century, Maude Hunter ran a general store at the corner of Shelbourne Street and Cedar Hill X Road that was a meeting place for Saanich farmers. This pub, popular with UVic students, appropriated Maude's name when it opened near the former site of her store in 1986 – even though she was a fierce prohibitionist.
3810 Shelbourne St., 721-2337

Prairie Inn

Originally built in 1893 to service travellers on the Victoria & Sidney railway, this hotel has since been renovated several times to become a store, a rooming house, a café, and (in 1974) the first licenced "neighbourhood pub" on Vancouver Island.
7806 East Saanich Rd., 652-1575

Stonehouse

Near the Swartz Bay ferry terminal, this Tudor-style home was built in 1935 by boatwright Hugh Rodd, who founded the Canoe Cove marina. Rodd hewed the beams and created the leaded windows himself. According to legend, the place is haunted by a boy who hanged himself because he didn't want to move from the house; the current owners say he often rattles pots and pans, and turns on the lights on the lawn.
2215 Canoe Cove Rd., 656-3498

Swans Hotel

The old pieces of machinery hanging from the rafters indicate the history of this former dilapidated feed warehouse, transformed from its "ugly duckling" status in 1989 by Michael Williams, a retired sheep rancher who creatively preserved numerous heritage buildings in Victoria's Old Town. Williams was also a passionate art collector, and there are hundreds of fine pieces throughout the hotel, including a Mfanwy Pavelić portrait of Pierre Elliott Trudeau (this one was PET's favourite) and Godfrey Stephens' mind-bending *Kluk Chiutl* totem pole in the foyer. Signature beer: a Black and Tan, mixing Swans' bitter and its rich Oatmeal Stout.
506 Pandora Ave., 361-3310, swanshotel.com

17 Mile House Pub

Originally a hotel for sportsmen, between 1940 and 1970 this dark antique pub was ruled by "Ma" Wilson, who upheld East Sooke's values by refusing to serve more than two beer to family men and closing the pub during the supper hour. (She also kept a shotgun under her bed in case customers gave her any guff.) The place was once haunted by an owner who hanged himself, but the ghost seems to have vanished; perhaps it was busted by Bill Murray and Dan Aykroyd, who stopped by in 1985.

5126 Sooke Rd., 642-5942

Country Rose Pub

A mahogany-panelled 1925 heritage home in Colwood that's been a pub since 1985. Featuring beautiful gardens, it's like visiting your grandmother's house, but with beer on tap.

592 Ledsham Rd., 478-4200

Six Mile Pub

BC's longest-running pub licence was first issued to the Parson's Bridge Hotel, built next to the Millstream River in 1855. Originally a watering hole for sailors from the Esquimalt naval base, by the 1880s it was a popular stagecoach roadhouse (six miles from Victoria on the way to Sooke, hence the name). An 1898 fire destroyed the building, and this mock-Tudor house replaced it, preserving some of the original's details such as its antique globed lamp standards and the old hotel sign, still visible in the bar today.

494 Island Hwy., 478-3121

MORE BEER HERE

Experts say Victorians produce some of the best microbrewed beer in Canada — thanks to a supply of soft mineral-balanced water and a faithful local clientele that keeps several excellent craft breweries afloat — so be sure to try some if you visit a pub. In business since 1984, **Vancouver Island Brewery** (vanislandbrewery.com) has established a local following for its crisp-yet-earthy Hermann's Dark Lager; for a brewery tour, call 361-0005. **Lighthouse Brewing** recently won gold Canadian Brewing Awards for its Race Rocks Amber Ale and Keeper's Stout, also sold in cans in local liquor stores, and **Phillips Brewing** bottles a citrusy India Pale Ale and a unique Longboat Double Chocolate Porter. If you want to sample them all, a great time to do it is at the **Great Canadian Beer Festival** (gcbf.com), held the first weekend after Labour Day.

In a category by itself, the **Strathcona Hotel** is a drinker's paradise, with seven bars spread over five levels, and more than 1,200 licenced seats. Originally an office building when it was constructed in 1913, in 1954 the hotel obtained the first licence in BC for a cocktail lounge, bringing public drinking back to downtown Victoria. In 1962, the hotel turned the lounge into **Big Bad John's** (see photo), designed to cash in on spillover traffic from the Seattle World's Fair. It was only meant to last a year, but BBJ's was such a hit that it survives to this day, delighting all with its tree-stump tables, peanut shell-littered floor, and a ceiling festooned with hundreds of autographed bras. The hotel's other theme rooms have come and gone (such as The Sting disco, which Paul Newman – yes, star of *The Sting* – once visited), and now sports predominate. Pub crawlers gather around an 19th-century ocean liner's bar in The Sticky Wicket, a dressier crowd meets in The Clubhouse, darts and pool players duel in The Games Room, and in summer the buff and beautiful head for the rooftop bar and its two beach volleyball courts.
919 Douglas St., 383-7137, strathconahotel.com

SOOKE RIVER HOTEL
The Castle Pub was built as a riding academy in 1902, became a drinking establishment in 1935, and since then has been the place for Sooke residents to conduct their off-hours business. Publican Don Rittaler is a well-known crusader for bar owners' rights, successfully fighting bans against dancing, recorded music, and the sale of spirits.
6309 Sooke Rd., 642-9900

Mass Romantic

Spend any time in Victoria nightspots and you're sure to encounter Alfred Sillem, a.k.a. **Alfred the Flower Man**, who visits more than 50 pubs and cabarets every evening with his basket of bouquets. Alfred's roots in the business go deep: he worked in the royal gardens of his native Holland before moving here in 1968, and (after stints as a welder and fisherman) has been selling roses in local bars since 1982. The secret to his perennial popularity? Always a tuxedo-clad class act, he never imposes on customers, sells on credit, and keeps mum about affairs and overindulgences he's witnessed. He also delivers flowers and singing telegrams (arranged via *alfredtheflowerman.com*), crooning one of the romantic jazz standards he's cut on CD.

WE MIND VERY MUCH IF YOU SMOKE

In 1999, Greater Victoria became the first city in Canada to enforce a total ban against smoking in all indoor public places and worksites, including restaurants, bars, and nightclubs. After slapping fines up to $1,000 on defiant individuals and even more on recalcitrant pubs, the bylaw's promoters now boast of nearly 100% compliance across the region – although the smoke may have merely drifted elsewhere. Tour around town and you're bound to notice an architectural feature likely pioneered in Victoria: the barely-legal smoking lounge, usually a once-outside patio that's since been roofed or tented over and filled with portable gas heaters.

Doctor No

Adrian Raeside

Without a doubt, the most controversial official around town is **Dr. Richard Stanwick**, Vancouver Island's public health officer. Best known for spearheading the capital region district's no-smoking bylaw, the good doctor also made headlines recently when he called for rules prohibiting kids under 18 from visiting tanning parlours or getting tattoos – a demand that even the temperate *Times Colonist* thought was beyond the pale. But such is Dr. Stanwick's practice: as part of the Canadian Paediatric Society's injury prevention committee, he's also spoken out against the dangers of snowmobiles, overly hot tap water, lawnmowers, all-terrain vehicles, bicycles, and cotton pyjamas. "Sometimes you want a big brother watching out for you," he once said. Perhaps he meant it in the Orwellian sense.

Fancy Footwork

Seven nights a week you can dance in style at **Café Casablanca** *(2524 Bridge St., 389-0222, cafecasablanca.ca)*, where west coast swing, salsa, and tango predominate on different evenings, often preceded by drop-in lessons. Much of the city's Latin-American community turns out to **Café Merengue** at the Victoria Event Centre *(1415 Broad St., 361-9433, vircs.bc.ca)* for its weekly salsa, mambo, and swing dances, occasionally powered by big live bands. Another cultural two-step that's popular locally is gumboot dancing, originated by black South African miners who stomped their boots to communicate: **Pamwe Gumboot Dancing** *(members.shaw.ca/pamwe)* welcomes new members to its free practices held at the University of Victoria. If you're fresh from the prairie, the **Frontier Twirlers Square Dance Club** *(652-2730, squaredance.bc.ca/clubs/ft)*, founded in 1959, do-si-dos at their twice-monthly hoedowns at the Colwood Community Hall (call first to confirm dance times).

Rave On

On Canada Day 2000, more than 4,000 ravers packed the Memorial Arena to dance to superstar DJs Sasha and John Digweed; today, the electronic scene seems to have faded faster than a rayon shirt. Or has it? Check out *ravevictoria.com* and you'll see that **underground parties** are still going off everywhere, although many are up-Island, such as the gigantic Soundwave festival every summer on the beach at Ucluelet. (If you're into the agro jungle and drum'n'bass scene, try *islandjungle.com* instead.) For a real trip, track down the SPEC (Society for Preservation of Empathogenic Celebrations) parties promoted exclusively by email and word-of-mouth. Govern yourself accordingly, however: a 13-year-old girl died after taking a mystery pill at one Victoria party in 2005, so look for the tables manned by IslandKidz, a group that does onsite testing so you know what you've bought.

Club Culture

In recent years, the BC government reduced the "training wage" for young employees and the city imposed a three-dollar minimum on drink prices, dampening Victoria's club scene — many are closed Sunday to Wednesday in the wintertime. But there still are plenty of places where you can let loose your caboose.

Blue Pearl

Residents of the western communities no longer have to drive downtown to party hearty, thanks to this 6,000-square-foot lounge named for its marine-blue tiles and 40-foot marble bar. The two-level dance floor occasionally accommodates live acts such as Nazareth and the Girls Gone Wild tour.
2835 Bryn Maur Ave., 391-8597, bluepearlnightclub.com

Purple City

Back in the '80s, when marijuana came from Colombia instead of the neighbour's backyard, local kids got a cheap, legal **hallucination** by staring into the sulphurous yellow lights situated in front of both the Empress Hotel and Vic High. Then, after a few minutes, they'd turn away – and all Victoria was rendered a deep purple as their retinas adjusted. Cool! Does it still work today? Try it for yourself.

Boom Boom Room

A rainforest-themed room as primal as its name, popular with American sailors when an aircraft carrier's in town. Ladies pack the joint when male strippers shake their things on Saturday nights before 11 p.m.
1208 Wharf St., 381-2331

Carlton Club Cabaret

Esquimalt's rowdy, top-40 party machine, thick with military types. If you're looking for a fight, this is the place: in 2003, police had to break up a brawl involving more than 70 drunken revellers.
900 Carlton Tce., 361-3666

Diego's

A 2001 fire toppled the clock tower of the Red Lion Inn and destroyed this club; now it's back in business with satellite sports, live bands on Fridays, and ridiculously cheap drink specials – which the club gets away with because it's just outside Victoria's city limits in Saanich.
3366 Douglas St., 475-7575

Old Boys' Club

For more than 125 years, downtown's most exclusive social establishment has been the **Union Club**. Formed in 1879 by the city's early plutocrats, Canada's oldest social club west of Winnipeg was first based over a butcher shop, and then in a grand residence the club built in 1885 at the northwest corner of Courtney and Douglas Streets. It wasn't completely posh, however; rats breeding in a livery stable next door constantly invaded the club kitchen, and tipsy members often amused themselves by bashing the rodents with their walking sticks. There was also a brothel across the street; when the old club building was razed in the 1950s, a collapsed tunnel was discovered heading under Douglas in the direction of the bordello, perhaps once providing a way for members to secretly patronize the painted ladies.

The club moved into its current building, a lovely Georgian Revival edifice on Gordon Street, in 1913. For decades, it was the meeting place for the city's male elite; women weren't allowed to become members until 1994. Even today, those wanting to join need a current member to vouch for them, and $2,500. (Fees thereafter are $95 a month.) But any plebe may enjoy the club's elegant lounge, games room, and dining room if you book into one of the 22 suites upstairs (cheaper than the Empress next door), and adhere to the club's dress code.
805 Gordon St., 384-1151, unionclub.com

I Need a Man

Despite Victoria's sizeable gay and lesbian population, official gathering places have always been few and far between. The only gay club that's currently out on the town is the **Prism Lounge** *(642 Johnson St., entrance on Broad; 388-0505, prismlounge.com)*, and though it's got a small and often-packed dance floor, it's more a friendly pub than a throbbing nightclub. For hotter action, **Steam Works** *(582 Johnson St., 383-6623)*, Victoria's only surviving bathhouse, is in the alley that leads up to Urge Tattoos. It's open 7 p.m.-9 a.m. daily, with anonymous "blackout" nights on Sundays.

That's So Kinky

Ever wonder what lurks beneath all that ivy? Just like Victorian-era Britain, peel back the vines here and you'll find a thriving fetish scene, principally organized by **Sagacity** *(sagacitygroup.net)*, a society that's swelled to include more than 800 members since it began in 2000. Every month they hold a theme party (pirate, wild west, back to school) or no-holds-barred "down and dirty" event where fetishists indulge in anything from bondage and flogging to hot wax and needle play. In 2003, Sagacity made international headlines for a "Bondage 101" seminar they organized at UVic, but they tend to remain publicly low-key: as spokesperson Ladyfish recently pointed out to *Monday Magazine*, despite laws against discrimination on the basis of sexual orientation, it's still scandalous to get caught doing kink.

Evolution

Located in former streetcar barns designed by Francis Rattenbury, Evolution is a loud and unpredictable club: industrial and metal some nights, punk and alternative others, and a sketchy crowd that takes advantage of the dark corners of the warehouse district north of downtown.
502 Discovery St., 388-3000

Hush

Victoria's finest electronic music club beats on. House, breaks, drum'n'bass, plus techno and trance, often spun by the world's best touring DJs. Check the online schedule to see who's in town.
1325 Government St., 385-0566, hushnightclub.ca

Legends

A former bowling alley in the basement of the Strathcona Hotel, converted into a vast, low-ceilinged room with DJs on weekends and the occasional live gig. Check the walls for memorabilia of homegrown stars (hence the club's name), such as Pamela Anderson's *Baywatch* bathing suit.
919 Douglas St., 383-7137, legendsnightclub.com

shake your money maker

The Fox Showroom Pub

Purveyors of fine flesh for more than 20 years, the Fox (part of the Red Lion Inn on Douglas Street) is the working man's nudie bar, as proven by the trucks parked out front, and its popularity with biker types who sometimes pack the joint after a road trip. After a 2001 fire consumed much of the adjoining hotel, the Fox reopened as a state-of-the-art show bar with huge video screens, a glassed-in smoking lounge, and waitresses in revealing tartan skirts.
3366 Douglas St., 475-7575

Monty's Exotic Showroom Pub

Still Victoria's first name in all-nude entertainment, this establishment on the ground floor of the Victoria Plaza Hotel got its name from a previous owner, Ron de Montigny, who took it over in 1984 and revamped it into a British pub; two years later he sold the business, but the new owners kept the Monty's name and started bringing in exotic dancers. Popular with college boys and sailors on shore leave, Monty's also attracts some big-name clientele: it's claimed that billionaire Bill Gates and NBA star Wilt Chamberlain have been spotted in the admiring crowds, although the most famous visitor was *Friends* and *Joey* star Matt LeBlanc, who tearfully confessed to the *National Enquirer* in the summer of 2005 that he got into a drunken entanglement with a Monty's stripper in a room upstairs. According to legend there are also a few ghosts around the joint, including one of a dancer who died after a performance.
603 Pandora Ave. (entrance at 1400 Government St.), 386-3631

Plan B

Saturday Night Fever enjoys a 21st-century revival on this club's LED-illuminated dance floor, set to the play-anything vibe of resident DJ Levi Hawk.
1318 Broad St., 384-3557

Red Jacket

Arsonists torched this space in 2000 and 2002, but it consistently returns to be one of the most popular rooms downtown. The current incarnation boasts a planet-sized mirror ball, and a chill-out lounge with fish tanks and a bar with a refrigerated strip of metal built into the counter to keep drinks cold.
751 View St., 384-2582

Tourists, sailors, visiting bureaucrats, Viagra-popping seniors – they all provide a relentless demand for sex. According to the **Prostitutes Empowerment and Education Resource Society** (PEERS), a Victoria outreach and counselling organization, there are as many as 700 sex-trade workers in the city, with about 80 walking the streets and the rest working out of their own homes or employed by the city's various escort agencies. A new twist in the biz is that some of their clients are now critiquing the strenuous work of many Victoria escorts on websites. One such site, *bcdarlings.com*, was started by a Victoria computer programmer who blew $16,000 over the course of a year, "reviewing" 59 different women; the site's drawn so much traffic that now he's working for one of the agencies himself, and escorts and johns use the site to set up dates. Communicating for the purpose of prostitution is illegal in Canada, however, so they rely on code: SP = service provider (escort), "donation" = fee, MISH = missionary position, BBBJ = bareback blowjob, DATY = Dining at the Y (use your imagination), and so on. Ain't the Internet wonderful? As PEERS points out, anything is better than walking the street, but agencies often take 75% of an escort's fees. And further consumer empowerment is probably not what a trade already based on exploitation really needs.

Unusual Societies

How's About a Pint, Guv?

Along with tweed and ivy, Victoria boasts the ***Coronation Street Fan Club***, where displaced Brits and indigenous fans discuss the comings and goings of the deathless UK soap opera, still broadcast nightly on CBC. They meet the third Wednesday of every month at the Chief and Petty Officers' Club in Esquimalt. *370-9960*

Barbie Grrrls

Mattel's plastic pixie was born in 1959, and remains source of timeless fascination to the First **Victoria Barbie Doll Club**, a society for adult collectors. Every month its dozen members discuss a new topic ("Travel," "Careers") and rally to promote their favourite doll. Not long ago they inspired creation of a Hudson's Bay Company Barbie, complete with the HBC's trademark point-blanket coat. It's only a matter of time until they open a museum to display their hundreds of dolls; to add your own, contact 388-6387 or debdav@shaw.ca.

Late-Night Nosh

The movie's over, the clubs have closed, and you've got the munchies. Where to go? **The Mint** *(1414 Douglas St., 386-6468)* is the hipster's choice, serving up Tibetan and Nepalese cuisine in a groovy candlelit room until 2 a.m. Ask for a table in back if you don't want to shout over the DJ. The **Fan Tan Café** *(549 Fisgard St., 383-1611)* serves late-night Chinese food, and the **QV Bakery and Café** nearby *(1701 Government St., 384-8831)* has cake and coffee around the clock. To hang out with other nighthawks at a diner – filled with modernist art – hike to the 24-hour coffee shop of **Paul's Motor Inn** *(1900 Douglas St., 382-9231)*.

GOOD QUESTIONS

Is God dead, or is He just nodding off in an Oak Bay retirement home? That's one of the subjects that could come up at **Café Philosophy**, Canada's longest-running salon of ideas, held every Wednesday evening at the Solstice Café *(529 Pandora Ave.)*. Michael Picard, who did his Ph.D. in philosophy at MIT, directs the proceedings, dealing with such big themes as Meaning, Sustainability, Wisdom, and Evil. Drop in for $4 plus the price of a drink.
385-4646, philosophy-shop.com

Drink, Without Driving

If you've had a few too many, a handy service is **Designated Drivers of Victoria** *(213-2901, givemeyourkeys.com)*. Call between 6 p.m. and 6 a.m. and they'll come to the pub and drive you and your car home. Slightly more expensive than a taxi, but you won't have to make a return trip in the morning – and it's far cheaper than tow trucks and lawyers. You can also get juiced without leaving home, thanks to **Dial-a-Bottle** *(475-2797)*, which will deliver booze to your door until 11 p.m. Be prepared to show ID: too often callers turn out to be kids hoping to sweet-talk a bottle out of the driver.

One thing the tourist bureau won't tell you: along with fine restaurants and beautiful scenery, Victoria is also a haven for paranormal phenomena, multimillion-dollar fraud, gruesome murders, and international terrorism. Here are some of the stories that give Victoria its gossip.

Bees in Their Bonnets

No protest in Victoria is complete without the **Raging Grannies**, a troupe of blue-rinsed radicals who've roused the city's rabble with satirical political singalongs since 1986. They originally began as a co-ed group, protesting against uranium mining and American warships landing in Victoria (US officials perpetually "neither confirm nor deny" whether there are nuclear weapons on board). The protesters wore lab coats and drew stares as they tested passersby for radiation. But after the men dropped out, a member suggested it might be better PR if they stood up for the world's grandchildren. They donned hoop skirts and bonnets, wrote witty new lyrics for nursery rhymes and old pop songs ("There's No Business Like War Business"), then boarded a visiting US destroyer, set out teacups on a tablecloth reading "Tea Not Tomahawks," and started to sing – enraging the captain, earning international headlines, and winning fans around the world.

Today there are more than 65 chapters of Grannies across Canada and the US, as well as in Great Britain, Australia, Greece, and Japan. Victoria's Grannies have been hosed, pepper-sprayed, and jailed; they've sung at the anti-logging demonstrations at Clayoquot Sound, and the anti-WTO rallies in Seattle. They also remain one of the few groups in this military town to protest against nuclear weapons in our waters. Up to nine Trident submarines regularly cruise back and forth along the Strait of Juan de Fuca to a base at Bangor, Washington (70 kilometres from Victoria) that reportedly stockpiles as many as 1,760 nuclear warheads – a frightening fact the Grannies point out in their ditty "Atomic Submarine." (Sung to the tune of "Yellow Submarine": "In the town where we reside / There are things we like to hide ...") Want to join the chorus? You'll have to put your name on a waiting list. Victoria's Grannies rehearse in living rooms, so they limit their membership to 12 at a time.

WARNING
NUCLEAR SHIP
NOW IN
PORT

Movie stars, criminals, retired politicians, hockey loudmouth Howie Meeker – Vancouver Island has always attracted reprobates, of whom the most famous was **Brother XII**. Originally a sailor named Edward Arthur Wilson, in 1924 at age 46 he saw an ankh and pentangle floating at the foot of his bed, and heard a voice announcing he was the 12th disciple of a great mystic brotherhood, destined to restore ancient spiritual traditions to the world. He feverishly wrote a book of prophecies that astounded London occultists, and was such a persuasive speaker that he convinced executives, professors, and socialites across England and North America to join a colony he was establishing on Vancouver Island to escape a "fire" about to consume western civilization. (Wilson had been to the island before: in 1907, he abandoned his wife and children in Victoria to start working on ships.) By 1928, his disciples had built a colony at Cedar-by-the-Sea located south of Nanaimo, containing a "house of mystery" he used for meditation – and for seducing female followers. One of them, a former Saskatchewan schoolteacher, became "Madame Zee," who enforced colony discipline with a riding crop.

After years of toil, expanding the colony to DeCourcy and Valdes Islands and enduring Wilson's increasingly bizarre behaviour (some say he was smuggling drugs), his followers decided to leave and sue for their contributions to the project. But they were scared: his past enemies had fainted in courtrooms or mysteriously vanished, and a *Colonist* editor had to give them an enchanted Native ornament to convince them to testify. They did, and in 1933 a Nanaimo judge ordered Wilson to grant the land and $36,500 to the followers. He and Madame Zee vandalized the property and disappeared, reportedly packing half a million dollars in gold. Wilson died a year later in Switzerland. But Brother XII achieved immortality: fortune-hunters still comb the colony's old buildings today, and his tale remains such a classic of Island lore that it was recently workshopped as an opera at the Victoria Conservatory of Music.

BAD WEED

One of the oddest trials in Victoria's history took place in 1988 when **Lion Serpent Sun**, a self-proclaimed Gnostic minister, sued the Christian TV program *100 Huntley Street* for defamation. The show ran an interview with Len Olsen, a Vancouver man who claimed he'd attended one of Sun's nude, drug-filled rituals – and been offered by Sun for human sacrifice. For weeks, the show's host called Sun a satanist, to which he took great offence. In the courtroom, however, it was revealed that Olsen seemed to have only suffered paranoid delusions brought on by strong marijuana and a profound flash of Christian guilt. The jury awarded Sun $10,000 in damages. If you want to ask Sun about the trial, he's still in town, providing tarot readings at the Angels of Avalon shop in Market Square.

KEEP WATCHING THE SKIES

Several years ago, conspiracy buffs burned up the Internet with talk about mysterious patterns of **contrails** caused by jet aircraft. In Victoria, you'll still meet people who talk about them today, thanks to local writer William Thomas, who's been largely credited (or blamed) for starting the panic with his books on the topic and his appearances on Art Bell's fringy *Coast to Coast* radio show. Thomas speculates that the contrails are a military experiment — the multiple crisscross patterns couldn't possibly have been caused by passenger aircraft — spraying a "sunscreen" of aluminum oxide into the upper atmosphere to reflect sunlight and reduce global warming.

Keeping the Faith

As befits their rough-hewn nature, some residents of Sooke show their religious devotion with hammers and nails. In the 1920s, a Christian sect moved to Sooke to await the Second Coming, and built a self-contained commune known as the **Star Construction Company** near Whiffin Spit, with its own sewing shop, dairy, and a huge meeting hall for its 400 followers; they dispersed in 1926. The sect also has a connection to the **giant rosary** (see photo) that stands at 5080 Sooke Road. Al Shepherd, the son of one of its members, converted to Catholicism, and in 1970 made a pilgrimage to Bayside, New York to see Veronica Lueken, a homemaker famous for her entranced channelings of the Virgin Mary. Shepherd went to her with a question, and was so struck by the answer that when he returned he had the ground blessed in front of his house, and built the rosary in tribute. (Veronica/Mary condemned modern culture, so an adjacent sign reads, "Rosary in, TV out, Honour our Queen.") The rosary has been stolen and set on fire several times, but Shepherd maintained it until he died in 2000, and his children protect it still — even though they never learned exactly what the question was that inspired it.

Fall from Grace

Brian Ruud

"I believe God's people should be the most successful in the world," **Brian Ruud** once said, and he lived as if it were true. A former speed freak and small-time thief in Saskatchewan, in the late 1960s Ruud had a revelation in prison, converted to Christianity, and wrote a book and recorded an LP (see photo) describing his "trip beyond." But his real talents lay in public speaking, and his tale of woe and halo of gold curly hair became trademarks on the Christian-school lecture circuit in the Œ70s. Gold was Ruud's colour: he wore diamond-encrusted gold chains and parked a gold Lincoln in front of Eagle's Nest, the grand Oak Bay mansion he moved into in 1977 and decorated with frescoes depicting his life. But Ruud ended up being a fatted calf for the tax man. In 1981, Revenue Canada slapped him with a $1-million bill, and in 1984 they dinged him again for $1.7 million. Ruud sold his palace in 1989. Today, he's working the fertile Christian terrain of BC's Fraser Valley.

Satanic Reverses

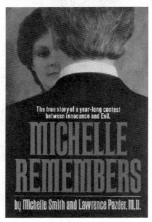

To this day, Victoria has a sinister reputation as a hotbed of crazed devil worshippers. Blame it on a book: *Michelle Remembers*, published in 1980 by the (devoutly Catholic) local psychiatrist **Dr. Lawrence Pazder**. The book told the story of Pazder's unearthing of a patient's buried "memories" of childhood abuse at Satanic rituals held in Victoria in the 1950s – including being lowered into a grave at the Ross Bay cemetery, eating the ashes of a dead woman, and stabbing a dead baby with a crucifix. The book became an instant bestseller, creating a career for Pazder and his patient (and soon-to-be wife) Michelle, both of whom appeared on talk shows as experts on the occult crime "epidemic" that was sweeping America in the '80s – an urban myth their book had largely created. (Apparently, no one cared that the purported events in the book had taken place decades earlier.) Pazder held himself out as a specialist in "ritual abuse" for years afterward, despite the lack of hard evidence that such murderous rituals ever occurred. He also ran Anawim House, a live-in drug and alcohol rehab centre at 973 Caledonia Avenue, until he died in 2004. Michelle, meanwhile, has gained a reputation as a fabric artist.

LOCAL LEGENDS

Victorians repeat all sorts of stories that are nearly impossible to verify, but too intriguing to ignore. Among them:

• Inca gold plundered by Spanish explorers is hidden in caves in the Sooke Hills.

• The bodies of the illegitimate children of nuns are buried on the grounds of St. Ann's Academy.

• A mysterious "flying cat" lives in the woods around Florence Lake.

• A vampire lives in the shadow of Craigdarroch Castle. Franciscan monks have a residence nearby on Joan Crescent to keep an eye on him.

• Donald Trump regularly comes to Victoria, to visit his aunt in a Rockland care home. Tom Selleck has a house in the Uplands. Danny DeVito has a house in Sooke. John Travolta has a house in North Saanich, and parks his planes at the Pat Bay airport.

• A submarine is parked at the bottom of the Inner Harbour, so the BC premier and his cabinet can escape in the event of an earthquake or nuclear war.

Here, Caddy, Caddy, Caddy

STILL MORE MONSTERS

Cadborosaurus isn't the only mystery creature sighted in waters around Victoria. The Cowichan Natives believed Shawnigan Lake was inhabited by **Sis-i-utl**, a huge double-headed snake. (Appropriately, the lake was used for the opening scene of the 1999 horror movie *Lake Placid*, although the monster in it was a giant alligator.) In 1972, two boys claimed they were chased from Thetis Lake by a **"gill man"** that sounded suspiciously like that creature from the Black Lagoon. And in 1992, writer Alison Griffiths (co-author of *Vancouver: A Novel*) told newspapers that while she was swimming in the Gorge waterway, she encountered a beast that was "almost round, medium grey in colour, with purply blotches." It was quickly dubbed **"Gorgeous,"** although biologists later said it was probably a sea lion. Spoilsports.

Not many aspects of First Nations mythology translate into modern pop culture, but one that certainly has is the belief that a **sea monster** lurks in the waters off Victoria. Over the past century, hundreds of people have claimed to see a creature with a head like a horse, a mane of seaweed, and a body like a snake, slithering through our seas. The first recorded observation of the creature occurred in 1881, when a 12-year-old boy claimed he fired a slingshot at it from a canoe off William Head. But sightings didn't start occurring frequently until 1933, when the first reports came in of a similar monster in Scotland's Loch Ness.

On October 1, 1933, the clerk of the legislature and his wife were out sailing near Chatham Island when they saw the monster, "nearly 80 feet long and just about as wide as the average automobile." The *Victoria Daily Times* ran their story on the front page, and within a few days more reports came in, including one that the creature had been seen in Cadboro Bay. That led a cheeky letter-writer to suggest that it should be called **Cadborosaurus**: "Besides, the name is euphonious, and, if too long, can be shortened to 'Caddy' as a pet name, especially for the lucky ones who see him from the nineteenth hole at [the] Oak Bay [golf course]."

News of the monster excited interest worldwide, which delighted Victoria's chamber of commerce. The sightings grew in number and in detail, from places all along the straits of Georgia and Juan de Fuca, and from as far away as California and Alaska. The reports dropped off in the '60s and '70s, when Caddy mainly became the subject of photo-contest hoaxes. But the creature may be resurfacing: a rash of sightings reported by the *Times Colonist* in the late 1990s renewed local interest, and today a project called "Caddyscan" has several 24-hour video cameras mounted at strategic points along Victoria's coastline to capture pictures of the elusive beast.

famous haunts

With its stone houses and oak trees, Victoria looks like a place that would be home to many ghost stories, and indeed it is. Here are some of the best-known, but for more hair-raising tales, try John Adams' excellent **Ghostly Walks** tours *(384-6698, discoverthepast.com)* and the Ghosts of Victoria festival he organizes every October.

Tod House

At 2564 Heron Street, a quiet lane in Oak Bay, sits Tod House, one of the oldest residential homes still standing in western Canada. Not all of its occupants have been alive, however. In 1944, a retired colonel and his wife purchased the house, and soon discovered that a benign but temperamental spirit had taken up residence. A door leading from the kitchen to a cellar would not stay shut, even after it was carefully latched. Also, objects suspended from hooks in the kitchen began rocking on their own. One Christmas morning, the colonel found all the decorations had been pulled off the walls and the tree and placed in a neat pile on the living room floor. On another night, two young airmen who'd stayed over fled from an upstairs room, claiming they'd seen a First Nations woman in chains, pleading for help. That story led some people to wonder if the ghost had been a victim of the house's first owner – a mystery that deepened in 1947, when the colonel was digging beside the house and came upon the remains of a headless skeleton.

Among the Stars

Every city lays claim to connections in Tinseltown. These are some of ours:

David Foster

This songwriter and Grammy-winning producer put together some of the biggest records of the 1980s and '90s for Lionel Richie, Neil Diamond, Kenny Rogers, Barbra Streisand, Whitney Houston, and Celine Dion, proving that no one knows his cheese like a Canadian. He still returns to his hometown (he's a Mount Douglas Secondary School grad) to oversee his foundation, which raises money for children in need of organ transplants, although he's relocated its annual celebrity-studded benefit to wealthier Vancouver. Most recently, Foster appeared in *The Princes of Malibu*, a reality TV show about his spoiled stepsons, as a gimmick to get them Hollywood work. It was a flop – and the day after the show premiered, his wife filed for divorce.

Meg and Jennifer Tilly

Best-known for wrapping herself around William Hurt in *The Big Chill* in 1983, Esquimalt Secondary School graduate Meg Tilly went on to earn an Oscar nomination for her role as a tormented nun in 1985's *Agnes of God*. Meg and her film-exec husband recently lived in an Uplands mansion (Colin Firth, with whom she has a son, visited occasionally), but they've since split and moved on. Her older sister Jennifer, who attended Belmont Secondary, is still onscreen: she was nominated for an Oscar in Woody Allen's *Bullets Over Broadway*, has lent her helium-squeak voice to numerous cartoons, and recently starred in Terry Gilliam's *Tideland*.

Pamela Anderson

The *Baywatch* star was born just over the Malahat in Ladysmith (on July 1, 1967, Canada's 100th birthday, making her the region's first Centennial baby) and passes through Victoria occasionally to visit her folks in Nanaimo. She occasionally makes noise about moving back to the Island, but recently became a US citizen.

The house had been built in 1851 by John Tod, one of first retirees from Hudson's Bay Company, who'd served the HBC for more than 37 years. He was famous for his explosive temper: one story had it that he'd saved Fort Kamloops from marauding aboriginals by holding a lit match over a keg of gunpowder, threatening to blow up the fort and them with it. He'd also had at least five wives, several of whom had been aboriginal. Tests proved that the bones discovered beside the house belonged to an Asian or aboriginal woman. Had she been a victim of Tod's fury? No one ever found out. After the remains were removed, the ghost disappeared and never returned. (People still reside in the Tod House, so don't go poking around. Unless you want to become its next ghost, that is.)

Phantom of the Links

Every spring at dusk, local students make a pilgrimage to the seventh fairway of the Victoria Golf Course to look for one of the most frequently sighted ghosts in North America. Doris Gravlin, a young nurse, was senselessly murdered there by her estranged husband (a sports editor at a local newspaper) in 1936, and ever since the 1940s people have claimed to see her apparition, sometimes wearing a white dress or simply as a floating ball of light, gliding over the bushes and along the shoreline, or occasionally flying toward and even entering cars on the roadway. One of the most detailed accounts was given by a pack of high school students who said they saw Doris's ghost on two consecutive nights in April of 1968, which gave rise to several local folktales. One suggests that the ghost will come out if you ring a bell next to the sixth green on the night of a full moon; another warns that the spirit is seen only by young couples. But don't go with your true love: the tale also says that couples seeing the ghost will never marry.

Bastion Square

From 1859 to 1885, the site of today's Maritime Museum of British Columbia (mmbc.bc.ca) was occupied by the city's police barracks and jail. In its yard, 11 men were hanged, several of whom were buried on the spot and never moved. The then-new courthouse (today's museum) was built right on top of the graves – which might explain why it and the surrounding square experience a great deal of supernatural activity today. Museum staff have seen sailor hats levitate in the gift shop, heard the rapping of a gavel in the heritage courtroom when it was empty, and encountered the floating black-robed figure of "hanging judge" Matthew Baillie Begbie on the stairway. Near the museum is Helmecken Alley (see photo above), a brick-arched passageway behind D'Arcy's Pub, in which some say it's possible to hear heavy boots and rattling chains. These could be the spirits of old convicts: between the 1850s and 1890s, chain gangs repairing streets were a common sight in Victoria, and at the end of an exhausting day they often trudged through this alley back to jail.

MINISTER OF CORRUPTION

Casinogate, Bingogate, Hydrogate – there are so many scandals involving BC politicians that it would be impossible to recount them all here. But the provincial capital's most famous government intrigue began in 1954 when **"Honest Bob" Sommers**, the minister of lands and forests, was rumoured to be taking loans and favours in exchange for licences to cut trees on vast territories of public land. The accusations grew louder, several witnesses to the deals came forward, and Sommers resigned from the cabinet in 1956, claiming he'd been defamed. But the police laid criminal charges against him, and after what was then the longest trial in BC's history (76 days), he was convicted and sentenced to five years in prison. Sommers will forever be remembered as the first minister of the Crown in the history of the British Empire to serve time for bribery.

Point Ellice House

Likely the most haunted home in town, Point Ellice House seems to be occupied by several long-dead members of the O'Reilly clan, who built the house in 1865 and owned it for more than a century. Guides swear they've witnessed the piano play all by itself, and heard footsteps in the empty attic and the voice of a boy saying "please, don't lock me in," when they go home for the night. One of the most unusual incidents occurred soon after the house opened as a museum in 1967. A mysterious woman in an old-fashioned blue dress took a visiting family on a tour of the place, and then vanished. The family approached a guide and asked who the woman was, but they were told that no one else was in the house at the time. They snooped around, and in one room found the blue dress laying on a bed — a dress worn by Kathleen O'Reilly, who had died in 1945. *2616 Pleasant St. 250-380-6506, heritage.gov.bc.ca/point_ellis*

Shelbourne Street

The late poet and occultist Robin Skelton said that on Sundays in October between 2 and 3 a.m., Shelbourne Street (just south of Hillside Avenue) reverts to what it was nearly a century ago: a gravel road with grass growing down the middle, fringed by trees and bushes instead of houses and shops. Skelton ascribed this to an "energy memory" of the old street, which apparently is so strong that it continues to appear. The pints at Maude Hunter's Pub, a few blocks to the north, have nothing to do with it.

Spiritual Cleansing

If a ghost is giving you grief, contact the **House Healers** *(477-3914)*, a team of three women who will channel and identify the spirit, and then persuade it to leave your home. Be prepared to have a bank balance in the material world, however. They charge $500 just for basic services, and co-founder Jacqueline Fraser says that in her five years in business she's encountered houses that are plagued by as many as a dozen entites at once.

Victoria was a virtually a second home for **Tallulah Bankhead**, the chain-smoking, outspokenly bisexual actress who dominated the London stage in the 1920s and '30s. A longtime friend of Dola Dunsmuir, the youngest daughter of coal baron James Dunsmuir, Tallulah visited Victoria frequently between 1949 and 1966, often with Dola bellowing "Make way for Miss Bankhead!" at the airport. (When asked once at customs to open her bags, Tallulah reportedly said, "You don't have to bother, darling. There's nothing in them but liquor and drugs." She was probably telling the truth: at various times, she had an appetite for cocaine, morphine, and entire pharmacies of pills.) While here, Tallulah attended art shows and the 1964 re-opening of the McPherson Playhouse, which was "selling" its seats as a fundraiser; she bought a few, and they still bear plaques with her name.

When she wasn't out on the town, Tallulah stayed at "Dolura," Dola's mansion on the grounds of her father's Hatley Castle, which was rented to the Canadian military and provided Dola with much of her income. (Dolura was torn down in 1997.) According to Dola's former maid, who's still alive and living in Langford, the women consumed prodigious amounts of booze: Dola drank a bottle of gin daily, and Tallulah had mint juleps at breakfast. They also threw lavish parties; at one, a soused judge couldn't get his car started, and the tow-truck driver was rewarded with a sip of champagne from one of Tallulah's shoes. Not that she wore them: Tallulah loved coming to Victoria for fresh air and sunlight, and spent nearly all her time at the house in the nude — a sight so upsetting to the in-house chef that he refused to serve her dinner until she got dressed.

THE ONE-DOLLAR MANSION

To live luxuriously in Victoria, you don't need millions; all you really need is a lot of nerve. In 1999, an Anglican women's organization leased their 17,000-square-foot mansion (a former nursing home) at 1322 Rockland Avenue to **Baron George von Bothmer zu Schwegerhoff** for the princely sum of a dollar per year for 99 years. The women believed the baron would use the 1894 house to exhibit his family antiques — until they discovered that he also was known as George Davis, a former teacher's aide from Oregon who'd quickly taken out a $600,000 mortgage on the property and then held several lavish parties. The women sued, claiming Davis had misrepresented himself. Davis replied that his baronial title was legit, acquired when he was adopted as an adult by his aunt. But he agreed to move out, and the mansion was later sold for $1.9 million.

Marilyn's Rock

Photo: Courtesy of David Conover Jr.

The blue recycling bins Victorians dutifully place in front of their homes figure in Canada's most famous case of **corporate espionage**. In April 2004, Air Canada launched a $220-million lawsuit against WestJet, claiming the rival airline tried to destroy the national carrier by illegally accessing its databases of flight-traffic info. As proof, Air Canada presented documents that private investigators took from a blue box at the Oak Bay home of WestJet co-founder Mark Hill. WestJet countersued for $5 million, claiming that Air Canada's agents had trespassed and stolen private records. Hill even had photos catching them in the act — to which Air Canada replied that Hill had planted the documents, hoping to embarrass its execs with the pics. The lawsuit is still unresolved. So much for the friendly skies!

If history had turned out differently, **Marilyn Monroe** might be living today in a Gulf Islands fishing lodge. In 1945, David Conover, a US Army photographer in Los Angeles, was given an assignment (by his commanding officer, Ronald Reagan) to photograph women helping to win the war. Conover snapped 19-year-old Norma Jean Dougherty working on an assembly line, and was so taken by her that they went off to the California desert together to shoot more film – and start an affair. They were both separately married at the time, and after the war Conover moved with his wife to BC's Wallace Island, just north of Salt Spring. But Conover's photos launched Norma Jean's modeling and acting career, and the two did more than stay in touch after she became Marilyn Monroe, carrying on a clandestine relationship for 17 years. (They did meet publicly on the set of *Gentlemen Prefer Blondes*; see photo.) Conover may have even hoped they would reunite permanently: as BC writer Margo MacLennan has written in her book *One Small Secret*, when Marilyn's marriage to Joe DiMaggio was falling apart in 1957, Conover bought another island near Salt Spring with the intention of giving it to her – and sold it when she later married Arthur Miller. Conover turned to writing, and after the star died of a drug overdose in 1962, told (nearly) all in his memoir *Finding Marilyn*, in which he maintained that she'd been murdered, a conspiracy he pursued until his death in 1983. Today, Conover's photos of Hollywood's greatest bombshell are prized by collectors, and when they were exhibited at Lunds auction house in Victoria in 1997, buyers from around the world turned up, although at the last minute the images were withdrawn from sale because of ownership questions. Even after her death, it seems, people fight over where and to whom Marilyn Monroe belongs.

You'd think that sleepy Vancouver Island would be the last place to have connections to international terrorism — but it seems our isolation makes us a haven for some of the world's most wanted. On December 14, 1999, customs officials in Port Angeles, Washington stopped Algerian-born Montrealer **Ahmed Ressam** as he was driving off the *Coho* ferry from Victoria. In the trunk of his rental car, they found four timing devices, two jars of nitroglycerine, and 54 kilograms of urea nitrate, the same material used in the 1993 World Trade Center bombing. And when the FBI learned he'd made a reservation at a hotel a few blocks from the Space Needle in Seattle, that city cancelled its millennium New Year's celebrations. Ressam is now serving a 22-year sentence. Victorians can be thankful he didn't have a fender-bender on Belleville Street.

Another explosive character is **Inderjit Singh Reyat**. An electrician and former director of the Sikh temple in Duncan, he's the only person ever convicted for the 1985 Air India bombings that killed 329 people off the coast of Ireland. Reyat built the bombs from components he bought at a Woolworth's store in Duncan. He's due to be released in 2008.

And then there's **Michael Scarpitti, a.k.a. Tre Arrow**: the man fingered as the ringleader of a band of "eco-terrorists" that torched logging trucks in Oregon in 2001. After 18 months on the lam, he was arrested at the Canadian Tire store on Douglas Street trying to shoplift a set of bolt-cutters. Currently he's housed in the Wilkinson Road prison and fighting extradition to the US, where he claims it will be impossible for him to get a fair trial. Once called an "environmental rock star" by *Rolling Stone* for his public activism, Brother Tre has become something of a Victoria folk hero, and coffee-shop benefits are held around town to raise money for his legal battles.

Too Good to Be True

Fraudsters operate everywhere, but it may be unique to Victoria that here they capitalize not so much on greed as good intentions. Perhaps the first was a prospector from California who announced in 1885 that he'd found gold in Beacon Hill Park: terrified that their beloved green space would be overrun, prominent Victorians bought out his claim, and then, after digging, realized there was no gold at all. But he certainly wasn't the last to engage in philanthropic flim-flammery, judging by recent cases.

Alice Goertzen

The prospect of employment with the United Nations appealed to noble Victorians, who gave this phony headhunter $40,000 to line up plum jobs in international relief. In 2004, a local court sentenced her to five years, her 34th conviction.

Lisa Hackney

This storyteller (a.k.a. Elisabeth Von Hullessem, one of her 16 aliases) spun lucrative tales about a writers' conference in Banff she was organizing, and an autism charity fundraiser featuring Elton John. In 2003, she was arrested in Oak Bay, and after repaying $7,000 and doing time in a psychiatric hospital, she was extradited to Arkansas where she was wanted for running over her mother with a car.

Robert Palm

In the 1990s, post-Communist Russia needed food, and this local (and self-proclaimed) Pentecostal minister made a deal to satisfy that hunger with wheat flour he obtained from poor farmers in Poland. The flour disappeared, and in 2003, a Victoria court ordered him to pay the farmers more than $37 million.

Den of Iniquity

Some say it was built with Nazi money as a hideout for war criminals. Others say it was a Mafia retreat where prostitutes entertained cocaine smugglers – and one girl who threatened to go to the police was pushed out of a helicopter over the Strait of Juan de Fuca. All kinds of creepy tales swirl around **Grouse Nest**, the waterfront resort at 1424 Gillespie Road in East Sooke. But are any of them true? What is known is that the property was developed in 1911 by a Victoria financier, was a family-run resort from the 1930s to 1963, and then was bought by Swiss investors and expanded to a 14,000-square-foot lodge – featuring a gaudy lounge (see photo) with a sealskin-upholstered bar right out of *Scarface*. Although floatplanes kept coming and going from the place, the Swiss claimed to have trouble attracting a regular clientele, so they sold off its surrounding land (creating Matheson Lake park), and auctioned the lodge in 1985 to the Tchividjian family, the Swiss in-laws of evangelist Billy Graham. One of the Tchividjian daughters hired former RCMP agent and convicted wife-murderer Patrick Kelly to do renos, and after he defrauded her of $40,000, the family sold Grouse Nest in 2005 to a California developer who plans to revive it as a resort. Perhaps it'll succeed this time: the rumours alone should draw curiosity-seekers for years to come.

infamous islands

Some of Victoria's dark tales involve the small bits of rock just off our shores.

Scorched Earth

Like many First Nations people of the BC coast, the local Songhees placed their dead on isolated pieces of land. A burial house once stood at the tip of Laurel Point, and bodies were often left on the tiny "coffin islands" at the foot of Robert Street in Vic West. Another common site was **Halkett Island**, next to the Selkirk trestle, on the Gorge waterway. "Up [its] trees were corpses of Indians fastened up in trunks," recalled Edgar Fawcett, in his 1912 autobiography *Some Reminiscences of Old Victoria*. But the bodies are long gone: Fawcett also confessed that in 1867, he and some swimming chums set the coffins ablaze as a boyhood prank. "Some time later we visited [Halket Island] . . . and found that all traces of the burying ground had vanished, the surface of the island being swept clean, with not a trace of boxes, bones or trees, and it has remained so till this day." The barren island was returned to the Songhees in 1993.

Gulf Island Gulag

Photo: BC Archives G00607

As the ferry headed for the mainland shoves off from the Swartz Bay terminal, the first rocky outcrop you pass on your left is **Piers Island** – a former penal colony for a radical sect of Russian pacifists. The Doukhobors, who arrived in BC around 1908, were communal-farming vegetarians who rejected all external authority, and

Michael Ruge

"You must give back to the community or we won't trade your money," declared this Shawnigan Lake bed-and-breakfast owner and stock promoter. In 2004, the British Columbia Securities Commission suspended him for 25 years for duping fellow members of Victoria's Rotary Club into investing $1.2 million in his worthless Chivas Growth Fund. He now offers Bigfoot safari tours and $10,000 "story selling" seminars featuring the visionary behind the *Chicken Soup for the Soul* books.

Ian Thow

In 2004, this high-flying mutual-funds salesman publicly pledged millions to Victoria hospital, university, and police charities. In 2005, he was hiding in Seattle from creditors claiming he owed them $42 million he'd purportedly invested in Jamaican banks. The charities are wondering what happened to the money too.

disrobed and burned their own homes and possessions to show their dissent. To deter such behaviour, in 1931 the Canadian government upped the penalty for public nudity to three years in prison. When the Doukhobors protested again, some 600 of them were rounded up and shipped to Piers Island.

The island had two compounds, one for men and one for women, surrounded by four-metre-tall barbed-wire fences. Discipline was enforced with bread and water diets, solitary confinement, and beatings with a "paddle." Children were placed in foster homes, and at times the laments of the mothers on the island were so loud that their cries could be heard in Sidney. In 1935, when nearly all the sentences had been served, the colony was dismantled and Piers Island was returned to its previous owners.

Quarantined Castaways

Photo: BC Archives F05163

In 1891, city officials trying to root out smallpox in downtown Victoria discovered five Chinese men afflicted with leprosy. Instead of treating them, the city exiled them to **D'Arcy Island**, directly across from Island View Beach. Over the next 35 years, several dozen leprosy patients were sent to the island, nearly all of them Chinese; they couldn't leave or have visitors, and relied on supplies shipped across every three months, including food, tools, clothing, opium, and coffins. (There are more than a dozen graves on the island today.) In 1924, its survivors were moved to a proper medical facility on **Bentinck Island** (near Race Rocks), which closed after the last patient died in 1957. D'Arcy is now a marine park, and the military uses Bentinck for weapons testing.

Housing Boom

If you're traveling on Highway 17 north of Mount Newton X Road, look east: the 316-hectare (780-acre) chunk of land just offshore is **James Island**. Once home to a hunting and horse-racing club, in 1913 Canadian Explosives Ltd. bought the island and erected a TNT factory there to capitalize on BC's railway and mining boom, as well as World War I. (James Island TNT was on the French ship that blew up in Halifax's harbour in 1917, killing 2,000 people.) As many as 800 workers lived on the island until the 1960s; the plant was dismantled in 1979. Today, the island is owned by Seattle cell-phone billionaire Craig McCaw. A few years ago, he put it on the market for $50 million US (it has a golf course designed by Jack Nicklaus), but he's now developing it into a ritzy 80-home eco-village. Among its rules: no insecticides, resident deer are managed by birth control, only electric cars are allowed – and no smoking.

Hostile Takeover

As deals go, this one was a steal. In 1850, Hudson's Bay Company agent James Douglas bought nearly all the land of today's Victoria from the Songhees, Clallam, and Sooke Natives for only £150, paying the equivalent of a labourer's wages for two weeks to the heads of 122 families. In return, the **Natives signed a treaty** stating (in English) that they retained only their villages and the right to hunt on unoccupied land, with everything else becoming "the Entire property of the White people for ever." (It's still debated today whether the Natives, not familiar with the British concept of property, knew what the treaty really meant.) Douglas also cut similar deals further north, and backed them up with force. In 1863, after a couple of settlers were found murdered near Kuper Island (north of Salt Spring), Douglas sent gunboats into the area and when they got into a shootout with militant Natives, the ships responded by shelling the island's village, reportedly killing eight people. Four of the militants were later tracked down, tried, convicted, and executed in Bastion Square.

Passing Through

Nearly four million tourists visit Victoria every year. A few have been historic figures.

Winston Churchill

Even in 1929, 11 years before he became prime minister, the British statesman had a famous reputation as an orator, and more than 800 people crammed into a hall in the Empress Hotel on September 5 that year to hear him speak. "Your green

Sugar and spice, everything nice – no one in Victoria will believe that cliché again after the murder of 14-year-old **Reena Virk**. On November 14, 1997, Reena was lured to a party by a pair of girls who were angry that she'd stolen an address book and was spending time with one of their boyfriends. At the party, she was attacked by eight teens – seven of them girls – who beat her up. She escaped and ran to the Gorge inlet, near the Craigflower Bridge. But Warren Glowatski, then 16, and Kelly Ellard, 15, pursued her, and when she told them that she'd turn them in, they beat her again. Ellard stood on Reena's back and drowned her in the waterway; the police didn't find her body for eight days.

When it was discovered that nearly all the attackers were girls, the story went global, and UVic prof Sibylle Artz – who'd just published a book called *Sex, Power and the Violent School Girl*, about Victoria-area teenage girls who used fear to gain respect and attention – became the media expert *du jour*. Glowatski and Ellard are now both serving life sentences for second-degree murder – although Rebecca Godfrey's 2005 book *Under the Bridge* implicates a second girl, who was merely convicted of assault and is now working as a stripper.

lawns and sturdy oaks, and hearts as British as the oaks, all remind me of the Mother Country," he told the audience, which greeted him with five minutes of thunderous applause. Churchill wasn't entirely at home, however: it was illegal to drink publicly in Victoria at the time, so the Empress staff had to serve his whiskey in a teapot. He also laid a stone for the northwest tower of Christ Church Cathedral (then under construction) and planted a hawthorn in the Mayor's Grove of Beacon Hill Park, near the Quadra Street entrance. Every year, Churchill fans gather around the tree on the Sunday closest to January 24 (the date of his death) to toast their hero, often played by Chris Gainor (see photo on previous page), a historian who bears a striking resemblance to the man who saved the world.

Ellard guilty of murder

Saanich teen Reena Virk was slain seven years ago

BY JOEL BAGLOLE
and IAN MULGREW
CanWest News Service

INSIDE ON VERDICT
• SUMAN VIRK GRACIOUS THROUGHOUT ORDEAL   A2
• CHRONOLOGY OF A MURDER CONVICTION   A3
• EDITORIAL: JUSTICE A LONG TIME COMING   A12

VANCOUVER — After seven years and three trials, 22-year-old Kelly Ellard was found guilty Tuesday of second-degree murder in the killing of Saanich teenager Reena Virk.

A jury that had deliberated since Friday returned the guilty verdict Tuesday afternoon. Supreme Court Justice Robert Bauman will sentence Ellard April 25. She faces a mandatory life sentence but could be paroled in either five or seven years.

Without a Trace

Every parent's worst nightmare became real for Bruce and Crystal Dunahee on Sunday, March 24, 1991. They were getting ready to play some touch football on the grounds of Blanshard Elementary School, when their four-year-old son, **Michael Dunahee**, wandered away from them. When they turned to look for him, he was gone. An immediate police search found no trace of the boy. Hundreds of volunteers combed the neighbourhood, and police interviewed several men who matched a sketch of someone seen lurking in the area; they also hypnotized a woman to find more clues, but ended up with nothing. National headlines and reports on TV's *America's Most Wanted* brought in hundreds of tips, but no solid leads. The case is still unsolved; although there have been alleged sightings of Michael from far away as New Jersey, no ransom note or message from the kidnapper has ever appeared. To remind the public about their son, who would now be in his 20s (see age-progressed photo), Michael's parents organize a Keep Hope Alive fundraising run for missing children every March.

Aleister Crowley

In his *Confessions*, the "great beast" of occult sex magic says he stopped here in 1915, on his way from Vancouver to Seattle. While ashore he met one of his former worshippers, transformed by Victoria's clean living. "[T]he flabby sensual debauched rake had become clean, muscular, trim, bright-eyed and self-controlled," Crowley wrote. "If I could have stayed a week in Victoria I might have rescued her." Other intriguing stories claim that he lived briefly near Victoria in a mansion owned by a German prince. Latter-day mystics maintain a shrine to Crowley on the lower floor of Market Square.

"The Great Impostor"

When the destroyer *HMCS Cayuga* sailed out of Esquimalt in July 1950 to join the Korean War, it had a notorious passenger aboard:

Ferdinand Waldo Demara Jr., an American who'd already worked as a psychology professor, a lawyer, a Trappist monk, and a civil engineer, all without any professional qualifications. On the *Cayuga*, he passed himself off as Dr. Joseph Cyr, a surgeon — and soon was tested on his self-taught skills. He pulled a tooth of the ship's captain, and treated three wounded South Koreans, removing a bullet near the heart of one man. These incidents got press, tipping off the real Dr. Cyr, and Demara was deported back to the US. In 1961, Hollywood made a movie based on his escapades entitled *The Great Impostor*, starring Tony Curtis. But the *Cayuga* crew didn't hold a grudge: the captain lobbied the Canadian government to let Demara return to Victoria for a reunion, and in 1979 the world's most famous resumé-padder was greeted here by his former shipmates.

Francis Mawson Rattenbury, the designer of the Empress Hotel and Victoria's Parliament Buildings, is the city's most celebrated architect. He's also its most famous murder victim. At a glamorous dinner at the Empress in 1923, Rattenbury met Alma Packenham, a beautiful young flapper. A brilliant but cruel man, he started flaunting her around town, much to the torment of his wife, who eventually sued him for divorce in 1925. There were more scandalous rumours, including one that Alma had gotten Ratz hooked on cocaine, so they fled to England in 1929 and holed up in a villa in Bournemouth. Rattenbury became besotted by drink, demoralized by impotence, and impoverished by failed land deals, and Alma started sleeping with George Stoner, their 18-year-old chauffeur. And then, on the night of March 24, 1935, somebody bludgeoned the architect to death.

Alma found Rattenbury's lifeless body, got drunk waiting for the police to arrive, and confessed to the beating. "I did it with a mallet," she slurred. "He has lived too long." Then she recanted, and Stoner confessed he'd done it, but had been under the influence of cocaine. They were both charged, and put on trial together. The case was a sensation in London, and crowds lined up for 12 hours just to get into the courtroom. After Alma testified against Stoner, the court found him guilty and sentenced him to death; Alma was acquitted, and thousands waiting outside booed as she left the courthouse. A few days later she committed suicide, stabbing herself six times and then falling into the Avon River.

The murder and subsequent events have been the subject of a play (*Cause Célèbre* by Terence Rattigan, made into a 1987 movie starring Helen Mirren); several English barristers have also written books, arguing that the evidence showed Alma committed the murder, and Stoner confessed out of love for her. If so, the chauffeur remained loyal. He received clemency, got out of prison after seven years, and went to his grave refusing to name the real killer.

On the night of January 18, 1943, 15-year-old **Molly Justice** stepped off a city bus and started walking toward Swan Lake. Skaters were playing on the ice, but the city had dimmed the streetlights for fear of a Japanese attack. No one saw what happened. A few hours later, Molly was found in the bushes, stabbed to death with a pen knife.

A city-wide manhunt began. The crime became an international incident when Victoria's mayor blamed it on the nightly dim-out, which BC's premier had ordered at the request of the US Army. Detectives found a pair of men's gloves near the crime scene, and went to the trouble of tracking down the owners of 96 similar pairs that had been sold in Victoria that winter. A break in the case finally came in May, when police arrested Frank Hulbert, a 15-year-old delinquent who'd assaulted a girl near Swan Lake and threatened that she'd "get the same as Molly Justice." Hulbert denied he'd had anything to do with the murder, but he said he knew who did it; the cops subsequently arrested a 50-year-old logger, but ended up dropping the charges for lack of evidence. The case remained unsolved for over 50 years.

Then in July of 1996, detectives announced that they'd cracked it. Hulbert was guilty, they said. In fact, documents indicated that he'd confessed to the killing, but his stepfather – BC's deputy attorney-general at the time – had declared the documents "confidential" and thwarted the prosecution. A retired judge appointed to investigate concluded that there was no evidence of a cover-up. But that still didn't answer the big question: did Hulbert do it? We'll never know. Hulbert died in Port Alberni in March of 1996, a few months before the detectives announced that he was the murderer.

Charles Lindbergh

At 4 a.m. on October 22, 1931, the famous aviator and his wife arrived by steamship at the end of a world tour. Lindbergh had heard en route that his father-in-law had died, and planned to fly home to New Jersey from Seattle. But *Victoria Times* editor Archie Willis told a friend of Lindy's that they could fly from here, and the friend had a plane waiting. At 6:22 a.m., Lindbergh took the controls of a speedy Lockheed Vega and lifted off from Lansdowne Field, soaring over a huge crowd of awestruck Victorians, many of whom had slept in their cars all night to see him.

Richard Nixon

After he lost the 1960 presidential election, "Tricky Dick" had some time on his hands. In 1962, he visited Victoria with his family (and Seattle lawyer and Watergate stooge John Ehrlichman), and ended up at Butchart Gardens. While a *Colonist* photographer snapped pictures, a small boy shook Nixon's hand and introduced himself as a fan and fellow American. Spectators reportedly fell into a hushed silence when the boy walked away and said, "Thank you, Mr. Kennedy."

Babe Ruth

The "Sultan of Swat" landed in Victoria on October 20, 1934 aboard a steamship loaded with baseball greats (including Lou Gehrig) heading to Japan for some exhibition games. According to the *Colonist*, "boys of all sizes and ages, yes, and of several colours" swarmed around the Bambino and his cohorts, who signed autographs while the ship was docked for 90 minutes at Rithet's wharves, the site of today's coast guard station.

Scott of the Antarctic

In the 1890s, Robert Falcon Scott was a lieutenant on the HMS *Amphion*, which was stationed in Esquimalt. He spent much of his time here dining and dancing with Kathleen O'Reilly, the beautiful daughter of the family at Point Ellice House. Scott and Miss O'Reilly continued to correspond over the years as he advanced up the chain of command, and eventually led an expedition to the South Pole. Tragically, Scott died during his second attempt to the reach the pole in 1912.

Catch Me If You Can

"I would not consider myself a criminal," said **Christopher Rocancourt**. "I steal with my mind." But police took a very different view of this French con man who scammed $60 million around the world before he was arrested in Oak Bay in April 2001. Born in 1967, the son of a prostitute and a drunken housepainter, he honed his smooth talk on the streets of Paris, and spent the decade of the '90s in LA and New York, passing himself off as (among other things) a Russian prince, a member of the Rockefeller family, and the son of Sophia Loren, promising the gullible fantastic returns on high-tech companies and movie deals, then taking their up-front cash and blowing it on $75,000-a-month suites at fancy hotels. But the heat was catching up with him, and in 2001 he travelled to Canada, where he fleeced $116,500 from locals at the Whistler ski resort, and started an affair with a woman he met in a clothing store. Although he was travelling with his wife (1988 Playmate Pia Reyes) and his toddler son Zeus at the time, Rocancourt chartered a helicopter, followed his new girlfriend to Victoria, and took a room in the Oak Bay Beach Hotel, where he hung out in the pub claiming he was a Formula One race car driver. He even got his portrait taken in a tourist photo shop downtown dressed as an outlaw with a gun and a bag of money next to a "Wanted" sign. He must have known the jig was up: a few days later, the cops nabbed him near the hotel.

Or was it? Rocancourt spent several months in the Wilkinson Road Jail writing his autobiography (published in France as *Me, Christophe Rocancourt: Orphan, Playboy and Convict*) before he was sent back to the US. In 2003, a New York court gave him four years in prison and ordered him to repay $1.2 million out of the proceeds from his book, which has been optioned by the screenwriter of *Monster's Ball*. Rocancourt's lawyer told reporters his client plans to get into the movie business when he's released in 2007: "He'll fit in right away."

Moi, CHRISTOPHE ROCANCOURT orphelin, play-boy et taulard

Treasure Maps

If you're scrutinized by the clerks at the BC Archives, cut them some slack. In 1995, Gilbert Bland Jr. – a thief as inconspicuous as his name – borrowed several rare atlases and **sliced out 30 maps** in the reading room without anyone noticing. Bland was later caught in the US with some of the Archives' documents (including a 16th-century map by Ortelius, maker of the world's first atlases) and others he'd stolen from 20 libraries across North America, comprising a collection worth half a million dollars. He plea-bargained away most of the charges, and spent 18 months in prison.

The Bank, the Thief, His Wife, and His Novel

Robbing banks is as addictive as heroin – just ask writer **Stephen Reid**. On June 9, 1999, addled from a two-week binge on booze and smack, Reid walked into the Royal Bank in the Cook Street Village brandishing a shotgun. He took $92,924, jumped into a car, had a shoot out with police during a chase through Beacon Hill Park, and was arrested a few hours later, passed out in a James Bay apartment. The town was stunned. Reid's conduct wasn't entirely out of character, though. In the 1970s, he'd been a member of a gang that stole more than $15 million from over 100 banks across the US and Canada. But many thought he'd reformed after he met Victoria poet Susan Musgrave who edited an acclaimed novel (*Jackrabbit Parole*) he wrote in prison in the 1980s and settled down with her to raise a family. For many years he'd been known around Victoria as a dedicated father, teacher, and actor. His old habits caught up with him in 1998, however, when he started messing with dope again (he'd been an addict as a teenager), eventually culminating in his desperate Cook Street heist. Reid pleaded guilty to armed robbery and attempted murder. Several Victoria poets testified in defence of his character, to little effect: he's currently serving an 18-year jail term.

Robert W. Service

In 1903 and 1904, the author of *The Shooting of Dan McGrew* worked as a clerk at the Canadian Imperial Bank of Commerce (now the Spirit of Christmas store) at 1022 Government Street. He slept in an apartment above the bank vault, with a loaded revolver on his bedside table in case of thieves. Service also attended parties and theatrical performances, and joined the South Cowichan Lawn Tennis Club (before he got the bank job, he'd tried farming in Duncan). The bank eventually transferred him to Kamloops and then to the Yukon, where he started composing his famous tales about the Klondike gold rush.

Books are Burning

In 1954, during the height of America's Communist witch hunts, the Victoria Public Library conducted a purge of its own. Only a few months earlier it had hired **John Marshall**, a 34-year-old librarian, to start a bookmobile service. But when the library board learned that Marshall had edited a leftist paper and attended peace conferences, it sacked him – and discussed removing subversive literature from the shelves. Mayor Claude Harrison then told a reporter he wanted all communist books burned, and the story went national: students torched Harrison's effigy in Pioneer Square, the House of Commons debated the case, and politicians accused RCMP officers of smearing Marshall by leaking his politics to the board. Marshall got a job at the University of Toronto, and worked there until he retired. The Victoria library publicly apologized to him at a ceremony in 1998 – ironically, while protests raged against the library for allowing Doug Christie's far-right Canadian Free Speech League to rent one of its meeting rooms.

John L. Sullivan

In the days when Victoria was a gold rush boomtown, the famed bare-knuckle prizefighter would often stop here for exhibitions. According to one account, the Irishman shocked the locals at a dinner by refusing to toast to the health of the Queen. But the incident he's best known for is threatening to "eat" the mayor, who voted against giving Sullivan a permit to fight in November of 1886. Sullivan was persuaded to abandon the idea after his friends convinced him it would have "serious international complications."

Our Man in Ottawa

Victorians can't say they've never been heard in the nation's capital: for four years, Prime Minister **Sir John A. Macdonald**, the founder of Canada, was also Victoria's member of parliament. In the 1878 federal election, Macdonald's Conservative party returned to power, but he was defeated in his own riding in Ontario, so he ran in a by-election for the Victoria riding and won. The Prime Minister was our Member of Parliament until 1882 when he ran and won back east. The only time he actually visited here was in 1886, to open the E&N Railway. But that was enough for a local Sir John A. society, which erected his statue outside Victoria's city hall in 1982. Recently they offered to move it – they didn't like the sight of the oft-drunk Macdonald staring longingly at the Douglas Hotel beer parlour – but the city council refused.

Canada's biggest parade, discount massages, certified organic medical
marijuana, freeze-dried dogs, Spiritualist churches, and burials at sea.
Only in Victoria, you say? Pity.

Municipal Mayhem

Why don't we have a
classy central library, a
modern performing arts
centre, or a light-rail transit
system? Some say it's
because we're a small
city. Others blame the fact
that "Victoria" is really **13
municipalities**, each with
its own city hall and
mayor – and in many
cases, police and fire
departments – as much
concerned about
defending their respective
turf as solving regional problems. These divisions began in 1906, when Saanich farmers
banded together to oppose the domination of Victoria's merchants, and incorporated their
own municipality. Later that year, Oak Bay incorporated after its residents asked to join
then-wealthy Victoria, and were spurned by a penny-pinching council that didn't want to
expand the city's sewer and electrical services. Ever since, such up-yours isolationism has
spread across the region like Scotch broom.

Twenty-two politicians from these municipalities (plus three vast electoral districts) sit on
the board of the Capital Regional District (CRD), which does a fine job with water,
sewers, and parks, but hopelessly squabbles over region-wide planning – leaving the City
of Victoria to deal with many of the region's social ills (homelessness, detox) largely on its
own. What's the solution? For at least 50 years, conferences and editorials have
proposed **amalgamation** of these fiefdoms into one big city. But most municipal politicians
(aside from Victoria's) reject it, and so do voters when given a chance: Saanich residents
voted against joining Victoria in 1962, and in 1978 and 1984 citizens of Colwood and
Langford twice voted against becoming one municipality. Some hope the BC government
will force amalgamation on the region, but voters howled when Ontario and Quebec
recently pushed it on Toronto and Montreal, and the University of Victoria's Local
Government Institute claims it would save little money (we'd need the same number of
police officers) and produce imperial, indifferent civic government. At the casino in View
Royal – which that municipality scooped up because Victoria didn't want it – you'll likely
get odds that we'll still be talking about "the A-word" 20 years from now.

unique legalities

The Dope on Pot

The way some people toke, you'd think **marijuana** is legal here. But it ain't. Victoria police laid 617 drug charges in 2004, and while only 10 were for the evil crystal meth, 310 were for cannabis – and more than half of those were for simple possession. So be discreet. Whether you get busted for sparking a fatty depends on where you are, the mood of the cop who catches you, and whether you're a clean-cut commerce type or a dreadlocked teen. In particular, do your doob away from Wharf Street's Reeson Park, a favourite ambush spot for bike cops, and never burn the stinky bud inside an automobile: police don't like drivers under the influence of anything stronger than coffee and donuts, and cars are easy to search.

Mom need help with her bursitis? She's in luck: Victoria's at the vanguard of the medical marijuana movement. The **Vancouver Island Compassion Society** (381-8427, thevics.com) supplies healing herb – largely without police harassment – to hundreds of clients who suffer from such conditions as cancer, AIDS,

Border Confusion

Many municipal boundaries follow the old property lines of long-vanished farms. Though invisible to passersby, these borders have strange consequences for those who live with them.

Shifting streets:
Why does Fort Street suddenly becomes Cadboro Bay Road when you cross the Victoria-Oak Bay line? Because the two cities couldn't agree what to call the route when it was completed. Victoria argued it should all be Fort Street, but Oak Bay refused because it never had a fort of its own.

Wacky elections:
The City of Victoria nearly went to court to overturn the results of its 1999 council election because dozens of people who lived in neighbouring municipalities voted in Victoria by mistake.

fibromyalgia, and chronic migraines. Growing it hassle-free is more complicated, but the folks at **Island Harvest** *(islandharvest.ca)*, the country's first supplier of certified organic cannabis, are happy to dispense advice and copies of their book, *Sell Marijuana Legally*. If you're pained by outdated laws, join the **International Hempology 101 Society** *(hempology.com)*, which has gathered on Wednesday evenings since 1995 for a march through downtown Victoria, enveloped in clouds of sweet smoke. If you need paraphernalia, look for the plant-sprouting bicycle on the sidewalk identifying **Sacred Herb** *(#106-561 Johnson St., 384-0659, sacredherb.com)*, the only head shop in town, with pipes, bongs, and a wall full of the latest legal news.

Getting Expelled

Long ago, if an aboriginal person committed a crime, one consequence a chief could impose was banishment from the tribe – a penalty that non-aboriginal judges use today. Drug dealers often get barred from the "**red zone**" of Victoria's downtown when they're sentenced, even though such a term may be unconstitutional because it impedes their ability to find work or catch a bus. Similar no-go restrictions exist in the Gulf Islands: courts have ordered outsiders who've caused trouble on a particular island to never return to it. BC Ferries has also been known to banish passengers: in July 2005, a guy from Mayne Island who jumped off a ferry and swam to shore to make a baseball game was barred from travelling on any ship in the fleet. So you literally can get voted off the island here – or be condemned to it, practically speaking.

Split development:
The University of Victoria straddles the Oak Bay-Saanich border, and has to get approval from both municipalities to install campus-wide facilities such as new lights or irrigation systems. The Olympic View Golf Club, which is partly in Langford and partly in Colwood, had to build half its commercial property in each municipality to win approval of the respective councils.

Crisis mismanagement:
In October 2005, a thief stole a van, robbed four banks in four different municipalities, and got away before the four police departments could figure out who should chase him. When he was arrested later, 12 cops had to meet to put together the case.

the first word

British Columbia's rugged, isolated terrain once spawned an extraordinary linguistic diversity: of the 54 **aboriginal languages** documented in Canada, 32 are in this province. Tragically, the residential school system forced First Nations kids to use English, and now their ancestors' languages are endangered, if not extinct. Around Victoria, there are no fluent speakers of T'Souke left, and only one or two of Lekwungen, the Songhees language. Fortunately, the First Peoples' Cultural Foundation, based at Bastion Square, has undertaken the FirstVoices project to record elders speaking these languages for future generations. Check out the dictionaries at *firstvoices.com* and you'll see that these languages are rich in meaning: in the same way that German has single words for psychological states (*schadenfreude*), First Nations languages have terms for familial relationships and the natural world that English needs several to describe. Languages reflect values, in other words – and Native languages show what English speakers are missing.

SENĆOŦEN

The language of the Saanich peoples. "Saanich" is derived from WSÁNEĆ, which means "emerging people" or "raised up" (the appearance of Saanich territory from the water). Only about 30 people speak SENĆOŦEN fluently, but it is taught intensively at the ŁÁU,WELṈEW Tribal School, which has published several excellent books, including one on the reef-net (SX̱OLE) technology the Saanich people used to catch salmon.

ÁLES	aunt in-law
ÁM,MEĆEN	to wade for crabs
ĆEĆÁLUSET	little one turning over
Ć,ĆÍ,EŁ	to gather wood
MEQŦINETEṈ	something that someone scrounged for someone else
NEĆITEL	paying attention to each other
ONEWEŁSET	to put oneself in the middle
OW̱SESOLEṈ	going on the road
SJEUWEŁ	canoes in the bush
STOLĆEŁ	far out at sea while loaded with possessions

CRD by the Numbers

In 2005, the Capital Regional District had an estimated 354,206 souls. Not including the Juan de Fuca electoral district and the southern Gulf Islands, here's how the region breaks down, by population and household income.

Central Saanich (incorporated 1950):
16,576
$69,461

Colwood (1985):
15,376
$62,341

Esquimalt (1912):
17,291
$46,490

Highlands (1993):
1,954
$78,061

Langford (1992):
21,914
$54,911

Hul'q'umi'num'

The language of the Quw'utsun (Cowichan) peoples, spoken on Vancouver Island from the Malahat to Nanoose Bay. There are currently around 200 fluent speakers. Malaspina University-College offers courses at its Duncan campus, and UVic has tutorials online at *web.uvic.ca/hrd/salish*. For more information, see *cowichantribes.com*

heen'ut	sing a lullaby
hwa'us	scare game out to hunters
kw'ulh	tip over in a canoe
lhiput	strip meat off the bone
p'ulh	to become sensible
puylthut	wiggle out of bed
sliim	V formation of Canada geese while flying
tsaal'uts	to go over a mountain
ts'akw'ul'tsus	changing hands while paddling or chopping wood
yem'qum'	ripples caused by moving fish

Chinook Jargon

The variety of aboriginal languages across the Pacific Northwest forced its peoples to evolve a common dialect so they could trade. The result was Chinook, a creole that later incorporated bits of English and Métis French. In 1875, more than 100,000 Natives and settlers across the Pacific Northwest spoke Chinook; a century later, it had almost completely disappeared. But academics continue to study the language, and words such as *saltchuck* (seawater), *skookum* (strong) and *tyee* (chief) are still used by many British Columbians today.

Biktoli	Victoria
Boston	American
cloosh	good
hayash puspus	cougar (literally, "big cat")
hayash mersi	thank you very much
kumtux	know, understand
laplash stik	cedar tree (laplash = board, lumber)
muckamuck	food; to eat
tamahnous	magic, spirits
tatoosh	milk, breast

Speaking Victorian

Ned Vukovic, a University of Victoria theatre instructor who's coached Oscar-winning actors on dialects, says there are several tell-tales to **Victorian speech**. We pronounce the letter o deeply, saying "Lohts of rohcks" as opposed to "Lahts of rahcks." We articulate medial consonants: we say "better," which is "bedder" in many parts of Canada. (Although r is stronger back East, where you're more likely to hear the pirate-like "worrk harrd" than you are here.) We also place words further forward in mouth, giving our speech a clipped, British rhythm. Vukovic says such details have disappeared in Vancouver, but they're still detectible here because a higher proportion of our residents have lived in the UK. Things are changing, though: un-British interrogative "uptalk" (in which? every statement? becomes a question?) is epidemic among Victoria youth, as it is everywhere else.

You Know You're Victorian When ...

You say you're "heading up-Island" if you're travelling north, refer to Ontario as "back East" even if you aren't from there, and call the Vancouver region "the Mainland." You say "peeler" instead of "stripper," and "logger" instead of "lumberjack." When you hear "scooter" you picture a motorized wheelchair instead of a Vespa, and you groan at mere mention of "amalgamation" or "two-sailing wait." Abbreviations such as ALR, CFB Esquimalt, CPR, CRD, DND, The E&N, NDP, OCP, P3, The *T-C*, and TFL turn up in your conversations. You know that the Colwood crawl isn't a swimming stroke, that Vic West and William Head aren't people, and that Hudson Mack isn't a type of truck. You say "thank you" to the driver when getting off the bus.

Bylaw & Order

In many ways, the capital region's municipalities are distinct societies, with their own personalities (tweedy Oak Bay, big-box Langford), and quirky bylaws to match.

• It is against the law to throw a snowball on any street in Oak Bay.

• In Sidney, it's illegal to play street hockey if the game is "likely to delay the passage of traffic."

• The sale of fireworks is prohibited in Langford, View Royal, and Colwood. (Fireworks torched a Colwood house and killed two dogs in 2004.) Sale is permitted in Victoria, only because fireworks are used ceremonially by Chinese residents.

• Saanich and Central Saanich have bylaws restricting light pollution (mainly from greenhouses) for better stargazing at the Dominion Astrophysical Observatory.

• No hemp store may do business within three miles of any Langford school.

Women's Issues

It's a man's, man's, man's world, and that's why there are several busy women's organizations in town. Best-known is the Victoria **Status of Women Action Group** (383-7322, pacificcoast.net/~swag), which runs workshops and a court-monitoring program, and can refer you to support groups, and woman-positive doctors, lawyers, midwives, and therapists. If you need shelter from a storm, contact the **Women's Sexual Assault Centre** (383-3232 for its 24-hour crisis line, 383-5545 for regular business, vwsac.com). At the university – where, as of this writing, only 57 of 281 full professors are women – look for the **UVic Women's Centre** (721-8353, uvss.uvic.ca/wcentre), which is also the office of *thirdspace* (née *The Emily*), English Canada's oldest university-based feminist newspaper.

Men's Issues

Life isn't always easier for men: they're more prone to stress-related illnesses, they're more likely to commit suicide, and they often get the short end of custody battles for their children. That's why hundreds of capital-region males have banded together to form the **Victoria Men's Centre** (370-4636, victoria.tc.ca/ Community/MensCentre), a group that holds regular meetings to discuss political and personal problems. If you seek professional help, therapists at the Victoria **Men's Trauma Centre** (#203-1420 Quadra St., 381-6367, mens-trauma.com) conduct counselling and group sessions for male victims of physical or emotional abuse, or car accidents.

Family Planning

We can talk about sex, but that doesn't mean we're any wiser when it comes to contraception. The non-judgmental staff of the **Island Sexual Health Society** (bcclinic.ca) provides referrals to doctors, tests for sexually transmitted diseases, and sells birth control at prices only slightly above cost at its four clinics (#200-1770 Fort St., 592-3479; 2170 Mt. Newton X Rd, 544-2424; 2782 Millstream Rd., 478-1757; and at

- Wearers of sandwich-board advertisements in Victoria must "continuously change locations" and remain completely silent.

- Video arcades are illegal in Sidney and Metchosin. If anybody operates one in Langford, they must ensure it does not become "a place of vice, drunkenness, profane swearing, or indecent, obscene, blasphemous or grossly insulting language."

- Victoria residents may keep chickens in their yards, but not roosters.

- It is illegal to hold a cattle drive in Oak Bay. This is permitted in Saanich, but only if the animals don't step on the sidewalk, and any bull or cow "known to be vicious" is tethered.

- If you run an escort service in Sidney, you must provide a list of your employees' names to the town.

- Leg-hold traps are *verboten* in Victoria.

- In Saanich, no one may keep fur-bearing animals, more than 25 pairs of pigeons, or nuclear weapons.

Camosun College's Lansdowne Campus, Richmond House, 592-3449).

Gays and Lesbians

Aside from Pride Week events, gay and lesbian life seems pretty quiet in Victoria – until you probe a little deeper. The website *gayvictoria.ca* provides a bulletin board of events and links to the comprehensive Vancouver Island Pink Pages directory. **UVic Pride** *(472-4393, uvss.uvic.ca/pride)* is an active GLBT student collective, and **Prime Timers Victoria** *(members.shaw.ca/primetimersvic)* is a social group for older gay and bisexual men. **AIDS Vancouver Island** *(1601 Blanshard St., 384-2366, avi.org)* offers education and street outreach services, along with a wellness program to improve men's sexual health and reduce HIV infections. (For clubs and sexual escapades, see Nightlife.)

Victoria lesbians haven't had a permanent home since The G-Spot club vanished, but the group that started it, the **Women's Creative Network** *(victoria.tc.ca/Community/WCN)*, is still active, along with the **Victoria Lesbian Seniors Care Society** *(vlscs.ca)*, which supports older women and holds movie nights and socials. **Lesbians on Vancouver Island** *(lovi.ca)* is a busy online forum with listings of events. Just for fun, **Musaic** *(598-2881, geocities.com/musaic_victoria)* is a choir for lesbians, gays, and allies that's been singing strong for over a decade. **Rainbow Campers** *(members.shaw.ca/rbcvi)* take to the outdoors, and **Ferry Riders** *(geocities.com/ferryriders)* is a motorcycle club for guys who love leather.

If you've found your soulmate, you can get hitched here: in July of 2003, British Columbia started to allow **same-sex marriages**, and more than 2,400 have been performed in the province since then. (Over half the participants are Americans.) Get a licence from the **Vital Statistics Agency** *(818 Fort St., 952-2681, vs.gov.bc.ca)*, hire a marriage commissioner (unlike priests, they're legally required to give equal treatment to same-sex couples), and contact a wedding planner like **Dennis Eyolfson** *(733-2415, gayorlesbianweddings.ca)* to arrange the flowers. For all-in-one planning and accommodation, try one of the city's open-minded B&Bs, such as the heritage **Earle Clarke House** *(1461 Pembroke St., 595-0944, earleclarkehouse.com)*.

Flower Power

Practically all Victoria florists buy from the gigantic United Flower Growers auction in Burnaby, so there aren't many differences between what they carry, but there are differences in what they do.

Daisy Chain Florists
Free consultations on wedding flowers, one of their specialties. Showcases work by Canadian artists in the shop as well.
950 Fort St., 382-2512, daisychainflorists.com

Flowers First
A wide variety of orchids imported from Singapore.
1025 Cook St., 384-2251, flowersfirst.ca

Dental Cases

One of Victoria's most enterprising dentists is **Donald Bays** *(115 Victoria Bay Centre, 381-6433)*, who makes house calls – occasionally while wearing a white spangled Elvis jumpsuit. Many people in Victoria who need dental care are bedridden or in nursing homes, and Bays helps them out with his mobile air compressor and power drills. If you suffer from acute dentaphobia, try **Deanna Geddo** *(404-645 Fort St., 389-0669)*, who uses relaxation techniques to calm sensitive patients. For preventative care on the cheap, check out the **dental assistants' program** at Camosun College, which does X-rays, cleanings, and flouride treatments for a fraction of what they'd cost at a professional office. Call 370-3184 for an appointment during the school year.

Flowers on Top
Hand-tied style bouquet techniques from Europe.
1005 Broad St., 383-5262, flowersontop.com

Harry's Flowers
A good source for orchids and vases, and more convenient parking than downtown shops.
1817 Oak Bay Ave., 598-3911

Zen Floral Studio
Yukiyasu Kato performs traditional *ikebana* (Japanese arranging), focusing on "negative space" by placing a few stems or flowers in shallow or narrow containers. He also delivers, and gives lessons.
3947B Quadra St., 727-0056

The Spa Life

The word *spa* comes from the name of a town that means "healing waters" – although "liquid assets" is more appropriate, judging by the profusion of pricy day spas in Victoria. Many of the city's big hotels have them, but the best is at the **Delta Victoria Ocean Pointe Resort** *(45 Songhees Rd., 360-5858, thespaatdeltavictoria.com)*, which has rooms overlooking the Inner Harbour along with gourmet lunches and a full fitness centre. For something more cozy, try the soothing **Spa 517** *(#1A-1218 Langley St., 480-1517, spa517.com)*; for natural healing, visit the **Ayurvedic Wellness Centre** *(523 Broughton St., 704-2222)* or **Silk Road** *(1624 Government St., 382-0006, silkroadtea.com)*, an aromatherapy and tea shop specializing in such herbal treatments as green-tea facials. Another unusual spa is **Fingers and Toes** *(209 Menzies St., 920-4247)*, specializing in diabetic and arthritic hand and foot care. If you're seriously into pampering, seek out the 7,000-square-foot **Le Spa Sereine** *(1411 Government St., 388-4419, lespasereine.com)*, offering more than 60 different treatments. On another chakra, students at the **West Coast College of Massage Therapy** *(#101-637 Bay St., 381-9800, wccmt.edu)* offer many services at a fraction of the cost of professional spas.

kidding around

Victoria's a great place to raise children, partly because there are many ways to keep them amused. These are a few favourite family-friendly attractions, but for more see *kidsinvictoria.com* or the free magazine *Island Parent*.

Animal Encounters

Touch the planet's once and future leaders at downtown's **Victoria Bug Zoo** *(631 Courtney St., 384-2847, bugzoo.bc.ca)*, which has giant beetles, assassin bugs, scorpions, and a mind-blowing leafcutter ant colony. More insects are up the Saanich peninsula at the **Butterfly Gardens** *(1461 Benvenuto Ave., 652-3822, butterflygardens.com)*, which has up to 35 species of flapping bugs from around the world and exotic birds you can meet up close. Open February to October, kids under five get in free. Children love to cuddle with the baby goats at the **Beacon Hill Children's Farm** *(381-2532; beaconhillpark.ca/childrenspark)*; if you're there at closing time you can help the staff chase the four-legged kids into the barn for the night. Open March to October, admission by donation.

Water Works

Many swimming pools have play areas and water slides, but the best is **Saanich Commonwealth Place** *(4636 Elk Lake Dr., 475-7600, gov.saanich.bc.ca)*, which has a wave tank, fountains, and an observation deck at pool level for parents who don't want to get

GETTING THE POINT
If you're looking to pick up a little local colour, look no further than **Urge Studios** *(586 Johnson St., 380-2989, urgetattoos.com)*, one of the finest tattoo shops on the entire west coast. Their internationally trained artists do excellent custom work at prices that don't make you wince. Other good places to make your mark include **Spitfire** *(522 Pandora Ave., 381-4471)*, the all-vegan **Tattoo Zoo** *(1215 Wharf St., 361-1952, tattoozoo.net)* and **Universal Tattooing** *(1306 Broad St., 382-9417, universaltattoos.com)*. If you want a little metal under your skin, Urge is also the best. All their piercers must make the pilgrimage to San Francisco to be trained by Fakir, the godfather of modern piercing. Urge also does professional branding and scarification, if that's your cup of tea.

wet. The Bruce Hutchison library branch is in the building too. During the summer, everyone can enjoy **All Fun Recreation Park** *(2207 Millstream Rd., 474-3184, allfun.bc.ca)* an amusement park with 16 waterslides, mini-golf and a driving range, batting cages, and two go-kart tracks. The whole shebang's next to Western Speedway, a kids' favourite on Saturday "hit-to-pass" nights (see Sports).

That's Entertainment

Parents on a budget will appreciate the free Children's Fun Hour in the food court at **Hillside Centre** *(1694 Hillside Ave., hillsidecentre.com)*, where clowns, singers, or puppeteers frolic every Wednesday at 10 a.m. The **Greater Victoria Public Library** *(gvpl.victoria.bc.ca)* also holds free storytimes at its various branches, although some sessions are so popular that you have to register in advance.

Great Outdoors

Victoria still has wildlife within its boundaries, and a good way to see it is with **CRD Parks' nature programs** *(478-3344, crd.bc.ca/parks)*, many of which are as free as the birds you'll learn about. The **Swan Lake Christmas Hill Nature Sanctuary** *(3873 Swan Lake Rd., 479-0211, swanlake.bc.ca)* is another popular look-and-learn destination with year-round activities, as is the **Goldstream Nature House** *(478-9414, goldstreamnaturehouse.com)*, in a provincial park that's home to bats, hummingbirds, and a fall salmon run that draws dozens of hungry eagles.

PLAYING DRESS-UP
Disguise the Limit *(3328 Metchosin Rd., 479-1156, disguisethelimitcostumes.ca)* has nearly 1,000 outfits for rent, including a full suit of armour, a Louis XIV ensemble with powdered wig, and a latex Batman body suit. Scottish formal wear too. A bigger selection of classic formal wear is at **Langham Court Theatre** *(805 Langham Ct., 384-2025, langhamcourttheatre.bc.ca)*, which also has medieval and masquerade items in its wardrobe.

gone to the dogs

Walkies?

One subject that's had the fur flying in Victoria lately is whether mutts should be allowed to run free in municipal parks. After many loud meetings, the City of Victoria has permitted a few **off-leash areas** (city.victoria.bc.ca/dogs), although the only one near downtown where canines may freely frolic year-round, at any time of day, is the Dallas Road waterfront between Douglas Street and Clover Point. Other municipalities have their own policies (see their respective websites), but rural areas generally have fewer restrictions: North Saanich, for example, is proudly leash-free. The situation is further confused when it comes to parks run by the CRD (crd.bc.ca/parks). Although pooches may go off-leash in some (Thetis Lake is a favourite), they're banned from nature sanctuaries and playgrounds, and many beaches and picnic areas during the summer. If you're ticked off by the rules, sniff out *citizencanine.org*, an advocacy group and forum of local dog news.

Behavior Modification

If Fido won't fetch, call **Wonderdogs** (133 Joseph St., 389-1876, wonderdogs.bc.ca). Ben Kersen's been training dogs professionally since 1979, and has appeared with his obedient pupils on the *Today* show. He does group or individual lessons, or you can board your pet with him and he'll train it while you're away.

Stay!

If you're too busy to walk Fifi, fear not: there are numerous services to help. **Club Dog Doggy Daycare** (480-0234, clubdog.ca) and **Pet Pampering** (381-5889, pet-pampering.com) can amuse your pooch for the day. If they need real caressing, **Top Dog Daycare and Spa** (602 Esquimalt Rd., 920-3647) and **Barking Lot Dog Spa** (103-1841 Oak Bay Ave., 592-2322) do

GAZE INTO MY CRYSTAL BALL

If you need a glimpse into the future — or clarification of the present — the best psychics in town work out of **Triple Spiral Metaphysical** at #106-3 Fan Tan Alley (380-7212, triplespiralmetaphysical.com) and **Angels of Avalon** in Market Square (#62-560 Johnson St., 380-1721, metaphysical.bc.ca). You'll also find readers of all manner and type scattered across town. Time-proven favourites include tarot readers Lion Sun (at Angels of Avalon) and Alison Skelton (alisonskelton.com), astrologer Jill Kirby (388-7905, holisticarts.ca) and spiritual counsellor/channeler Lynne Shields (598-2391). For more, see the back page of *Monday Magazine*.

BIDDING AROUND

Kilshaw's *(1115 Fort St., 384-6441, kilshaws.com)* has been around for more than 50 years, auctioning household furnishings on Thursday nights. While they also handle antiques and fine art, you're much more likely to leave with a steal on a sofa than a deal on a Degas. **Lunds** *(926 Fort St., 386-3308, lunds.com)*, on the other hand, has carved out a niche as Vancouver Island's luxury auctioneer, so you'll hear prices into the thousands at its weekly events and occasional theme auctions (jewellery, toys, weapons). They often run past midnight, so deals can be had if you wait it out. **BDF Auction** *(6678 Bertram Pl., 652-0064, bdfauction.com)* features good vehicles at great prices at their Saturday car auctions, while real deals on just about everything are up the Malahat at **Whippletree Auctions** *(#5-4715 Trans-Canada Hwy., 746-5858)*. An amazing selection of stuff appears at their Sunday "bid and buys," from vehicles to building supplies and household goods to sporting equipment.

show-quality grooming and massages. For longer stays, try such spiffy rural pet hotels as the **Halliford Canine Country Club** *(4339 Happy Valley Rd., 478-4082, hallifordkennels.com)*, which has five acres of park-like grounds, a play penthouse for cats, and a doggy "beautique." **Puppy Love and Cat's Meow Pet Care Centre** *(2918 Lamont Rd., 652-2301, puppylove.ca)*, conveniently near the airport, also has a canine "playschool," climate-controlled buildings for cats, and full-service grooming.

Animal Crackers

Every good pet deserves a gourmet treat. **Woofles: A Doggy Diner** *(#102-560 Johnson St., 385-9663, wooflesadoggydiner.com)*, at the entrance to Market Square, serves up snacks that look so tasty that tourists often order some for themselves by mistake. They also create cakes for dog birthdays and weddings (no kidding), and sell snacks for felines and organic catnip too.

Oh, Poo!

Nearly all municipalities impose fines for failing to pick up after Rover, so carry baggies when you're out for a walk. If he's messed your yard and you can't bear to clean it yourself, call the brave folks at the **Poop Patrol** *(386-POOP)* or **Scoopy-Doo Residential Pet Waste Removal** *(744-5474)*.

Doggone Mortality

If your animal friend passes on, **Family Pet Services Ltd.** *(479-3343, bc-biz.com/familypetservices)* has cremation services and hardwood urns. To preserve them in more than memory, call **Angler's Taxidermy** *(1-800-409-3474, anglerstaxidermy.com)*, which can freeze-dry a deceased cat or small dog in any pose you choose. (Laying down costs less than standing up.) Although their usual subjects are fish and game, they've immortalized pet iguanas, snakes, and spiders, too.

Greens to Your Door

You can find organic produce in most supermarkets, but if you want to make sure you've always got some in the icebox, subscribe to services that'll deliver the goods. The blue ribbon for local commitment goes to **Saanich Organics** (818-5807, saanichorganics.com), which fills its weekly boxes only with certified organic fruits and veggies from farms on the Saanich peninsula. You get what's in season – berries and figs in summer, leeks and king cabbages in the winter – but year 'round there's braising and salad greens, beets, carrots, potatoes, onions, and garlic. **Share Organics** (595-6729, shareorganics.bc.ca) and **Small Potatoes Urban Delivery** (383-7969, spud.ca) buy first from local and BC organic growers, and then import from elsewhere when necessary, enabling them to provide grapefruit, strawberries, and tomatoes in mid-winter. Also, going organic doesn't mean you have to be a raving vegan: Sidney's **Kildara Farms** (11293 Chalet Rd., 655-3093) sells certified organic chicken and pork, but you have to visit them to pick it up.

Alternative Therapies

Victoria's alternative healing network is vast. From aromatherapists to practitioners of Traditional Chinese Medicine (TCM), from pranic healers to somatoenergetic consultants, in Victoria it's the MDs who often get relegated to the place of second opinions. To find the practitioner for you, check out the annual Victoria Health Show (usually in January) or the back page of Monday Magazine. If you,re looking for a path more than a cure, the city's also full of alternative healing schools such as the **Canadian College of Acupuncture and Oriental Medicine** (551 Chatham St., 384-2492, ccaom.com) and the **Oshio College of Acupuncture and Herbology** (114-1595 McKenzie Ave., 472-6601, members.shaw.ca/oshio), whose students provide treatments (overseen by a clinical supervisor) at bargain prices.

Festival City

Victoria is more than Ye Olde England, and it's proven by a variety of parades and cultural festivals. (For art, music, and theatre fests see Arts and Literature.)

Chinese New Year

The lion dancers parade along Fisgard Street and snap the beast's jaws to gobble up lettuce and little red envelopes hanging from every building. Be sure to rub Buddha's belly while wishing the latest animal year well.
February; 384-7352

Christmas Truck Parade

This always brings out a crowd: 75 or more semis, decorated with lights, roar across the capital region collecting food and cash for local charities. Go to Ogden Point at sunset to see the trucks before the parade begins. Sponsored by the Island Equipment Owners Association.
December; 382-4362, ieoa.ca

Diwali

This "festival of lights" sponsored by the Victoria Hindu Temple is like New Year's and Thanksgiving rolled into one for Victoria's South Asian community, which gathers for a Bollywood-quality music and dance show at UVic. Tasty refreshments.
October; 652-6626

FolkFest

The biggest event in downtown Victoria: ten days of live world music on the waterfront, for one low all-admission price. Many come just for the food, prepared by the city's numerous ethnic and national associations.
First week of July; 388-4728, icafolkfest.com

Latin-Caribbean Fest

Victoria's Immigrant and Refugee Centre takes over Market Square with food, crafts, and a visual art show celebrating Latin and Caribbean culture — but the real highlights are reggae and salsa bands that keep crowds dancing long into the night.
Late July; 361-9433, vircs.bc.ca

A Clean Conscience

Many dry cleaning establishments pump out toxic effluents worthy of a pulp mill, but not **Elite Earth-friendly Drycleaners** *(1019 Cook St, 381-2221, greendrycleaner.com)*. It's the only business in Western Canada using environmentally friendly citrus oils instead of poisonous solvents to clean clothes. Holland America was so impressed by Elite's work that it now uses nontoxic dry cleaning on all its cruise ships. If your home needs tidying, call on **Dusting Divas** *(391-4058, dustingdivas.com)*. They use cleaning products made only from all-natural ingredients like vinegar and washing soda, and can provide feng shui and aromatherapy advice so your household can be cosmically and cosmetically clean at the same time.

Waste Not

Victoria has cleaned up its act somewhat since the first half of the 20th century, when the city literally dumped all its garbage into the Strait of Juan de Fuca. (After the trash started littering beaches, officials "solved" the problem by compacting it so it would sink.) Today it goes to the Hartland Landfill at the rate of 150,000 tonnes per year, or 429 kg per citizen. Fortunately, there are programs to reduce this waste. Some 45,000 tonnes of our annual trash is organic matter, and though Hartland captures the methane it gives off (burning it to generate electricity for 1,600 homes), it can also be put to use with tips from the **Compost Education Centre** *(1216 North Park St., 386-9676, compost.bc.ca)*. Practically anything, from clothes hangers and tires to batteries and appliances, can be taken to the **Hartland Recycling Area** *(1 Hartland Ave., 360-3030)* or certain businesses listed by the CRD *(crd.bc.ca/es)*. Electronic "e-waste" like that old 386 computer can be reclaimed by companies such as **Break Down Recycle** *(859 Devonshire Rd., 381-2373)*.

unreal estate

In 2007, Victoria was branded among the 25 most unaffordable real-estate markets in the world: since 1981, the average house price here has increased 229 percent, to $400,000. That's partly due to the global housing bubble, but it's also because Victoria's got some very expensive properties.

The region's most extravagant estate lurks on the northwestern tip of the Saanich Peninsula. At 670 Land's End Road sits **Villa Madrona**, an 11,500 square-foot Italianate residence (3br, 7bath) built by the former CEO of Sunkist, fitted with plaster niches from New York's Vanderbilt mansion, an office with oak panelling from the S.S. *Britannic* (sister ship to the *Titanic*), a teahouse, a glass menagerie for parrots, and a grove of orange trees. In 2007, it was assessed at $13.7 million, making it the most expensive house on Vancouver Island.

More high-end waterfront huddles in Oak Bay near the Royal Victoria Yacht Club. The grandest is a **15,800 square-foot palace** at 3195 Humber Road once owned by Frank Hertel, a German petroleum engineer who fleeced Victorians in the early 1990s with dubious high-tech investment schemes. His former residence, which

Lavender Harvest

The folks at the Happy Valley Lavender & Herb Farm invite the public to visit as they gather their fragrant crop, and to sample some lavender cosmetics, baking, and ice cream. It's one of the sweetest ways to spend a summer day. *July; 3505 Happy Valley Rd, 474-5767, happyvalleylavender.com*

Luminara

A soft parade of candle-lit lanterns, sculptures, and performances throughout Beacon Hill Park. To become a participant instead or just a rubbernecker, join the lantern-making workshops that start in late May. *July; 388-4728, luminaravictoria.com*

has doors covered in gold leaf, a desalinization plant, and 19 TV sets, has been assessed at $11.6 million – although recently it went on the market for $25 million, setting a record asking price for the city. On the same point, at 3160 Humber Road, is a modern $10.5-million home (5br, 7bath) designed by Victoria mayor and architect Alan Lowe, proving that he doesn't just do McDonald's franchises.

Other costly estates line the nearby promenade of Beach Drive. **Eagle's Nest**, a 10,000 square-foot Tudor mansion (5br, 7bath) at 3125 Beach Drive, was built in 1930. Canada's ambassador to Japan owned it in the 1940s, and in the 1970s it was home to the evangelist Brian Ruud (see page 199). A Vancouver tech wiz bought it in 2003 for $7.5 million, but it's worth more than $10 million today. At 3175 Beach Drive stands **Riffington**, built in 1911 for a director of the Uplands development; the mansion has 10 fireplaces, and a tide-controlled pool once swum in by Princess Margaret. Several years ago it was assessed the second-most expensive property in the region, but in 2001 the owner (newspaper baron David Black) got it classified as a lower-tax "farm" because his family sold plants from the property. Now you know how the rich stay that way.

Palace Tours

When it comes to residences, Victoria boasts an incredible architectural diversity. That's partly because it never suffered a land squeeze (unlike rapid-growth Vancouver) so big lots survived – and partly because in the 1920s, Victoria had the highest density of millionaires in the country. If you're curious about how the upper 0.1% lives today, join the luxury house tours organized every fall by the **Art Gallery of Greater Victoria** (aggv.bc.ca/info-volcom.asp).

New Year's Day Levees

According to colonial traditions dating to the fur trade, officials throw their doors open and toast the New Year with the great unwashed. The practice continues today at many municipal halls and at Government House – providing excellent opportunities for Victorians to grouse about their taxes.

January; look for times and locations in local media

Oak Bay Tea Party

There once really was a "tweed curtain" separating Oak Bay from the rest of the region: it was stitched together as a joke for an early incarnation of this municipal festival, going strong since 1963. Includes an airshow, fireworks, a midway at Willows Beach, and (of course) tea.

June; 388-4457, oakbayteaparty.com

Christ Church Cathedral

Victoria's grandest house of worship is a tribute to patience. It was designed in 1896, but Anglicans didn't have enough money to lay the foundation stone until 1926. The northwest tower wasn't finished until 1936, and the southwest not until 1954. But that patience has been rewarded with a church – one of Canada's largest – that's rich in detail.

A pillar in the southeast corner is adorned with a robin (see photo), the stonemasons' charming tribute to a bird that built a nest on the pillar while it was under construction; Winston Churchill, an experienced mason himself, laid a stone in the northwest tower in 1929. Visitors may explore the subterranean crypt, which holds the ashes of more than 1,000 of the faithful, or examine the spectacular stained glass in the east chapel, depicting St. John's ecstatic (or psychedelic) visions of the New Jerusalem. Time your visit to hear a concert on the new $2-million pipe organ, the largest in BC, or climb the northwest tower Tuesday evenings to watch the Cathedral Guild of Ringers rehearsing (see photo) on Christ Church's 10 huge bells, produced by the same London foundry that cast the Liberty Bell and the chimes of Big Ben.
930 Burdett Ave., 383-2714,
christchurchcathedral.bc.ca

Pride Week

Victoria's gay, lesbian, bisexual, and transgendered communities show their size and strength – much to the surprise of tourists – with a movie night, a tattoo-a-thon, an art show, the Marcus Tipton memorial softball game (played entirely in drag on Canada Day), and a rollicking parade through downtown.
June or July; victoriapridesociety.org

Saanich Fair

One of the oldest country fairs in Canada (it started in 1868), with pie-eating contests, 4-H displays, milking demos, and a midway. Take a convertible and a bottle of whisky, and you've got the makings of a Larry McMurtry novel.
Labour Day weekend; saanichfair.ca

places of worship

Victoria Day Parade

Since 1899, Victoria's commemorated the monarch's birthday with Canada's longest-running parade. It also claims to be the country's biggest: the 2004 version had 156 entries, including many marching bands from US schools.
First Monday preceding May 25; 382-3111

Victoria International Flower and Garden Festival

The pruning shears get drawn as the city's green thumbs compete to see who has the best show garden, window box, or floral arrangement. Plus speakers and demonstrations that dig the dirt.
Late July; 381-7894, flowerandgarden.ca

God has more big shrines downtown that are worth a peek.

The Church of Our Lord

The all-wood church (near the Marriott Hotel) was the product of an Anglican dispute. In 1872, dean Edward Cridge spoke publicly against Catholic-type "ritualism" practiced by the bishop at Christ Church Cathedral; Cridge was put on trial by an ecclesiastical court, and kicked out. Most of the congregation followed him down the hill to build this "Carpenter Gothic" edifice in 1876, using Douglas-fir beams and walls of California redwood. One prominent member was HBC man James Douglas: he provided the 1827 organ (purportedly from a shipwreck), and his daughter hand-carved the oak pulpit.
626 Blanshard St., 383-8915

St. Ann's Academy

Victoria is the oldest Catholic diocese in Canada west of Toronto, and for many years its most visible presences here were the Sisters of St. Ann. The nuns started arriving from Quebec in 1858, and began teaching in a cabin (it stands next to the Royal BC Museum); by 1871, their order had grown so large that they started building this convent and boarding school. Today, it's all government offices, but you can visit the chapel, designed by a multitalented priest in 1858 for the hospital across the road, and later moved as one piece and built into the academy.
835 Humboldt St.

St. Andrew's Roman Catholic Cathedral

When this gothic shrine opened in 1892, its spire (see photo), measuring more than 50 metres, was the tallest point in the city. (A tin statue of St. Andrew also stood atop the centre pinnacle, but was demolished in a storm.) St. Andrew's is the oldest Catholic cathedral in BC, with some lovely stained glass and silkscreen prints on its stonework replicated from the Book of Kells. Around the corner at 740 View you'll find the bishop's residence (cathedral = seat of a bishop) and monuments to pioneer missionaries (their remains are in the crypt inside) including Archbishop Charles John Seghers, who was shot to death by a lunatic in 1886.
1202 Blanshard St., 388-5571

Temple Emanu-El

The brick building at is the oldest surviving synagogue in Canada, built in 1863. There were only a dozen Jewish families in Victoria at the time, but other religious denominations helped pay for the construction because they believed the city would grow if all were welcomed. Visitors include Rachel "Ray" Frank, the first female Jewish preacher in the US; she officiated at high holiday services here in 1895, drawing Jews from across the Pacific Northwest.
1461 Blanshard, 382-0615

Spiritualism

Sufism

Faith of the beloved poet Rumi and the mother religion from which Islam split, Sufism's still going strong after a thousand years. The first Tuesday of every month, Sufis practice their chants and whirl like dervishes at 1831 Fern Street.
385-3378

Theosophy

Theosophists promote their central premise — that we are all one — by welcoming everyone to their quest to understand our place in the universe. They meet monthly in Victoria, and help run Camp Indralaya, a 78-acre retreat founded in 1927 on Orcas Island that's an ongoing experiment in applying theosophical principles to daily life.
655-9471, indralaya.org

resting places

With its reputation as a residence for the "newly wed and nearly dead," Victoria has more than its fair share of cemeteries. Here's a rough guide, but for the real skinny on the skeletons in our closet, contact the Old Cemeteries Society *(598-8870, oldcem.bc.ca)* and catch one of their tours.

Pioneer Square

Victoria's first graveyard was located at the southwest corner of Douglas and Johnson Streets (which might explain why the Blenz coffee shop there today draws a weird nocturnal clientele). Its ground was muddy, though, and locals were creeped out by pigs rooting around the graves, so in 1855 the city's churches got together and consecrated a burial ground at the corner of Quadra and Meares. Today known as Pioneer Square, this leafy park is filled with the bodies of 1,300 fur traders, fortune-seekers, and Royal Navy men. Many of the graves are unmarked: though headstones were later moved to Ross Bay, few of the bodies were exhumed. (The office workers who lunch on the grass probably don't know it, but they're likely eating atop a corpse.) To appreciate its spooky atmosphere, join the nightly lantern tours during the summer.

Ross Bay Cemetery

Victoria boomed with the Fraser River gold rush, and by 1872 the Pioneer Square graveyard was nearly full. Following an English trend to put cemeteries in picturesque settings, the city bought a waterfront farm east of the city, and began creating a burial ground with winding carriageways and ornamental trees. Japanese and Chinese graves were relegated to a corner so close to shore that in 1909, before Dallas Road existed, a storm unearthed their coffins and littered the beach with corpses. Some 28,000 people are interred in the

cemetery today, including such BC luminaries as James Douglas, Emily Carr, the Dunsmuirs, and gold rush legend Billy Barker, who laid 100 years in an unmarked grave until the Old Cemeteries Society provided a headstone. It's not easy to find particular graves without a map, so get one from the society's website or buy John Adams' excellent guidebook.
1516 Fairfield Rd.

Chinese Cemetery

In 1903, Chinese mourners had to confront an enraged white neighbour with a shotgun before they could use this isolated cemetery, on a rocky point jutting into the Strait of Juan de Fuca. Fortunately, a policeman enforced their rights, and today the graveyard at the end of Crescent Road is the oldest Chinese cemetery in Canada. Few buried here thought it would be their final resting place: Chinese immigrants believed their souls would remain homeless unless their bodies returned to China, so their bones were exhumed after seven years and stored in a charnel house until there were enough to fill a boat for the journey. The tradition faded, and the bones of 849 pioneers still awaiting shipment were re-interred at a ceremony in 1961. Their descendants burn offerings in the stoves flanking the altar (see photo), built in 1907.
Harling Point located on Crescent Rd.

Jewish Cemetery

Like Victoria's Jewish community itself, the cemetery tucked away at Cedar Hill Road and Acton Street often gets overlooked. It was consecrated in 1860, when there were only 76 Jewish families in town; the first person buried in it was Morris Price, a former Berliner killed by Natives at Lillooet in 1861. Other residents include prominent local merchants such as Simon Leiser, and Samuel Schultz, the first Jewish judge in Canada. It's also worth a visit to get a sense of the natural beauty

Wicca

Vancouver Island boasts Canada's largest per-capita population of witches, pagans, and Goddess worshippers: estimates range up to 5,000 devotees. The trashy '70s book *Michelle Remembers* gave the world the false impression that Victoria was a hotbed of satanism (see Notoriety) and tarred local witches with the same bad brush. Since then they've worked hard to prove they're about respect, not blood-soaked rituals. Wiccan ministers

that existed in the Hillside area before it was built up in the 1950s.

Veterans' Cemetery

Another unusual graveyard sits in the middle of Esquimalt's Gorge Vale golf course. The Veterans' Cemetery was originally a piece of farmland owned by a subsidiary of the Hudson's Bay Company. The admiralty purchased it in 1868 for deceased officers from the nearby naval base, and since then it's become the final resting place for more than 2,590 military personnel and their families. (The HBC sold the surrounding land in 1927, and the golf course opened in 1931.) The cemetery is a national historic site, and a tribute to the hard life on tall-masted ships – as proven by the numerous memorials to sailors who "fell from aloft." To see it, turn off Colville Road at the yard for the motor pool, and drive up the hill. Park at the gravel lot and walk in. The road continues across the 12th fairway, and a tee shot might dent your car.

offer spiritual outreach to the William Head prison and the Victoria Hospice, and conduct legally recognized marriages (via the Wiccan chaplain at UVic's Interfaith Chapel) and burials (via the Aquarian Tabernacle Church). Of the city's myriad covens and moon circles, the busiest is the Thirteenth House Mystery School, which offers classes and private rituals. If you're curious, visit Triple Spiral Metaphysical (see "Gaze into My Crystal Ball") or the Victoria Pagan Alliance, a Yahoo! chat group.

Dust in the Wind

Despite its cemeteries, Victoria has the highest **cremation** rate in North America, being the preferred way to go for 85 percent of the city's recently departed. One wonders what happens to all the ashes, though. Soon many may end up at Ross Bay: the City of Victoria recently sold 200 unused plots in the graveyard for up to $17,500 apiece, and will use the revenue to build underground vaults for the cremated remains of up to 5,000 more. But some people can't afford a vault, and others don't want an urn in their living room. You could bury them in the yard, but that's a problem if you sell the house, and it's illegal to scatter ashes in many parks. So what to do? One option is to commit them to the deep. Rev. Ryan Knight, a retired United Church minister, conducts services on his 42-foot sloop, sailing mourners to quiet sites where they may scatter a loved one's remains.
866-947-7282, marinememorialservices.com

further reading

Numerous books provided facts and details for *Victoria: The Unknown City*. These are the best of them.

The British Columbia Parliament Buildings edited by Martin Segger (Arcon, 1979)

Brother Twelve: The Incredible Story of Canada's False Prophet, by John Oliphant (McClelland & Stewart, 1991)

Emily Carr: A Biography by Maria Tippett (Oxford University Press, 1979)

The Empress: In the Grand Style by Terry Reksten (Douglas & McIntyre, 1997)

Exploring Victoria's Architecture by Martin Segger and Douglas Franklin (Sono Nis Press, 1996)

The Forbidden City within Victoria: Myth, Symbol and Streetscape of Canada's Earliest Chinatown by David Chuenyan Lai (Orca Book Publishers, 1991)

The Geology of Southern Vancouver Island by C.J. Yorath (Harbour Publishing, 2005)

Looking at Totem Poles by Hilary Stewart (Douglas & McIntyre, 1993)

More English Than the English by Terry Reksten (Orca Book Publishers, 1986)

More Victoria Landmarks by Geoffrey Castle (Sono Nis Press, 1988)

Old Langford: An Illustrated History, 1850-1950 by Maureen Duffus (Town and Gown Press, 2003)

On the Street Where You Live: Pioneer Pathways of Early Victoria by Danda Humphreys (Heritage House Publishing, 1999)

Only in Oak Bay: 1906-1981 edited by Fred C. Barnes (The Corporation of The District of Oak Bay, 1981)

Saanich: An Illustrated History edited by Geoffrey Castle (Corporation of the District of Saanich, 1989)

Saltwater People by Dave Elliott Sr. and Janet Poth (School District No. 63 Saanich, 1990)

The Ships of British Columbia: An Illustrated History of the British Columbia Ferry Corporation by Patricia and Gary Bannerman (Hancock House Publishers, 1985)

Shoot Shoot Shoot: A History of the Victoria-Esquimalt Coast Artillery Defences, 1878-1956 by R. Lovatt et al. (Rodd Hill Friends Society, 1993)

Songhees Pictorial: A History of the Songhees People as seen by Outsiders, 1790-1912 by Grant Keddie (Royal BC Museum, 2003)

The Story of Butchart Gardens by Dave Preston (Highline Publishing, 1996)

The Story of Sidney by Peter Grant (Porthole Press, 1998)

The Terror of the Coast: Land Alienation and Colonial War on Vancouver Island and the Gulf Islands, 1849-1863 by Chris Arnett (Talonbooks, 1999)

Vancouver Island Railroads by Robert D. Turner (Sono Nis Press, 1997)

Victoria Landmarks by Geoffrey Castle (Sono Nis Press, 1985)

Victoria's Streetcar Era by Henry Ewert (Sono Nis Press, 1992)

A Voice Great Within Us: The Story of Chinook by Charles Lillard and Terry Glavin (New Star Books, 1998)

Wings Across the Water: Victoria's Flying Heritage, 1871-1971 by Elwood White and Peter L. Smith (Harbour Publishing, 2005)

index

index

index

index

index

index

index

index

index

index

ROSS CROCKFORD is a journalist and photographer based in Victoria. A former Vancouver trial lawyer and staff writer for *The Prague Post*, from 1998 to 2001 he was the editor of Victoria's *Monday Magazine*. He has received a National Magazine Award for sportswriting, a Western Magazine Award for business writing, and a Jack Webster Award of Distinction for investigative reporting. His freelance work has appeared in *Western Living*, *explore*, *Adbusters*, and *The Globe and Mail*.